P9-DNF-338

Swim WITH THE DOLPHINS

HOW WOMEN CAN SUCCEED IN CORPORATE AMERICA ON THEIR OWN TERMS

CONNIE GLASER and BARBARA STEINBERG SMALLEY

WARNER BOOKS

A Time Warner Company

If you purchase this book without a cover you should be aware that this book may have been stolen property and reported as "unsold and destroyed" to the publisher. In such case neither the author nor the publisher has received any payment for this "stripped book."

Grateful acknowledgment is given to Molly Ivins to quote from her book *Molly Ivins Can't Say That, Can She?*

Warner Books Edition
Copyright © 1995 by Connie Glaser and Barbara Steinberg Smalley
All rights reserved.

Warner Books, Inc., 1271 Avenue of the Americas, New York, NY 10020
Visit our Web site at http://warnerbooks.com
Ⓦ A Time Warner Company

Printed in the United States of America
Originally published in hardcover by Warner Books, Inc.
First Trade Printing: March 1996

10 9 8 7 6 5 4 3

Library of Congress Cataloging-in-Publication Data
Glaser, Connie Brown.
    Swim with the dolphins : how women can succeed in corporate America on their own terms / Connie Glaser and Barbara Steinberg Smalley.
        p.   cm.
        Includes bibliographical references (p.   ).
        ISBN 0-446-67184-3
        1. Women executives—United States.   I. Smalley, Barbara Steinberg.   II. Title
    HD6054.4.U6G58   1995
    331.4′816584′00973—dc20

Book design by Giorgetta Bell McRee
Cover design by Rachel McClain
Cover photograph by Joanne Savio

ATTENTION:
SCHOOLS AND CORPORATIONS
WARNER books are available at quantity discounts with bulk purchase for educational, business, or sales promotional use. For information, please write to: SPECIAL SALES DEPARTMENT, WARNER BOOKS, 1271 AVENUE OF THE AMERICAS, NEW YORK, N.Y. 10020

Writing a book is never a solo project. Nor, as in our case, is it limited to the efforts of these two co-authors and soulmates.

We are grateful to the many women in management who graciously shared their stories and tips with us and made this book possible.

We are indebted to our editor, Joann Davis, for her keen insights and her firm belief in women's ability to succeed on their own terms. Heide Lange, our agent, played a key role in the development of this book. Her support and enthusiasm far exceeded her job description. And special thanks to Larry Kirshbaum, who clearly demonstrates that dolphins have no gender.

On a personal level, there were many who lent us support and friendship during the course of writing this book: Carol Deutsch, Bogie Ethridge, Avra Hawkins, Judy and Dan Hees, Marty Johnston, Krys Keller, Sharon Loef, Sue Rains, Ann Smith, Gail and Kim Stearman, and Dale Steinberg.

We are especially grateful to our families who encouraged and helped us to maintain a sense of balance in our lives throughout this project. Our heartfelt thanks to our husbands, Tom and Tim, and our children, Rusty and Max, Logan and Benjamin. And to our parents, Dolly and Bernie Brown and Zelda and M. K. Steinberg, for their unconditional love and guidance.

Companies Included in *Swim with the Dolphins*

ABC Television Network*
AT&T Business Communication Services
Aegir
Aldus Corporation
Avis
Christine Anderson & Associates
Anheuser-Busch
American Express Personal Financial Planning
Atlanta Committee for the Olympic Games
Atlanta Gelatin (General Foods)
Bank of America
Baptist Hospital of Miami
The Barter Corporation
Ben & Jerry's Homemade
Borden*
W.H. Brady Company
Browning Management
Butterick/Vogue
CBT Training Systems
Cape Cod Community Newspapers
The Carlson Group
Center for Creative Leadership

Central Fidelity Mortgage Corporation
Century Publishing
Chrysler Corporation
The Coca-Cola Company
Communication Seminars
Compaq Computer Corporation
Adolph Coors
Coors Ceramicon Designs
Corning Incorporated*
Detroit Receiving Hospital
Dow Corning
Dorsey Trailers*
Eastman Kodak Company
A.G. Edwards
EDS (Electronic Data Systems)
ESPN
Endymion Company
Epstein, Becker & Green*
Ewing and Thomas
Federal Express
Fel-Pro Incorporated
First of America Bank–Northeast Illinois*
First Republic Bancorp
The Fontayne Group

Ford Motor Co.
Gartner & Young
General Electric
Gerber Plumbing Fixtures
Great Plains Software
Hallmark Cards
Heinz U.S.A.
Hewitt Associates
Hewlett-Packard*
Hi-Fi Buys
Hoechst Celanese Corporation
Holiday Inn Worldwide
Honda Motor Co.
Intel
Jimmy Dean Foods
Johnson Wax
Kenetech Windpower, Inc.
Eastman Kodak Company
Land O'Lakes
Levi Strauss
Lotus Development Corporation
MECCO
MTV Networks
Mazda Motor of America*
Meredith Corporation
Meridian Travel
Metro Atlanta Rapid Transit
    Authority
I. Miller Shoes
Monsanto Company
Mrs. Fields Cookies
Nordstrom
Odetics
Ogilvy & Mather Worldwide
Phelps County Bank
Alain Pinel Realtors
Playfair

Preston Trucking
Procter & Gamble
The Prudential Referential
    Financial Services
Quad/Graphics
The Quarasan Group
Rosenbluth International
The St. Paul Companies*
Schering-Plough
Scios Nova
Shadco Advertising Specialties
Silicon Graphics
SmithKline Beecham
Southwest Airlines*
Super Wash
Systems Service Enterprises
Tellabs*
Tennant Company
Tenneco Minerals
Texaco
Texas Instruments Incorporated
3M (Minnesota Mining and Mfg.)
Toyota Motor Corp.
Turner Broadcasting System
USAir
U.S. Committee for UNICEF
U.S. West Communications
Viking Freight System
Wal-Mart
Walt Disney Imagineering*
Warnaco, Inc.
Westin Hotels and Resorts
Westin William Penn
Westinghouse Electric*
Xerox
YWCA of the USA
Zep Mfg. Co.

Denotes profile

Contents

Introduction

In 1982, Sharon gave herself an ultimatum. Twenty-nine at the time, she had worked her way up to director of human resources within a midsized corporation in three years' time. "But I wanted more," she says. Sharon's ultimate goal was to become a senior vice president of the company by the time she reached thirty-five. No woman had ever risen higher than associate vice president in Sharon's company. "Never mind that," she recalls thinking. "I'll be the first to crack that glass ceiling."

And so she was—at age thirty-seven. But she paid a hefty price. "I knocked myself out getting there," she admits. "The pressures to adopt a masculine style of management were constant and inescapable. And every step up the career ladder, they got worse. Nevertheless, if learning how to play hardball meant becoming a contortionist of sorts, I was game. I took all the projects that no one else wanted and rarely got credit for my achievements. I put in twice as many hours as my male counterparts, taking only two vacations in five years. And with my hard-nosed attitude, I alienated subordinates and colleagues alike.

"Now what have I got to show for it? On the positive side, lots of material things and a hefty savings account. But on the dark side, two children who ask 'Who are *you?*' whenever I spend a quiet weekend at home, and a husband who's on the verge of filing for divorce because he claims I'm not the 'loving, caring' person he married.

"If only I could turn back the clock . . ."

We Swam with Sharks

Sharon's ordeal is typical. It used to be that for women to penetrate the upper echelons of corporate America, they had to "fit in." More often than not, fitting in required an extensive makeover in style—from caring to tough, from motivating to controlling, from empowering to overpowering. For most women, it wasn't a comfortable fit—and no wonder! We couldn't swim with sharks because we're *not* sharks. We're different. We're more like dolphins.

Granted, some like Sharon found success. But emulating sharks also left the majority of women—Sharon included—feeling empty, lost, and out of sync.

Moreover, despite the fact that they had sacrificed their femininity to become "male clones," many of these women found themselves caught in a vicious Catch-22. If, like her male counterparts, an executive woman was aggressive, she was called "bitchy." If, like her male colleagues, a female manager was persistent, her subordinates labeled her a "nag." Straightforwardness in males translated into abrasiveness when it came from females. And if *he* was authoritative, no problem. But if *she* was, they called her "power mad."

We couldn't win!

The Times They Are A-Changin'

Fast forward to the 1990s, and a different picture is emerging. A new breed of women is succeeding on their own terms. Not only are they celebrating—and flaunting—their strengths, they are revitalizing the workforce. The deck has been shuffled, and feminine equals competence.

What gives? Unlike the feminist revolution of the 1970s, this movement is more of an *evolution*. It's come about slowly, but surely; quietly, but inevitably. It's not something any one person, or group of people, orchestrated. Rather, its catalyst has been a myriad of sweeping changes. And, thankfully, women just happen to be in the right place at the right time with the right skills to take advantage of it.

Money Talks

This evolution was sparked in large part by the economy. In the 1980s, the United States shifted from an industrial to an information society and joined the global economy. Stiff global competition has, in turn, changed the rules of business. Staying afloat in the 1990s means raising productivity. And that means motivating the workforce, something women have traditionally excelled at.

Today's workers have also changed. Better educated and more highly skilled than workers of past decades, they have higher expectations of the companies they work for. What's important to them is not the same as what was important to earlier generations of workers. Today's workers crave more than a paycheck. They want to be nurtured and empowered. They want to make a contribution. They want a voice.

This trend is proving to be particularly true for young employees fresh out of college. With them, automatic company loyalty is no longer a given. The company has to earn their loyalty. Moreover, a command-and-control style of management doesn't sit well with them.

Farewell to the Old Boy Network?

Tough economic times have driven corporate executives to listen to the needs and desires of today's workers. As a result, in corporations nationwide, hierarchies have now been flattened or molded into circles—with managers reaching out from the center instead of perched on top looking down. "Me" companies are becoming "We" companies, and "Do-it-my-way-or-else" attitudes are dissolving into "Let's-work-together" approaches. Bosses are now cheerleaders/coaches/facilitators/mentors/friends. And concerns for the bottom line now go hand in hand with concerns for people.

The good news: Being female is no longer a hindrance; it's an advantage. Because what today's corporations and workers need in order to succeed are the very characteristics that come naturally to women. Empowering and nurturing others. Showing appreciation. Sharing the workload. Building consensus.

A New Map for a New Era

Because the corporate waters have changed so dramatically over the last decade, the navigational maps that led to success in the 1980s are now obsolete. Seasoned executives like Sharon, for example, are increasingly finding themselves on unfamiliar turf. They climbed the corporate ladder at a time when success meant emulating men. Now they're discovering that to remain effective managers in the 1990s and beyond requires switching gears.

If, like Sharon, you're an experienced manager, this book will provide you with a blueprint for success in a changing work world. *Swim with the Dolphins* is based on interviews with over two hundred successful female managers working in corporate America today. We're going to introduce you to these women and show you how their management styles are not only right for the times, but feel right to women. *Swim with the Dolphins* also encourages you to reexamine your strengths and values and to take pride in who you are. And if, like Sharon, in your quest for success you were forced to compromise your femininity—and came up feeling lost, lonely, and disconnected—you will not only easily identify with this book, you will embrace its free-to-be-me philosophy and approach.

If you're a new manager, *Swim with the Dolphins* will help you navigate through the new corporate waters—guiding you through the safe areas as well as the danger zones. Throughout its fifteen chapters, we provide you with specific strategies and hands-on advice that will help make you, as a woman, a better manager—both for yourself and for your company in these changing times.

If you're an aspiring manager, you will also benefit from *Swim with the Dolphins*. We'll show you how to seize the moment and take advantage of women's ascending influence in corporate America.

Most importantly, however, we show you how to succeed in business without selling out.

Finally, it's important to note that the cataclysmic changes that have been shaking corporations across America for the last decade are still evolving. Which means that some companies, while aware of new and more effective styles of management, are clinging steadfastly to the old ways of doing things. In *Swim with the Dolphins*, we address this issue and arm those of you who work for these dinosaur companies with the skills you need to survive—and succeed.

In sum, this book shows *all* managers—from trainees to executives—how the dolphin approach applies to *all* managerial skills. Attracting, hiring, and keeping good employees. Building and coaching effective teams. Sharing the workload. Motivating and inspiring your staff. Managing conflict and difficult employees. Setting the stage for win-win negotiations. Bouncing back from adversity. Working smarter, not harder. Getting noticed and promoted. Overcoming obstacles that female managers still encounter in corporate America.

You will also learn how to apply the dolphin approach internally . . . to keep you from falling into the trap of perfectionism, to avoid the fear of failure—or success, to manage your time more efficiently, and to prevent stress from managing you.

Building Blocks of a New Archetype

Swim with the Dolphins shows you how to master these skills by introducing you to a new archetype. An archetype that taps and celebrates both male *and* female strengths and one that blends the best of *both* styles to form a coalition based on talent, mutual respect, and *human* traits and values.

In short, *Swim with the Dolphins* is a new model for managerial success that works because it's not necessarily gender specific. It's simply good management.

Enjoy!

—Connie Glaser and Barbara Steinberg Smalley

CHAPTER ONE

The Shark Attack Is Over

"The number one question children always ask me is, 'Can a dolphin beat up a shark?' And my answer is always, 'Yes. They do it all the time. And they do it by working together cooperatively.' "

—David Nathanson, Ph.D., a psychologist who uses dolphins to administer therapy to his handicapped patients in Grassy Key, Florida

Until recently, working as a manager in corporate America was like swimming in a pool of sharks. Command-and-control was the watchword of the day, and perched at—or circling near—the top of most hierarchies were the cold-blooded sharks. You know the types. Tough. Arrogant. Ruthless.

Maybe you even tried to mimic them—and if so, you weren't alone. Many women, in their efforts to climb the corporate ladder, attempted to emulate the sharks. But for most, it wasn't a comfortable fit. And with good reason. The mentality of sharks is simply foreign to the majority of women.

The Model Shark

Sharks are stern taskmasters who relish power. Their approach is strictly top-down, leaving no doubt whatsoever about who's in charge. They bark orders to their subordinates, expecting obedience and loyalty in return. And despite the fact that most who work for them loathe them, sharks could care less. Their concerns are with the bottom line, not with people.

In fact, because sharks think with their heads, and not their hearts, they are oblivious to employees' needs and desires. Rigid and hard-nosed, they are quick to criticize, but rarely take the time to offer positive feedback. And if *they* should be criticized? Close-minded sharks simply ignore it. After all, owning up to mistakes is not in their nature.

Not surprisingly, sharks prefer to act alone. Consequently, they are known for hoarding responsibilities and rarely delegating anything but the mundane tasks. Moreover, with their "Do-it-my-way-or-else" attitude, they are unresponsive to new ideas, and discount their employees' strengths.

A Changing Climate

Fortunately, this once prevailing climate in corporate America is rapidly changing. Stiff global competition has led to rampant downsizing and mega-mergers. As a result, savvy organizations are now realizing that a command-and-control, top-down management approach just doesn't cut it anymore. Instead, turning a profit in the 1990s and beyond hinges on companies making the most of the staff they have. And that requires motivating and empowering workers, not controlling and dominating them.

Bottom line: The shark population is dwindling. Not to say that some managers don't equate "lean" with "mean" and continue to cling to the old ways of getting things done. But for the most part, we are witnessing the extinction of the shark in corporate

America, and finding in its place a new archetype that more closely resembles the dolphin.

Enter the Dolphin

Supremely gifted motivators. Excellent communicators. Acutely intelligent. Warm-blooded and friendly. While researchers frequently use these characteristics to describe dolphins of the sea, they are traits that just as easily describe the new breed of managers succeeding in corporate America today.

In contrast to the sharks, dolphins prefer operating in webs rather than in hierarchies. They seek respect (rather than obedience) from subordinates and recognize that loyalty cannot be demanded; it must be earned. Like the sharks, dolphins are concerned with the bottom line, but they are equally focused on the people who work for them.

Dolphins are extremely intuitive and constantly tuned in to employees' needs and desires. As a result, they make decisions from the heart as well as the head. Firm, but fair, dolphins offer continuous feedback—both positive and negative—to subordinates. And should *they* be the objects of criticism, dolphins are quick to admit their mistakes—and to take any necessary steps to correct them.

Dolphins are comfortable with power, but rarely abuse it. They view themselves as "leaders" rather than "bosses." With their "Let's-work-together" attitudes, they eagerly share power with their subordinates, often using it to build on others' strengths. Dolphins also delegate tasks whenever feasible and continually welcome new and better ideas. Moreover, while they *prefer* to build consensus, dolphins are confident enough to act alone when necessary.

Dolphins Are Not Guppies

Granted, the dolphin approach to management is "softer" than the shark's. But dolphins are not to be confused with guppies, who misunderstand the concept of power and are uncomfortable exercising it. Or who are so intent on building consensus that they lack the confidence to make decisions on their own. To them, being popular is far more important than gaining respect. Consequently, guppies are typically pushovers and totally ineffective as managers.

Unlike the guppies, dolphins are strong and tough. Yet, unlike the sharks, dolphins are gentle and caring. And with their tough but caring ways, dolphins are not only revitalizing the workforce, they are changing the way America's companies do business.

A Sigh of Relief

In response, women in management who, for years, have revolted against the shark mentality are breathing a collective sigh of relief. After all, the shark's practices and habits have always felt foreign to them. Moreover, the traits of this evolving new management approach are far more compatible with women's styles. The pressure is off to squeeze into the ill-fitting mold of a shark. And with the green light to do what comes naturally, women are uniquely positioned to change the managerial icon in the 1990s—and beyond.

New Men with New Attitudes

Of course, dolphins are not exclusively female. Many male managers, equally disillusioned with the status quo, are also relieved to be granted "permission" to exhibit a leadership style that is less tough and more caring. This is particularly true for younger men, who have graduated from college within the last decade—at a time when men and women were equals. After all, what they want is the same thing women want: challenging and satisfying jobs *as well as* time to spend with their families.

One recent survey by Yankelovich (a market research firm), for example, reported that an increasing number of men were refusing corporate transfers in order to have more time for themselves and their families. In another survey, this one involving four hundred economics students at Stanford University, both women *and* men rated a happy marriage as more important than a successful career for attaining "the good life." So, in essence, these "new" men have likely helped to reinforce a more caring management style by demonstrating to their superiors a changing set of priorities and lack of interest in joining the rat race.

Nevertheless women are the chief beneficiaries of this changing environment, because the very characteristics that are in demand in corporate America today come more naturally to them. And just as we have tried to win through intimidation—and *only* because that has been the corporate axiom of decades past—maybe sharks can now learn a thing or two from us.

At last, women can acknowledge the fact that we *are* different, because different is good. Finally, we have no reason to hide our softer side for fear of being perceived as weak and powerless. And finally, the corporate climate is just right for us to make it on our *own* terms.

CHAPTER TWO

Steel and Soul: Power Tools of Dolphins

PROFILE

GRACE PASTIAK
DIRECTOR, NEW BUSINESS DEVELOPMENT
TELLABS
LISLE, ILLINOIS

*"I try to get people to connect with what they're doing
and where they are in the world. It's really important
to me to give people the opportunity to excel."*

Her subordinates call her "Amazing Grace"—and with good reason. A champion of worker empowerment, Grace Pastiak, Director of New Business Development at Tellabs, firmly believes that "the old practice of beating on people to get things done doesn't work, and that people do a far better job when they are happy about what they are doing."

A shining example of the new management paradigm, Pastiak exudes a "Let's-make-it-happen" spirit, which has endeared her to superiors and subordinates alike. "Instead of giving directions, Grace asks for input and lets the team help make decisions," reports one employee.

Case in point: In the fall of 1991, Tellabs, which designs, manu-
factures, and markets sophisticated telecommunications equipment, received an important order that needed to be completed
by year's end. Rather than post overtime notices—as would happen in most factories—Pastiak, then Director of Manufacturing,
called a meeting of the plant's workers. "I knew it was getting into
the holiday season and many of the people would have family
demands," she recalls. "So I gave them choices. I said we could
tell marketing that we could fill only half the order before the
deadline. I offered to bring in contract labor or to shift some
production outside. I also told them that I thought *they* should
make the decision. So we talked about it, and they said, 'Go for
it!' "

It figures that Pastiak would have an undergraduate degree in
applied behavioral science. Her people skills are top-notch, and
despite the fact that she was the first professional staff woman
ever to be hired by Tellabs, she has never felt—and *still* does not
feel—like a token. "I've never thought of myself as being a woman
at Tellabs, except for about fifteen minutes last year, when I was
asked to give a short presentation on being a woman at Tellabs,"
she quips.

When Pastiak started out at Tellabs, in 1979, she says the company was "pretty much the same as other American companies,
in that we asked our employees to come to work and do the job.
But what we really meant was, 'Come to work, sit on the line,
put parts in, and look busy anytime your supervisor walks by.' "
However, once Tellabs began embracing the concept of employee
empowerment—a movement Pastiak helped spearhead—that
message changed. "The new message we began sending was, 'Your
viewpoint is important,' " she says. "In fact, we began to look at
employees in terms of their whole lives and decided, 'These people
have all kinds of leadership responsibilities *outside* of the corporation. They go home at night and are deacons of their churches and
presidents of their PTAs. They also have tremendous problem-
solving skills. Why don't we give them the opportunity to use those
talents *inside* the corporation?' "

In 1986, Tellabs decided to do just that by promoting Pastiak and challenging her to implement a just-in-time (JIT) manufacturing program. JIT involves streamlining the manufacturing operations in a way that improves employee productivity and product quality. "With JIT, the company receives materials just in time, and we deliver products just in time. In essence, *everything* happens just in time," Pastiak explains.

When she was first given this assignment, the company's goal was to convert 10 percent of Tellabs's manufacturing facility to JIT by way of a pilot program involving a dozen employees. If the pilot went well, the company's master plan was to eventually convert the entire Tellabs factory to JIT. "The twelve employees chosen for the first pilot were initially skeptical," Pastiak recalls. "They didn't know a whole lot about the process, and frankly neither did I. But once we cut over our first pilot, we literally changed the way we manufactured. We went from assembling a product in twenty days to doing it in six and a half hours! It was like, 'My God! Let's never manufacture the old way again!' "

The dramatic results of Pastiak's first pilot created an interesting cultural phenomenon. "People were afraid to be involved in the first pilot; then, when we began cutting over another pilot every sixty days, people were afraid to be asked *last*—kind of like the old softball game. And what happened was, it gave us a tremendous momentum in the factory."

Along with the implementation of the JIT philosophy at Tellabs came the introduction of a total quality management program designed to give employees the tools they needed to take an active role in achieving the goals of JIT. "This program is basically a team approach to problem-solving," Pastiak explains, "and everyone in the company—from top management on down—takes classes in it."

In fact, Pastiak herself teaches the total quality management problem-solving classes at Tellabs. While many managers would eschew this responsibility, offering excuses from "I'm too busy" to "It's not my job," Pastiak feels that teaching these classes sends a critical message to her employees. "I'm modeling that this is important," she says. "Basically I tell my student-employees, 'I don't have someone from the training department doing this. I'm doing this myself—not only because I want to make sure that you have these skills, but also because I'm trusting *you* to run the business.' "

Pastiak says that the benefits she enjoys from teaching more than make up for her investment of time. "The role of educating employees is often delegated to someone who doesn't have the authority to carry out the new procedures. But whenever the boss leads, explaining *why* something is important and what must be accomplished, successful change follows. Moreover, before I started teaching total quality management, I probably spent 80 percent of my time running the business, and 20 percent coaching. Once I started teaching, however, 80 percent of my time was spent teaching, 20 percent was spent running the business, and the business was running *better* because people realized that I was holding them accountable."

Tangible results after implementing JIT and the total quality management program were equally dramatic. Pastiak and her teams began meeting production targets 98 percent of the time, compared to an industry standard of about 90 percent. Moreover, employee suggestions for solving problems had soon saved the company over $160,000.

Tellabs's original goal was to convert 10 percent of the factory to JIT between June and December of 1986. In fact, 55 percent was converted within that six-month period, and by the end of ten months the entire manufacturing facility was converted. "And not because we were on any kind of let's-get-this-done kick, but because once your eyes were open to what waste was, you couldn't *stand* it. It was like, 'Wait a minute. Over here, I'm manufacturing a product start to finish in a day; whereas just five feet away, it's taking me fourteen weeks. What's wrong with this picture?' "

Not surprisingly, the two programs quickly spread to other units and departments at Tellabs. "When we started working through the system in manufacturing, it exposed problems with purchasing, which forced us to go out and work with our vendors. It also exposed problems with our internal sales system—how we took sales orders from customers. Consequently, when we finished with manufacturing, we began making the same changes to inside sales, product control, and forecasting. And again, we saw the same kind of gain. Instead of reducing inventory like we had done in the factory, we reduced the time it took to process an order, which then reduced more inventory in manufacturing. At the same time, we increased the skills of all the workers in each of these three areas, because now they were cross-functional and could understand the bigger picture."

These days, employees at Tellabs report that their work is exciting, that every day brings a new challenge. Morale has skyrocketed. So have levels of productivity and feelings of loyalty to the company. Employees are also more open with their feelings. "Everyone puts their two cents in now, because they know they will be listened to," remarks one employee. And because they're calling the shots, Tellabs employees take more responsibility for their work and feel important to the company.

Pastiak has since moved up to a new position where she negotiates contracts for new business development, a responsibility that she says reveals her tougher side. "In my efforts to carve out the best deal possible for Tellabs, I've been criticized by my opponents for driving a hard deal. But that's my job."

Pastiak's office has no walls and no doors—by choice. It's a U-shaped marketing and engineering environment, and because it lacks doors and windows, Pastiak often jokes that she has the largest office in the company. But how does she get any work done? "Quickly!" she laughs. "In this kind of environment, you solve problems instantly. We have a big round table in the center, so when there's an issue or problem that needs to be discussed, we convene right there and take care of it immediately. Otherwise, you learn to focus at your table when you need to be focused."

Focused. Disciplined. Organized. Determined. Perhaps that's why someone once called Pastiak an iron butterfly. "I think that sometimes people perceive you as tough when you're consistent with one view," she says. "My style has always been, 'We *are* going to do this. Now, if you have a better idea, I'm willing to listen. But if you don't, move over. Because I've got to get this done.' "

Pastiak says she doesn't consider herself an iron butterfly, but also doesn't think that men get the same kind of backlash for getting things done as women do. Nor does she offer any excuses or apologies for her just-do-it style. "I'm definitely action-oriented," she admits. "My attitude is, 'Okay, let's try it.' I'm *not* going to plan for six years and then do it. My philosophy is, the more action you take the more chances you have to get things right."

• • •

Across the nation, women like Grace Pastiak are gaining clout as effective leaders and managers. They are making their mark not by adopting a command-and-control style of management, but by treating employees as their most precious resource. Their priorities lie in creating effective and supportive environments where workers feel inspired and empowered to do their best.

Unlike many of their female predecessors, these women don't feel the need to masquerade as men. But neither is their management style exclusively female. Recognizing that managing people is a science as well as an art, these leaders demonstrate a repertoire of skills. Like dolphins, they are decisive, yet flexible. Self-confident, yet empowering. Firm, yet fair. Strong, yet compassionate. In short, they are tough enough to be caring, yet caring enough to be tough.

Dolphins: The Balanced Management Style

The Shark	The Guppy	The Dolphin
Lacks compassion; often arrogant; stern taskmaster	Takes on role of social worker; strives to be everyone's friend	Compassionate; treats subordinates with respect
Prefers operating in hierarchies	Uncomfortable with hierarchies	Prefers operating in webs
Aloof; rarely pitches in; isolates self in office	Goes overboard pitching in	Highly visible; hands-on; pitches in when necessary
Task-oriented	People-oriented	Task- *and* people-oriented

The Shark	The Guppy	The Dolphin
Analytical	Expressive; sometimes overly so	Analytical *and* expressive
Rarely delegates	Gives away too much responsibility	Delegates whenever feasible
Emphasis on competition	Eschews competition	Emphasis on cooperation
Unresponsive to new ideas	Overly accommodating	Welcomes new ideas
Fosters dependency in subordinates	Likes to be one of the group	Fosters independence in subordinates
Concerned primarily with the bottom line	Concerned primarily with people	Concerned with bottom line, but focused on company's people
Rational	Intuitive	Rational and intuitive
Rigid; no-nonsense	Uses self-deprecating humor	Uses humor when appropriate
Relishes power; sometimes abuses it	Uncomfortable with power; misunderstands it	Comfortable with power; uses it to accomplish tasks
Discounts employees' strengths	Overly dependent upon employees' strengths	Builds upon employees' strengths
Seeks obedience	Seeks popularity	Seeks respect
Prefers to act alone	Consensus-builder; rarely acts alone	Prefers consensus-building, but acts alone when necessary
Critical; hard-nosed; abrasive	Likes to give compliments; is rarely critical	Straightforward; firm but fair
Hidden agenda/ vision	Agenda/vision unclear	Shares agenda/ vision
Moody, unpredictable	Almost always cheerful	Consistent

The Shark	The Guppy	The Dolphin
Overconfident	Lacks confidence	Confident
Coldhearted	Softhearted	Objective, sensitive, caring
Oblivious to employees' needs, desires	Tends to give in to employees' needs, desires	Tuned in to employees' needs, desires
Rarely offers feedback; quick to criticize	Reluctant to give negative feedback	Offers continuous feedback, both positive and negative
Manipulative	Overly accommodating	Open, honest
Makes decisions from head	Makes decisions from heart	Makes decisions from head and heart
Close-minded; believes "Do it my way or else"	Believes "All for one, and one for all"	Open-minded; believes "We can do it working together"
Ignores criticism; rarely admits mistakes	Takes criticism personally	Open to criticism; admits mistakes and takes steps to correct them
Intimidates employees	Bends over backward to keep everyone happy	Inspires employees
Expects loyalty from subordinates	Hopes for loyalty	Recognizes loyalty must be earned
Aggressive	Passive	Assertive
Thinks of self as the "boss"	Thinks of self as a "friend"	Thinks of self as a "leader"

In essence, swimming with dolphins is a blending of styles (see chart, "Dolphins: The Balanced Management Style," beginning on page 17), a balance that enables managers to respond more effectively to a wide variety of situations. It takes the best of the old—and traditionally male—management practices and instills some new—and traditionally female—ones to meet the needs and demands of today's corporations and workers. It allows managers to lead with their heads as well as their hearts. Best of all, it provides both men *and* women the opportunity to move beyond the expectations and constraints of sex role stereotypes. Like the misconception that women, like guppies, have no clout or tend to be indecisive. Or the notion that men are like sharks: insensitive, lacking compassion, and obsessed with power.

The Leadership Equation of the Future

It's true that dolphins are more likely than sharks to adopt a leadership style that encourages employee participation, involves sharing power and information, and relies on strong interpersonal skills. But to label these qualities exclusively female would be a mistake. In fact, according to recent research, the number of male managers who have incorporated such "caring" characteristics in their leadership styles is burgeoning. James Autry, former president of Meredith Corporation, is a good example. In his book *Love and Profit: The Art of Caring Leadership*, Autry explains how and why he chose to abandon a traditional management approach in favor of a more caring style.

"I flew jet fighters in the Air Force for four years back in the 1950s," he writes. "I was as macho as anyone who ever drew a breath. I came into business thinking command and control was the only way to get the job done. But what I've come to realize, after 29 years of management, is that what works most often is what is most responsive to people's needs and gives them the freedom to make choices."

Autry admits that through the years he has been regarded with skepticism by colleagues for his dolphin-like management style. But in response he has simply pointed to the numbers. "When I took over this magazine group, we had four magazines; now we have 17. We grew from $150 million in revenues to $747 million today. We have low turnover, high morale, and good performance. My credibility has silenced most of the critics."

Nor should leadership qualities like being dominating, authoritative, competitive, and aggressive be considered exclusively male. We have all worked for, or alongside, female managers who adhere to the traditional corporate model and who prefer this sharklike style of management.

But from our own experience working with managers, as well as numerous and extensive interviews we conducted to write this book, truly successful managers appear to mix and match a repertoire of styles, depending on what is most appropriate for a given situation or employee. Some tasks, for example, call for toughness. Balancing a budget. Freezing employee pay raises. Meeting deadlines. But toughness alone won't work. Without the respect and cooperation of the people who work for them, managers can easily overshoot a budget, face massive turnovers, and miss important deadlines.

Therein lies the beauty of the dolphin approach. It's flexible. It's comfortable. It's personalized. It's tough *as well as* caring. And it's as individualized as the managers who endorse it.

In fact, *because* this tough and caring approach encourages women to succeed on their own terms, managers who swim with dolphins are as different as they are similar. Most, however, appear to share certain characteristics and rely on specific tools, both to achieve their own personal goals and to create goal-driven environments for their subordinates.

Positive Attitude

Dolphins prefer to lead by example. Recognizing that employees tend to mirror their manager's attitudes, they demonstrate enthusiasm and a strong work ethic. These managers are also well aware that they cannot control their subordinates. At best, they can inspire and influence them—with a can-do attitude that is, hopefully, contagious.

Solid Job Knowledge

Dolphins make it a point to know not only what is expected of them and their divisions or departments, but to know the exact job requirements of each person working for them. They also go out of their way to master their corporate culture—how things get accomplished in their companies, and who *really* counts in the decision-making process.

A Personal Touch

In *The 100 Best Companies to Work for in America*, Robert Levering and Milton Moskowitz say that one of the major factors on their list of twelve themes for successful companies is that the excellent ones "make people feel part of a team . . . or a family." Yet in a recent study by the Conference Board, a New York–based research organization, more than half of the 216 companies surveyed characterized their relationship with employees as a business-financial arrangement rather than a close, family one. Which, according to many of the managers we spoke to, may be exactly what's wrong with much of corporate America today.

Management is a people business, and savvy managers typically believe that relationships between supervisors and their employees can be positive and friendly, yet still remain professional. So while they are sticklers when it comes to getting the job done, dolphins also boast a personal touch. They realize that showing concern for those who work for them—not like social workers, mother hens, or best buddies, but by treating people with respect—can ultimately make or break their careers.

Harriet Gerber Lewis, Chairman of the Board of Gerber Plumbing Fixtures in Chicago, is a perfect example. When her father died, Lewis took the helm of his multimillion-dollar company and became the nation's first female CEO in the plumbing industry. Sharing responsibilities with her brother and husband, this mother and homemaker managed to steer the manufacturing company through decades of financial and marketing growth. Since 1953, the company's sales volume has increased tenfold—from $7.5 million to approximately $90 million at the close of 1993. Yet despite her—and the company's—success, Lewis, now seventy-four, still talks about the company as if it were a big family rather than a big business.

"I'm a real people person, and relationships are important to me," she says. "The best thing you can say about the Gerber/Lewis Family is that we work together as a family, and everybody who works for us is part of the family."

Described by colleagues and subordinates alike as "a rare combination of compassion and competence," Lewis prefers a first-name relationship with employees and business associates. And her personal touch works. "Many of the company's nine hundred employees have spent their entire careers at Gerber, and many others represent second or even third generations as members of our own extended 'family,'" she reports.

Generosity

What do today's workers crave most? Many managers assume "more money" and "better benefits." But according to scores of surveys, topping most employee wish lists is "information-sharing." In a Harris poll, for example, 40 percent of respondents indicated that information-sharing was important to them. Yet only 33 percent felt it was happening on their jobs.

Sharks are typically reluctant to share too much information, for fear they will lose power. But, as Diane Tracy suggests in her book *10 Steps to Empowerment: A Common-Sense Guide to Managing People*, reluctance to share information is usually a sign of insecurity. "The insecure manager feels that he must 'have something over' the people who work for him, and all too often that something is valuable information that the people need to do the job."

Dolphins, however, recognize that sharing information not only creates loyalty among subordinates, it sends them a powerful message: "I believe in you and your abilities and will do all I can to help you do your job well." Besides, withholding information that employees need to achieve company goals is self-defeating.

Laura Martin, Director of Administrative Systems for Westin Hotels and Resorts, agrees. "Sharing information enhances employees' sense of being part of the team. I'm amazed how often managers just don't think to pass on information that would truly be beneficial to their subordinates because they are only focused on 'who needs to know,' " she says. "This is not only inefficient, it is also demoralizing and can erode an employee's sense of belonging and commitment."

Dolphins are equally generous at sharing power by delegating tasks and authority and including employees in the decision-making process whenever feasible. Doing this, they believe, not only boosts subordinates' self-confidence, it gives employees an opportunity to expand their skills and better understand the organization as a whole. It also makes jobs more satisfying and increases workers' commitment to the organization's goals.

Karyn Marasco, General Manager for the Westin William Penn in Pittsburgh, says, "I usually try to involve as many people as I can in the decision-making process. I find that it is far easier to have them buy in to and take ownership of a decision they believe is best for the organization than it is to make a command decision or bulldoze them into accepting what *I* want."

But dolphins share more than information and power. They share glory as well. When a job well done receives accolades from above, they are quick to give credit where credit is due. They know that recognizing good work spurs employees to do even better work. "I have an exhibit coordinator who recently put together a huge interactive project," says Carole Kitchens, Manager of Business Services for the Sunette Division of Hoechst Celanese Corporation. "It was a project that required months of hard work, and I just gave it to her and let her go. I told her I'd be there if she needed me, but otherwise it was her project. When she presented it, everyone applauded, and I just stepped back and let her bask in all the glory." After the presentation, Kitchens says she received several congratulatory notes from higher-ups. "Even then, I made sure that my employee got full recognition by telling my superiors who was responsible for the project," she adds.

In fact, dolphins are typically emphatic about giving feedback, both positive and negative. They know that keeping employees in the dark regarding their progress breeds insecurity or, worse, apathy. "The best motivator of all is direct one-on-one feedback," believes Christine Anderson, President of Christine Anderson & Associates, a public relations firm in Los Angeles. "Far too many employers forget to congratulate success and, instead, reprimand mistakes. I always thank my employees for a job well done as soon as I can."

A Sense of Direction

In a survey conducted by *Working Woman* magazine, more than half (58 percent) of the 7,800 respondents complained that management did a poor job of setting goals. Not dolphins, who tend to be visionaries. They set clear goals—both for themselves and their subordinates—and do everything in their power to make sure that everyone is aware of those goals.

Suzanne F. Jenniches is a good example. In 1990, when top management at Westinghouse Electric formed its Imaging and Data Systems Division, Jenniches, a seventeen-year veteran at Westinghouse, was tapped to direct the new division. One of her first goals was to develop and communicate her vision of where she wanted to lead the new division's workforce. "One problem I wanted to avoid was making the vision too nebulous," she says. "If it was too broad and sweeping, employees might understand it with their hearts, perhaps, but not their heads. What we needed was to have a vision that was communicated so that each individual could see how he or she could contribute and become involved in that vision. I worked hard at breaking down the vision for individual 'ownership' and at empowering individual employees to take responsibility for their actions and their contributions to the overall success of the company."

At Compaq Computer Corporation, Karen Walker, Vice President of Operating Services, took the process a step further by including her subordinates in the vision-setting process. "A couple of years ago, I took my staff—mostly architects and engineers—off-site and invited a human resources specialist to join us," she says. "We put a poster on the wall, gave everyone a marker, and asked them to draw where we were going to be in ten years. Then we asked one of our architects and one of our engineers to turn those drawings into words, and they did. Next, I took what they had come up with back to my department, where I pitched it to smaller groups and got feedback. I said, 'Here's where we think we're going. What would you like to add? What doesn't work for you?' Then I took that feedback and turned it into a vision statement and a vision poster. Everyone now has a copy of that poster, which we review every year. And since our vision is something *everyone* had a hand in creating, everyone here is working for the same goals."

Dolphins also provide subordinates with the training and knowledge they need to fulfill these visions. They recognize that a good training program requires a substantial investment of time and money, but they also realize that a good training program *saves* them substantial time and money in the long run. Well-trained employees not only require less supervision, they also give better customer service and are more loyal to their organizations.

Consistency

Surveys of employees show that even when subordinates are privy to the company's goals and priorities, these seem to change frequently. "Goal setting changes on a daily basis," complained one respondent in the *Working Woman* survey. "We've become 'reactive.' And 'reactive' probably isn't as productive as it could be."

Ditto said a respondent in another similar survey: "My boss is like a pancake. She flip-flops back and forth."

Employees also complain that there is frequently a delay in communicating priority changes to the workforce, which they find particularly frustrating.

Dolphins strive for consistency and avoid changing goals and priorities without good reason. Moreover, when circumstances do dictate changes, these managers make sure everyone is aware of them—as well as the reasons behind them—as promptly as possible.

Flexibility/Adaptability

In her book *Mary Kay Ash on People Management*, Ash tells a story of shifting a member of her public relations staff to a new position when after two years of trying the employee could not address large audiences. "I will not discard an employee as if she were yesterday's newspaper," Ash writes. "I would rather err to the 'people side' than err to the 'hard-core business side' of this issue."

Dolphins always keep a keen eye on the bottom line, but they also make it a habit to be flexible when it comes to making people decisions. Individual workers have different needs, and when managers can accommodate these needs, it will almost always result in a more productive workforce. Says Laura Martin of Westin Hotels and Resorts, "I make it a point to keep up with the details of people's lives that are important to them. I can be a more effective manager if my employees and I can talk candidly about the personal toll of an illness of their child or parent. Then we can plan together how that will impact their work or work schedule."

A manager's flexible attitude can also reap rewards from workers down the line—when circumstances dictate that a manager adopt a more rigid approach. As Ash points out, "If you're good to your staff when things are going well, they'll rally when times go bad."

Dolphins also possess flexible communication styles. They are well aware that achieving desired results in such areas as problem-solving, motivating, and negotiating depends not on communicating and acting *one* right way, but on adopting a managerial style that best suits the situation and the person they are dealing with.

In her best-seller *You Just Don't Understand: Women and Men in Conversation*, Deborah Tannen confirms this notion. "The most important weapon a woman has in her arsenal is her own perceptiveness about other people and styles. If she can understand who the boss or subordinate is in terms of his or her own styles, she'll have a much better chance of getting what she wants. It's not a matter of finding the one right way to behave. Anyone who wants anything in any kind of situation has to be flexible."

Open-mindedness

Sharks typically think they have all the answers—or at least they like for their employees to assume that they do. Dolphins, on the other hand, are far less presumptuous. In fact, they are always looking for ways to improve and to learn from others. And whereas sharks rarely admit they don't know something—for fear they'll be viewed as less powerful—dolphins actively seek advice and help. They are also open to criticism, quick to admit mistakes, and equally quick to take steps to correct—and learn from—their errors.

Trustworthiness/Reliability

Trust is important to dolphins. They know that trusting workers not only breeds confidence and self-esteem, it often results in higher levels of productivity. As Diane Tracy points out in *10 Steps to Empowerment,* when workers feel trusted, they are more likely to focus all of their efforts on completing the tasks at hand and less likely to worry about justifying their actions.

On the flip side, dolphins know that lack of trust fills subordinates with anxiety and self-doubt, often causing them to become sneaky and manipulative. "Managers who are basically untrusting usually make snap judgments based on outward appearances. They don't take the time to gather the facts and objectively evaluate situations," Tracy adds. "Consequently, the people who work for them spend enormous amounts of time and energy manipulating outward appearances, since that's all that matters."

By the same token, these dolphins strive to *earn* subordinates' trust—by honoring commitments and delivering on promises, regardless of how small. They also make it a point to be there for their employees when it counts—always ready and willing to go the extra mile to support them in terms of higher pay, better benefits, and greater visibility.

Firmness/Decisiveness

According to stereotype, female managers are often wishy-washy and have a tough time making decisions on their own, particularly unpopular ones. Not the managers we encountered! While many *preferred* presenting problems to their employees and reaching consensus on a solution, they also acknowledged that taking such steps can sometimes be cumbersome and often impossible due to time constraints. Moreover, in such instances, none appeared to be reluctant to make decisions on her own or to go against the will of the majority when necessary.

A Sense of Humor

Dolphins typically take their jobs seriously but themselves lightly by incorporating a sense of humor into their management style. They believe that humor not only fosters good relationships with those they direct, but also motivates employees to be more productive. They also recognize that humor and creativity go hand in hand, and that sharing a laugh together from time to time improves communication and morale.

"Creating an environment where people can have fun is important," believes Candy Obourn, Vice President and Director of Information Systems and Business Processes at Eastman Kodak Company. "We are currently having budget reviews with soft-tipped dart guns, cans of bullshit repellent, and other assorted useful tools."

Randi S. Brill, President and owner of the Quarasan Group, which develops textbooks for educational publishers, also finds humor to be one of the most useful tools in her workplace. "This is a high-pressure industry," says Brill. "Humor can be a great buffer and an important release. I *like* humor, so I hire humor."

Strength/Confidence

According to stereotype, when the going gets tough, female managers tend to fall apart. Yet in our research we couldn't find a shred of evidence to support this notion. On the contrary, we found the managers we interviewed to be exceptionally strong and confident, regardless of the obstacles they faced.

One case in point is Nancy Singer, President and CEO of First of America Bank–Northeast Illinois, headquartered in Libertyville. From 1989 through 1991, when Singer merged the five banks in her holding company into one large bank, she took charge of the transition, meeting with each of the five CEOs, five senior loan officers, "five of almost everything," she recalls. "There could be only one incumbent in each category, so I sat down with each person, all within a single four-or five-hour period. We talked about what they might do, where they would fit. I had a memo out the same day so everybody would know what was going on." Singer's honest and up-front approach, she believes, "cut off the grapevine. Those meetings also cut out insecurity and uncertainty—the two elements of change," she adds. As a result, Singer proudly reports that not a single person left during the two-and-a-half-year merger.

The practices and philosophies of the managers we interviewed defied another stereotype as well: that female managers are "push-overs." On the contrary, almost none of the managers we spoke with seemed fearful of taking an unpopular stand *or* to be held accountable for the results of their decisions—right or wrong.

Visibility/Accessibility

"My door is open . . . so is my mind" read the hand-lettered sign posted on the door of one manager we interviewed. "An open-door policy can be very disruptive," she acknowledges, "but I believe its advantages far outweigh its risks. Ultimately, it makes my division more productive because people don't waste time sitting around waiting for my input before proceeding with their work." Most of the managers we interviewed echoed this manager's thoughts: that accessibility, while time-consuming, should be a priority—even if it means making personal sacrifices.

In addition to being accessible, dolphins are also highly visible, making daily contact with as many employees as possible. Tommye Jo Daves, a plant manager for Levi Strauss & Co., and one of just a handful of female managers in her company and her industry, says, "Since most of the best ideas come from employees on the floor, I try to get out into the plant as much as I can every week to talk about whatever ideas and concerns people might have."

And Katherine August, Executive Vice President of First Republic Bancorp in San Francisco, recommends: "Spend as much time as you can with the people in your organization, getting to know them and making them feel good. One cannot do too much of this. People have to like you and respect you. They have to think you're fair and feel comfortable with you." August believes that sometimes women are so focused on mastering and demonstrating competency that they may overlook these important interactions. "They demonstrate competency, which is necessary but not sufficient. So show up for office parties, go out to lunch, and stop by and chat."

According to psychologist Judith Komaki, Ph.D., of New York City's Baruch College, this kind of visibility makes managers more effective leaders. In her extensive studies focusing on leaders' abilities to maintain high-quality worker output, Komaki found that managers who monitored their employees most consistently were rated highest by their superiors. "A major complaint of employees is that bosses make judgments without adequate information about what the employees are doing," Komaki says.

A number of surveys also show that employees prefer bosses who wander around and who are concerned about subordinates' personal lives, so long as they don't pry or invade an employee's privacy.

Motivating

Savvy managers recognize that motivation to do a good job is not something they can instill in their employees; rather, it must come from within an individual. What managers *can* do, however, is set the stage for self-motivation by providing a positive climate and conducive stimuli. They can also spur self-motivation by recognizing and building upon employees' strengths, by providing constant encouragement, proper training and incentives, and by always looking for ways to make subordinates' jobs more challenging and interesting.

Susan Groenwald, President of the Barter Corporation, the Midwest's largest business-to-business trade exchange, believes that recognition for doing a good job can be extremely motivating, and that recognition *and cash* for doing a good job can be even more motivating. Groenwald recently purchased a pull-tab board and launched an incentive program to reward trade brokers who have day-to-day contact with Barter's member companies. When pulled, tabs on the board reveal instant $5, $10, or $20 bonuses. Employees who fulfill the company's service pledge, as well as those who meet their weekly sales goals, have the opportunity to select one of the mystery tabs. Each month, all of the tab-pullers from the previous four weeks participate in a $250 grand prize drawing.

"Our brokers are the first line of contact for our member companies," says Groenwald. "If *they* do well, *we* do well, so it makes sense to encourage good service and to express our appreciation for their good work."

The Communication Connection

Nearly all of these "power tools" rely on strong communication skills, something worker surveys repeatedly claim that managers lack. In a 1992 survey conducted by *Industry Week*, less than half (46 percent) of the respondents said their bosses were good listeners. And a whopping 55 percent complained that their supervisors were "poor" or "average" in providing direction, in their knowledge of subordinates' jobs, and at communicating goals.

Happy Campers:
The Dolphin Approach Makes Sense

A different—and prettier—picture emerges from a six-month study conducted by *Inc.* magazine in conjunction with the Hay Group. This survey of the Inc. 500—the fastest growing small and midsized private companies in America—included a sample size of 2,800 employees. Despite the fact that their pay and benefits lagged well behind those employed by publicly held corporations, Inc. 500 employees were found to be more satisfied with their jobs and to have more respect for their companies.

Their sources of satisfaction? Challenging jobs. A sense of accomplishment. Companies that valued initiative and ideas. Being treated with respect.

Michael Cooper, president of the Hay Group's Research Division, commented, "These companies are not successful simply because they have a good product or a brilliant founder, but because they have managed their people in ways that keep their involvement and sense of partnership high. The positive attitudes of the Inc. 500 employees give them a great competitive edge. If I were a fortune 500 CEO, I'd be worried."

The Dolphin Approach Makes Cents

Since the United States joined the global economy, many Fortune 500 CEOs *are* worried about increased competition. As a result, they have had little choice but to focus on increasing productivity. That, of course, requires hiring the best and brightest managers—regardless of gender. But as Jerry R. Junkins, Chairman, President, and CEO of Texas Instruments Incorporated, writes in *21st Century Leadership: Dialogues with 100 Top Leaders*, "It's important to realize right now that only 15 percent of the incoming work force in the year 2000 will be white males; the balance will be females and minorities. Women are already beginning to fill key leadership positions in computer science, human resources, financial markets, sales and many other fields. So the raw material for leadership exists. Yet far more women and minority leaders will have to be developed. And we'd better begin right away to be prepared for the next century."

Increasing productivity also requires involving and motivating the workforce. Which in turn requires hiring—and promoting— managers who are capable of inspiring and influencing employees, who treat workers as people, not performers, and who are willing to share the power and the glory.

General Electric is a good example of a company doing that. In the 1980s, Jack Welch, CEO of G.E., earned the nickname "Neutron Jack" after closing plants and laying off nearly 100,000 employees. But in one of the company's recent annual reports, Welch wrote, "In an environment where we must have every good idea from every man and woman in the organization, we cannot afford management styles that suppress and intimidate."

Not to say that this shift in preference for tough and caring managers is a move CEOs like Welch personally relish. On the contrary, when so many corporations turn about-face, as G.E. has done, it's strictly a bottom-line strategy. And one that seems to be working. In an interview with *Working Woman* magazine, Welch confessed, "To be open to ideas from anywhere and empower people isn't easy at first if you've been accustomed to another way of doing business. But the results [such as increased worker creativity] make it addictive."

Women in Power: All the Right Stuff

As American corporations reinvent themselves, many believe that there's never been a better time for women to make their mark as managers. Steven Berglas, a Harvard Medical School psychologist, concurs: "In an era when the need to motivate is so important, women will do better because they are nurturers and value-driven. And at a time when the corporation needs restructuring, women will be able to do so because they operate in webs rather than pyramid-shaped hierarchies."

Women also appear to have an advantage over men because they value relationships and are far more likely to show compassion toward those who work for them. In their book *The Healing Manager: How to Build Quality Relationships and Productive Cultures at Work*, clinical psychologist William Lundin and his wife, Kathleen, argue that to survive and thrive in the 1990s, corporations must shift their thinking from a "no-brainer to a learning environment." How? By creating what the authors call TQR—total quality relationships—in the workplace. "What you feel about your company depends on where you are, how you feel about yourself, and how you are being treated," the authors write. And American workers, for the most part, they add, are being killed emotionally, spiritually, and intellectually by "friendly fire"—in the form of endless attempts to restructure, reorganize, and downsize.

Critics, on the other hand, argue that in times of organizational crisis, participative management is not the answer. What's needed instead, they insist, are managers who are in control, and who are not afraid to make decisions without seeking consensus.

The bottom line is: Both masculine *and* feminine traits are necessary for managerial excellence in today's business world. That's why the dolphin approach works. Dolphins know when to seek consensus and when to be "Lone Rangers." They are able to maintain control, yet still empower and inspire their employees.

Best of all, the dolphin approach doesn't require women—or men—to squeeze into some ill-fitting mold, which can be exhausting, self-defeating, and often impossible. Dawn Steel's story is a good example. Steel, who has no college degree, managed to climb from receptionist to president of a Hollywood studio—and the first woman at that. When recently asked by *Mirabella* magazine about her worst—and most treasured—mistake, her reply was, "Trying to be one of the boys.

"For all those years that I was a girl member of the boys' club, I had no concept that I was out of balance. But I have to tell you that it did get exhausting after a while, because being part of the club just isn't possible. No matter how good I am, or was, it's just not possible. . . . But the truth is, I never aspired to be a man. I wanted to be part of the boys' club, but I wanted to do it as a woman."

"I Gotta Be Me!"

Dolphins have learned not to waste their time trying to be something they are not—or cannot possibly ever be. Having discovered that authenticity equals effectiveness, they prefer leading with their true selves and finding success on their own terms.

"Our management styles develop out of personalities and life experiences, and they are what we're comfortable with," agrees Lawrence J. Gartner, who with Naomi Young founded the Los Angeles law firm Gartner & Young. What's interesting about this partnership is that Gartner is more of a consensus-builder, while Young's style is more direct. "From a get-somebody's-attention standpoint, it has been beneficial for me to be no-nonsense, get on the table what you want, and get it done," Young said in an interview with *Nation's Business*. "It's very complementary to my personality, and it's a style that I've had a long time."

Yet both partners said they are capable of trading styles whenever necessary. Gartner can be direct; Young can be accommodating. "We each have a predominant style," explains Young, "but the other aspects of leadership must be present as tools to use when you need them."

That's precisely what the dolphin approach is all about. It's a win-win management style in which everyone gains. Employees prefer it because it places a premium on their input. It's also a strategy that has proven to be bottom-line effective. But above all, it gives women the freedom to succeed in business on their *own* terms.

CHAPTER THREE

Great Beginnings: When You're the New Boss

KAREN HIMLE

VICE PRESIDENT, CORPORATE COMMUNICATIONS
THE ST. PAUL COMPANIES
ST. PAUL, MINNESOTA

*"I found my first year on the job to be one of the best experiences
I've ever had professionally. It's not that I didn't have some
management problems—I had to downsize the department and
make some personnel changes. But I have a great group, so I'm
lucky."*

Mission Impossible." That's what Karen Himle's employees claim
she accomplished when she took over the leadership of the Corporate Communications Department at the St. Paul Companies in
1992. "She transformed our department into a highly respected,
well-organized, and efficient operation," says one subordinate.
"And she did it by treating each new member of our twenty-
person staff with respect and fairness."

Himle also did it with no formal background in journalism and
no professional writing experience. In fact, in 1991 Himle was
working for the St. Paul Companies as an attorney and lobbyist
when this international property and casualty insurance company

not only changed its leadership, but its vision as well. The corporation's new chairman, Doug Leatherdale, sought to raise the profile of the corporation locally, nationally, and ultimately, internationally, and he asked Himle to be a part of that.

"From a corporate perspective, we had been in business for 140 years," she reports. "Out of that history, I think, was born a view that we could afford to be quiet, and people would still buy our products. Having enjoyed tremendous success for so long, the company more or less subscribed to the old adage, 'If it ain't broke, don't fix it.' And along with the philosophy came a view that public relations and communication with external audiences was more of a nuisance than a necessity. Naturally, this view had a negative impact on those who worked in corporate communications."

Enter Doug Leatherdale, who decided to shake things up a bit. "Not to throw everything out," says Himle, "but to retain the good history while molding the company into one that was much more aggressive, that would be ahead of the times, and that wouldn't rest on its laurels."

As part of his master plan, the company's new chairman issued Himle a challenge she couldn't refuse: "Create a world-class public relations organization." Before accepting the position, however, Himle issued a challenge of her own. Well aware that the insurance industry had long been male-dominated, and recognizing that she would be one of just a handful of female mangers at the St. Paul Companies, she decided to be candid with her boss. "I told him, 'If you see public relations as fluffy, I'm not interested in the job.' In response, he said, 'Public relations—or the absence of it at this point—has an effect on our bottom line.' "

From the outset, Himle was granted total managerial freedom to do what she thought best. "Given that corporate communications had long been viewed as a necessary—or unnecessary—evil, my first challenge was to bring my department up from a view that they were the ugly ducklings of the corporation. And I did that by telling my staff: 'You are in a position of prominence. You will be responsible for assisting the chairman in making his vision become reality. You have a right to demand and command respect.' "

When members of the department first heard that a new corporate communications vice president would be named, no one suspected that Himle would be tapped for the position. And no one envied her either. "At the time, our department was operating in total turmoil," explains one employee. "There was not much cohesion, and people in the department were not working together. Also, our manager at the time had had some major differences with senior management, which made things difficult for all of us. Yet Karen came in and turned everything around."

How did Himle do it? "The first thing I did was set up one-hour appointments with every person in the department," she says. "Certainly that's easy to do with a staff of twenty, but I think even in a larger organization I would figure out a way to meet face-to-face with as many employees as I possibly could." These one-on-one meetings were basically an information-gathering opportunity for her in terms of how the department operated. "But I was also very interested in what made these people tick."

Following these meetings, Himle's notion was that corporate communications was in dire need of a major reorganization. "The way business had been done, whoever happened to pick up the phone had to do the media call, write the speech—or whatever," she reports. "There was no sense of strategic communications planning and no sense of the marriage between communications and business marketing. In fact, the overall attitude was 'Just another day of drudgery' or 'Where's the next crisis coming from?' And since we are the largest providers of medical malpractice insurance in the world, the department had definitely had its share of crises. So, of course, there were days when *nobody* wanted to pick up the phone."

Reorganization, however, spells change—something employees are known to dread, loathe, and often resist. Yet Himle was sensitive to the psychological ramifications of change and went out of her way to avoid being the kind of new boss who charges into the workplace and turns everything upside down. "I took a course at a local college called 'Dealing with the Staff You Inherited,' which gave me the tools I needed to do some of my own in-house training," she says. "The course also dealt with change—the sense of loss and different phases everyone tends to go through during the change process. So I was able to walk my staff through the reorganization. I told them up front, 'We're going to go through this together, and we're going to go at our own pace. I'll try to keep you posted in terms of what my instincts tell me regarding when we have gone through one phase and are moving on to the next.' "

This kind of hand-holding is unusual for Himle, who otherwise operates as a hands-off manager. "I have been blessed with good bosses my entire professional life. Nobody ever micromanaged me, so in turn I don't micromanage anyone who works for me. I basically said to my new staff, 'Look, you're all adults. You were hired to do a job, and you know what that job is. If you feel that you are most functional at three o'clock in the morning, then work at three o'clock in the morning. I have a couple of minimal requirements, and one is that there are people to answer the phones during business hours. But don't expect to punch a time clock. And don't expect that to prove yourself you have to be here all day Saturday and Sunday. I'm *not* going to be here, so I won't know if you are or not."

What Himle *does* expect her employees to do is tell her when they've done good things. "I'm a firm believer in tooting your own horn," she says. "So we have a policy around here that we call SSP—Shameless Self-Promotion, which is designed to inspire people to ask for recognition. I think it's very difficult sometimes for people to say, 'Gee, I think I did a really good job on this.' And given that I'm a hands-off manager, I think we need something like this to allow people to develop self-esteem, to feel as if they *have* done a good job, and to realize that somebody *is* paying attention."

But Himle also has a tough side. "One of the first things I had to do as a new boss was to terminate someone, and I had never done that before. The reason for the termination was poor performance, but it took a lot of soul-searching." Since then, Himle has had to let other employees go as well. She says it's never easy, but she likes to think that her people realize and understand the fact that she thinks through all aspects of a situation before taking such drastic action. "Fundamentally, my view is that the whole department needs to work well together, and if people aren't pulling their weight, others will not only resent them, but me as well, for not having the managerial courage to take a difficult action."

Managerial courage is certainly not something Himle lacks. When she first took over the Corporate Communications Department at the St. Paul Companies, she didn't hesitate to admit her ignorance of standard Associated Press style and media relations. "As a lobbyist, my media relations had always been in the heat of political battle, so I had some things to learn." Now, three years into her new position, Himle is described by her staff as a "quick learner" and a "real pro at corporate communications."

Indeed, Himle has managed to orchestrate a major restructuring of corporate communications in her first few years on the job. And as a result she's feeling pretty good about herself and her department. Especially now that the rest of the departments within the St. Paul Companies intend to follow suit. "That's good news for us," she says, "because we did it as a department before the rest of the company did it. Now we're in a perfect position to help the rest of the corporation through its own restructuring."

• • •

As a new boss, Karen Himle won rave reviews from her subordinates and superiors alike. But not all new bosses fare so well.

In 1989, Rosabeth Moss Kanter made headlines when she was named the first female editor of the prestigious *Harvard Business Review*. Three years earlier, the world-renown sociologist-turned-management-consultant had become only the second woman in Harvard's history to win a tenured faculty position in the university's business school.

Harvard had wooed Kanter from a teaching position at Yale when her visibility was already on the rise. A prolific writer, Kanter was author of a dozen books—including the award-winning *Men and Women of the Corporation* and the highly acclaimed *The Change-Masters: Innovation for Productivity in the American Corporation*. She was also earning hefty sums consulting for Fortune 500 companies and upward of $25,000 per speaking engagement.

The business philosophy Kanter preached involved improving communications with employees and distributing power throughout an organization. Yet in 1992 Kanter made headlines once again when she left her position at the *Harvard Business Review* following a walkout by the majority of her staff. Kanter, they claimed, did not practice what she preached.

What really went wrong depends on whom you ask. (Kanter herself has refused to discuss the ordeal.) But on this much everyone appears to agree: Kanter was never one to hide her desire for power, fortune, and fame—an attitude that probably didn't sit well at Harvard, especially coming from a female. Indeed, according to *Working Woman* magazine, one Boston high-tech executive labeled Kanter a "pushy broad."

Her staff claimed that Kanter never tried to build a team and rarely solicited their opinions. They also accused her of monopolizing meetings and said they were insulted as well by Kanter's policy of handing out rewards—gift certificates and bottles of wine—for good work.

Kanter's advocates, on the other hand, argue that she inherited a staff accustomed to running the magazine alone and who were predisposed to dislike her from the start. The fact that Harvard is a tight insiders' world, and Kanter was an outsider, probably didn't help matters either. Moreover, Kanter's supporters claim, she was never given any clear instructions as editor. She was simply commanded: "Take over and run it well."

One of Kanter's clients went on record insisting, "She has a real sense of what you need to do to energize a corporation." And a colleague of Kanter's hinted that the whole incident smacked of sexual stereotyping. "I can't shake off the feeling that some piece of it is that she didn't do some of the TLC that is expected of women," the colleague told *Working Woman* magazine. "I've seen so many men who had her style. She just wasn't giving warm fuzzies when people expected it."

Regardless of who's right or wrong here, Kanter's story illustrates just some of the problems that new bosses—male and female—typically face on the job.

Great Beginnings

What can *you* do to get started on the right foot as a new manager? That, of course, depends on your particular situation—whether you're an outsider or were promoted from within, the popularity of your predecessor, your age in relation to your subordinates' ages, whether or not your appointment was a controversial one, and whether you're one of many female managers in your company or the "token" one. We'll delve into each of these situations shortly, but first let's discuss some general pitfalls *any* new female boss should avoid.

10 Deadly Sins of a New Female Manager

(1) Misunderstanding—or underestimating—the psychology of change.

(2) Expecting too much too soon.

(3) Taking charge too quickly.

(4) Not taking time to get to know the people you'll be working with.

(5) Failure to set—and share—your goals and priorities.

(6) Being a "pushover" or a "pushy broad."

(7) Inaccessibility to subordinates.

(8) Pretending to know it all.

(9) Placing your own career aspirations ahead of your organization's needs.

(10) Not taking time to explore your corporate culture.

The Psychology of Change

Starting off on the right foot as a new manager is no easy task. From a subordinate's perspective, there are a lot of psychological factors at play—particularly the notion that change is inevitable. Because change makes workers nervous, their natural tendency is to resist it. Nothing personal, they'd just feel safer and more secure keeping things the way they are. And until they get to know you, you'll simply be perceived as someone whose mission it is to rock the boat.

A major challenge for new managers, then, is to find ways to help subordinates view change as an *opportunity* rather than an *obstacle*. But to accomplish this requires understanding why employees feel threatened by change in the first place.

Fear appears to be the number one reason workers resist change. Fear of uncertainty. Fear of failure. Fear of discomfort. As a new manager, you can calm employees' fears with open and honest communication. For example, keeping everyone informed of changes on the horizon, and explaining the reasons behind each change, should calm fears of uncertainty. And if changes will be made in your employees' job descriptions, you can also assure them that they will be properly trained to meet any new challenges.

To help your staff conquer fears of failure, start small by initiating changes that you *know* your subordinates will handle well. If they start off feeling like winners, they will be less resistant to future changes. Next, gradually introduce tasks that require learning new skills, then mix and match these with tasks that require tapping old skills. That way, you'll convince your subordinates that many of the skills they already possess are transferrable. Also, make yourself available to give immediate (and constructive) feedback. According to Tom Payne, author of *From the Inside Out: How to Create and Survive a Culture of Change*, "Research shows that as much as fifty percent of performance problems occurs because employees don't get the feedback they need."

"We've tried that before." "That will never work." "Your approach is way off base." All of us tend to grow attached to our work routines, so naturally, when someone threatens to shatter these routines, we resist. One of the best ways to soothe employees' fears of discomfort is to tell them what's in it for them—new skills, more challenge, higher pay, and so forth. But be sure to deliver on your promises. Otherwise you risk losing your subordinates' trust.

Employees also resist change when they are not involved in the decision-making process. As mentioned earlier, surveys show that today's workers want to feel in on things. They want to be empowered. They want a voice. Armed with this knowledge, the savvy manager will seek subordinates' input on changes.

Helen Dahlander says when she took over as Manager of Sales and Marketing Systems at Westin Hotels and Resorts, she listened first. "I did not come in and make changes immediately. Instead, I allowed each employee a chance to help identify what needed to be accomplished."

And when Cynthia Danaher was promoted to General Manager of Imaging Systems at Hewlett-Packard, she sent a personnel liaison to her new staff to ask a series of twelve questions—among them "What do we know about Cynthia?" "What do we *want* to know about Cynthia?" "What do we worry about with Cynthia?" "How do we like to celebrate successes?" According to Danaher, "People were just blown away that I would want to do this. But I wanted my new staff to get the message loud and clear that, 'I want to hear what you think, and I want to hear the truth.' "

Even if their ideas aren't used, employees will feel as if they contributed to the decision-making process. Moreover, involving workers in the change process not only encourages them to think long-term, it lessens their fears of—and their resistance to—future changes.

Gwendolyn Calvert Baker, Ph.D., the first African-American and the first woman to serve as President and CEO of the U.S. Committee for UNICEF, agrees. Before assuming her current position in September of 1993, Baker spent nine years as National Executive Director of the YWCA of the USA. "When I took that job, the YWCA was about 126 years old and plagued with problems. Morale was low, and the organization lacked unity," she says. Faced with a major reorganizational task, Baker took the time to reach out and include volunteers and staff from YWCAs across the country.

"The first thing I did was call in experts to help me conduct a two-year study to figure out how we could all come together with one logo. At the time, we had over four hundred logos—and sometimes double that amount, since some of the associations changed logos every season. What that told me was, we were not yet united in purpose and mission. Later, at the national convention, we were able to vote and adopt one logo with almost no discussion. And that was my first step in restructuring the organization."

Baker acknowledges that while it takes longer to involve people in the decision-making process, it's usually well worth the effort. "Even when the ultimate decision turns out to be one that you would have made in the first place, taking another six months—even a year—to inform people and to organize small groups so that the decision-making is shared, whatever comes out of that process is going to last for a long time."

Still another reason employees resist change is because they are leery of it. Many mutter, "Here we go again . . . how long is *this* plan going to last?" But probably one of the best lessons managers of the '90s can teach their employees is that change is inevitable in corporate America today, and that it's far smarter to learn to adapt to it than to waste precious time and energy resisting it.

"The first problem we tackled when switching from a traditional manufacturing program to just-in-time, was that this was 'management du jour' short-lived," acknowledges Grace Pastiak of Tellabs. "The second was a basic resistance to change. We looked for ways to convince people to accept that this is a normal process, that one thing that *was* going to be constant at Tellabs was change. Then our goal was to find ways to get people excited about it instead of resistant."

Great Expectations

"I'll turn this department around in no time." "My subordinates will adore me." "I'm going to do such a good job, that I predict I'll be promoted within the year."

It's natural to start a new job with high hopes and great expectations. But *too-high* hopes and *unrealistic* expectations can make you overconfident and lead to disappointment when things don't work out as you had anticipated. Starting a job with too much confidence can also cause you to misjudge—and underestimate—the obstacles you'll face as a new boss. This in turn can quickly lead to panic and make you feel like a failure.

So don't start out expecting to make an immediate impact. Don't count on being treated a certain way by your subordinates. And don't expect immediate recognition from your superiors. That way, you'll avoid setting yourself up for disappointment and/or feelings of failure.

Steamrolling Your Way into a New Managerial Position

Naturally, you'll want to make a big splash as the new boss. But it's a better idea to get your feet wet gradually by easing into your new role. Otherwise, in your eagerness to get ahead, you may become impatient and move too quickly. This can alienate your subordinates and sabotage your efforts to win their respect and cooperation. In fact, moving too quickly—without thinking about and preparing for things that can go wrong—is one of the major reasons new bosses fail.

By all means, go in with immediate goals. But knowing how employees feel about change, wait until you've had a chance to analyze your situation and forge alliances with subordinates before taking any significant action. Then, when the time seems right to begin initiating change, spend time *beforehand* carefully analyzing what might go wrong, and be ready with a backup plan.

Women have a tendency to spend too much time trying to do— or redo—other people's jobs, so be careful, too, about getting bogged down in too many details. "Don't make the same mistake I did in my last job," cautions Alice Lusk, now a Corporate Vice President and Group Executive for the Insurance and Health Care Industry Group at Dallas—based EDS (Electronic Data Systems). "I felt I had to go in and learn what all 1,800 people knew who reported to me. You need to know enough about the business to run it, but don't spend time doing other people's jobs. My style now is to go in and learn the *people*, not their jobs."

Get to Know Your Staff

Your employees can make or break your career, so do all you can to make a good first impression. Host a get-together to introduce yourself, but don't stop there. Make it a point to spend time with every employee. Find out what each one does, his or her feelings about the job as well as the company, and what it's going to take to win each one over to your side. Determine the mood of your team. Ask members what *you* can do as their new boss to make their jobs better and more productive. Ask them what changes they'd like to see occur. Figure out what motivates them—what their "hot buttons" are. They'll appreciate your interest, and you'll learn a lot.

When Kathleen Williams was promoted from controller (a staff position) to Manager of Manufacturing and Engineering (a line position) at Atlantic Gelatin, a division of General Foods, she knew she had to gain credibility quickly. "I made sure I recognized workers for what they did well," she says. "And if there were people who I sensed were not happy, I tried not to let things fester."

Williams believes that one of the most important things a new manager can do to get people on her side is to empower them. "My company offered an early retirement program, which was designed to eliminate nearly 20% of the salaried work force," she writes in a "How-I-did-it" article for *Working Woman* magazine. "I decided the only way to deal with restructuring the remaining staff was to let all the department managers in on the decision making. It would have been just as easy to sit in my office and draw up a list, but by talking things over, you give people a chance to have input and to know that they were part of the process. Not everybody will like the decision, but at least they had some say in it."

Setting and Sharing Priorities

Once you've had a chance to build rapport with your staff, your next goal is to build commitment. Share your vision with them, and challenge them, as Williams did, to help you realize it. Explain your goals in clear terms and exude enthusiasm. By letting everyone know exactly what you want—and how you plan to get there—subordinates are far more likely to share ownership of your action plan.

Attitude Is Key

To write *Becoming a Manager: Mastery of a New Identity*, Linda Hill followed the development of nineteen new female managers during their first year on the job. She found that many made the mistake of trying to forge friendships with their subordinates instead of good working relationships. "They were too eager to be liked, when it was far more important to be respected," Hill says.

Indeed, many female managers start off on the wrong foot by being too nice and overly accommodating. Their rationale: "If I'm nice to my staff and try to please them, they'll like me and work harder." In reality, when you bend over backward to please your employees, many will peg you as a pushover and try to take advantage of you.

On the flip side, Hill found that another obstacle to earning trust and building commitment was female managers' tendency to be pushy, particularly in response to challenges and criticisms. "In the early months, it's next to impossible to avoid defensive reactions," Hill acknowledges. "There's always that urge to say 'I'm the boss,' and get upset. But calm is best."

A better way to respond to subordinates who challenge you early on? "Try saying, 'You have the right to express your opinion, and I have the right to do it differently than you suggest,'" Hill offers. "Then explain why you did it the way you did, and that's it."

In fact, as a new boss, it's probably better to start out a bit more tough than caring. Not mean, not macho, and certainly not command-and-control. But firm, somewhat serious, and decisive. Then, once you and your subordinates get to know one another, you can show your caring side—without having to worry about being taken seriously.

Ultimately, though, you must go with a management style that is most comfortable for you and is best suited to your particular workplace and employees. And sometimes finding just the right style calls for experimentation.

While Manager of Editorial Services at the Coca-Cola Company, Julie Culwell first tried distancing herself from her subordinates and keeping the relationship she had with them strictly professional. "I'd read a lot of management books that warned me not to get personally involved with my team," she says. "But that was very difficult for me, because I have a very warm and nurturing personality. In fact, I was miserable, and so was my staff." Culwell finally decided to just be herself. "I broke all the rules and became close friends with my team members. We laughed a lot together. We helped pull each other through professional and personal crises. We spent time together after hours. And what happened was, the more I nurtured them, the more they produced. In fact, they became passionate about their work—putting in long hours at the office and often taking projects home with them. Nobody ever missed a deadline, and the feedback we got from our clients was consistently outstanding."

The close relationship Culwell developed with her staff offered another benefit. "Because I knew my people so well, I was able to zero in on their strengths. I could see who gravitated toward certain assignments, or who always requested to write certain types of stories. And that's how I would make assignments. I think a lot of managers don't bother to do this. Instead, they delegate with no rhyme or reason. Worse, some even hand out tough assignments to people they know probably won't handle them well, just to see them sweat. But I believe that if you take the time to figure out what your people *enjoy* doing—and let them go with it—you can bet that their work will be top-notch."

The Visible Manager

In Hill's study, one of the most significant factors that spelled success for new managers was the amount of time and resources they invested in their employees. "Almost constant accessibility and active one-on-one involvement with individual employees was critical in developing effective relationships," Hill reports.

She adds that small things and personal touches—working alongside subordinates on special projects, treating employees to lunch—also made a difference.

When Janet Reno assumed her post as Attorney General for the State of Florida, for example, she has said that one of her top priorities was to remain accessible. "I tried not to be remote, not to close my door," she told *Time* magazine. "I think it's important that people feel that the Attorney General can be accessible to them so that I know what's happening on the streets of America and not just what's happening in the halls of the Department of Justice."

Reno had a knack for looking after her staff as well—by attending subordinates' family funerals and birthday parties. She also allowed her staff extra leave for such things as seeing their children in school plays.

Nobody Likes a Know-it-all

On one hand, your staff needs to believe that you know what you're doing. On the other, they don't expect you to have all the answers. As Debra Benton points out in *Lions Don't Need to Roar: Using the Leadership Power of Professional Presence to Stand Out, Fit In, and Move Ahead*, "Most of us don't trust and are reluctant to be led by people who seem too sure of themselves." Tellabs's Grace Pastiak agrees. "To me the best thing to do as a new boss is to listen and to bring a real sense of optimism to the job. The worst thing to do is to come in with the 'right' answers to everything and expect people to fit the mold you want them to, instead of finding ways to value their diversity."

So while it's fine to be confident in your abilities, it can also be advantageous to be humble. In fact, when you don't have all the answers, it not only sharpens your sense of learning, it helps you see more possibilities.

In the beginning it's also a good idea to listen a lot more than you talk. Ask lots of questions—particularly if you don't understand the specifics of your subordinates' jobs—and pay close attention to the answers. "By demonstrating that asking questions is acceptable and not a sign of weakness or stupidity, you create a climate where others will feel free to ask questions themselves," believes Benton.

In November of 1993, when Susan Insley was named manager of Honda's two-thousand-employee engine plant in Anna, Ohio, she became the highest-ranking woman in American automotive manufacturing. Insley, a lawyer by profession, had been working at Honda since 1985 after helping to negotiate the purchase of the land on which the engine plant is built. While her dealings with Honda's parts and materials suppliers had familiarized her with manufacturing issues, Insley admitted to *Working Woman* magazine that she had a lot to learn about the process and that one of her first moves as manager would entail "being out on the floor listening hard."

As a new manager, what can you do if you're unsure of your abilities in one or two areas and feel too uncomfortable winging it? Consider hiring a private tutor, or taking a course. Better yet, do as Grace Pastiak does. "I make it a *point* to hire people who know more than I do," she says, "then I try to get the most out of them. The real value of a manager at any level comes in bringing the best out of everybody on the team. In fact, the teams I'm working with right now—I'm *not* the subject matter expert. I also believe that beating the defects out of ideas—just as we beat the defects out of manufacturing—is critically important. But you really need to recognize people's knowledge base to do that."

First Things First

In the beginning, forget about what *you* want from your new position. Instead, focus on what the *organization* needs. After all, your worth to the company will ultimately be measured by what you've done to help it succeed. Alice Lusk of EDS suggests pinpointing three to five goals for your first year as the new boss. "If you try to do more than that, you won't be able to focus on your top priorities. You'll get very fragmented and end up not doing anything. For every new job, I stop and say, 'What's my vision for the organization, and what are the things I need to accomplish?' I try to determine those priorities fairly quickly—probably in the first week or so. Then I make sure I focus all my attention on doing those things."

Adds Gwendolyn Baker of UNICEF, "I think that anyone who is successful in management and provides leadership can only be so and do so if they are really committed to the organization's mission. Leadership is not about power. It's about success at getting people to move with you for the good of the cause."

At the start of her efforts to reorganize the YWCA's national organization, for example, Baker found a mission statement that hadn't changed much in over a hundred years. "The national organization was not providing adequate technical assistance to the individual YWCAs or branches across the country," she reports. "There were many complaints. I wasn't happy with the quality of the work. And we were suffering financially."

With the help of outside consultants, Baker surveyed YWCA staff members and volunteers throughout the nation, asking them what they expected of the national organization and what they wanted to see happen. "As a result, we completely redesigned the national organization by literally closing out the old structure one day and launching a new one the following day. Unfortunately, under the new structure, I was the only one left with a job."

Working with completely revamped job descriptions, as well as new titles, Baker was able to interview and rehire some of her old staff immediately. "Nevertheless, there were still seventy people left without jobs, because we needed fewer people to run the new structure."

To soften the blow, Baker devised an attractive early-retirement plan to take care of nearly a third of those laid off. She also hired a career transition team to be on site the last day of work and to help those in need find new jobs.

"Still, for about two weeks, as people were preparing to leave, they would come to my office, and we'd hug and sometimes cry together," Baker recalls. "Many offered, 'Whenever you can use me, I'd be glad to help,' and I've since been able to hire quite a few on a part-time basis. I think the only reason we all handled the situation as well as we did was because everyone was so committed to our mission and our new vision. We had talked about it a great deal, and since the staff was involved from the very beginning, we all knew that what was happening was best for the organization."

Exploring the Corporate Culture

Of course the best way to find out what your organization needs is to do your homework. Dee Soder, Ph.D., President of Endymion Company, an executive assessment and advisory firm in Manhattan, frequently offers this advice to her clients: "Think about walking into a new job as if you were walking into a foreign country. That's the degree of sensitivity you'll need to pick up the nuances of a new corporate culture."

In other words, your goal should be to find out how things *really* get done in your company, so take time to figure out the unwritten rules, and determine who's got the real power in the organization. You won't find the answers to these questions in the corporate handbook. Your best bet is to find a mentor to show you the ropes, ask smart questions, and nurture the right people.

On the Outside Looking In

There are both advantages and disadvantages to being hired from outside the company to fill a managerial position. On the plus side, you're not expected to know everything, so there's not as much pressure to prove yourself—at least initially. Consequently, your honeymoon will be longer than if you were promoted from within. Since you're not privy to your department's or division's political past, you can be more objective. Also, if the individuals you'll be overseeing have recently experienced a lot of turmoil, you'll likely be welcomed as a fresh—and neutral—addition.

On the flip side, you may be resented for not "working your way up" within the organization. Nanci O'Neill found this to be the case when she was hired from the outside to take over as Manager of Training, Development and Performance Systems at Westin Hotels and Resorts. Her first goal was to build internal credibility. "I held orientations designed to expose myself to as many people within the organization as I could as quickly as possible," she says.

As a new boss from the "outside," it's likely that your every move will be carefully scrutinized as employees try to figure out your style and their position in this new environment. Anxious to please and impress you, subordinates may give you one-sided views of workplace problems. For the big picture, you may also want to talk to customers, suppliers, managers from other departments, and neutral board members.

Finally, remember that you're not expected to know every detail of every person's job. So don't make the fatal mistake of trying to bluff your way through *anything*.

The Inside Track

When you're promoted from within, you have the advantage of being familiar with all of your players as well as their responsibilities. You also have the inside track on who's good at what they do, and who's not.

But there's also a downside to being promoted from within. For starters, you may initially have trouble thinking of yourself as "the new boss." Consequently, you may come across as timid or lacking confidence. Or you may take your job too seriously and come across as too bossy.

Your subordinates, too, may have trouble thinking of you as their new boss. Managing old friends can be especially tricky. But it's up to you to reassure them that while your working relationship has changed, they are still important to you. And if they make jokes or snide comments about your new role, it's your responsibility to put a stop to this kind of behavior immediately.

Can you still socialize with your former buddies after you've been promoted? Betty Forbes, Senior Vice President of Central Fidelity Mortgage Corporation in Richmond, Virginia, thinks so. "I still see my former colleagues socially," she says, "but not one-on-one. You don't want people to think you're playing favorites." Socializing with *groups* of old cronies, however, is perfectly appropriate. "I've had employees over to my house for cookouts, and I remember their birthdays," adds Forbes.

If you've moved up the ranks, resist the urge to hold on to your old responsibilities. Granted, doing this might make you feel more secure, but you'll be perceived as weak.

Finally, there will likely be some employees who will resent your success and, as a result, not support you. If this happens, you'll have to show your tough side by making it clear to them that their behavior will not be tolerated.

When You're the Young Boss

When you're the new boss and younger than the majority of your subordinates, some may be less than thrilled with your appointment. After all, your career is racing ahead faster than theirs—and at an earlier age. Consequently, they may resent having to report to you. They may also resist your ideas or try to patronize you.

Lisa Resnick, C.L.U., now general manager of the Prudential

Preferred Financial Services in Chicago, says, "When I landed my first job in management, I was assigned three salespeople—two of whom were about ten years older than I was. I could sense their skepticism, and winning their respect was an uphill battle. The first thing I did when I came on board was to talk to each person individually to find out what each one liked about the job or didn't like and how we could improve things. I knew I wasn't going to go in and change them and that the best way to make improvements was to work together."

Resnick adds she spent her first two months as the new manager proving that she would be there for her associates when they needed her. "I worked very hard doing whatever was needed—taking an appointment for someone who wasn't feeling well, keeping promises, going above and beyond. But on the road to proving yourself, avoid the mistake of taking on too much—you must learn how to delegate and how to say no," Resnick cautions. "Otherwise, despite your good intentions, too many things just won't get done."

Adds Tellabs's Grace Pastiak, who also speaks from experience, "The best thing to do as a young new boss is to focus on listening and making sure that everybody understands that you have no interest in taking credit for their contributions. Instead, convince them that your goal is to help *everyone* shine."

Keep in mind, too, that older and more seasoned employees are often great sources of information on everything from company history to corporate politics. So try to tap them for their expertise. Then, chances are, you'll not only uncover valuable information, you'll also win their respect and cooperation.

Filling Big Shoes

Replacing a "legend" (particularly a male one) presents special challenges, and the pressure to prove yourself can be overwhelming. No matter what you do, expect to be compared to your predecessor. Just don't take it personally.

It may be worth your while to find out exactly what your predecessor did that people liked—and didn't like. You don't have to mimic his style, but if you can continue some of his beloved traditions and make his weaknesses your strengths, it may help you gain acceptance more quickly.

Early in her career, Victoria Ogden, now President and Publisher of Cape Cod Community Newspapers, took over a paper that had been run by an editor who was a legend. "It didn't work out," she reports, "and it was my fault. I didn't understand his magic or his ties to the community. I didn't have enough respect for his ability to teach me the ropes. He had retired, but was still around, and I didn't spend enough time at his knee. It was my first big job, and I thought I knew it all. My attitude was, 'Who needed these old guys anyway?' and 'Oh geez, do I *have* to sit and listen to all these old stories?' They were trying to teach me, but I just wasn't listening. As a result, I learned a hard lesson: that I should have been quiet, listened more, and *welcomed* all the help and advice I got."

When You're the Token Managerial Woman

"When I took a job as marketing manager three years ago, there were comments made to me like, 'Well, you just got this job because you're a woman,' " says Cynthia Danaher, who as General Manager of Imaging Systems at Hewlett-Packard heads up a staff of about five hundred—mostly males. "But with my recent promotion, I didn't hear that at all. Most people were very accepting. Besides, I'd been in the business long enough to have proven myself."

In fact, after just four weeks in her new position, Danaher's subordinates began responding in positive ways to the change in style she brought to the department. "They told me it seemed like a calmer, gentler approach," she reports. "And since many of my staff are parents of young children, they said they especially appreciated my sense of flexibility."

If you're the only—or one of few—female managers in your company and haven't had the opportunity to prove yourself, expect to be greeted with caution and/or to jump through hoops to be accepted. As Gary Powell points out in his book *Women and Men in Management*, tokens often get a lot of attention because they are so different, but it means working twice as hard to have competence recognized.

Karyn Marasco agrees. "Being the company's first female general manager in Pittsburgh, a very male-dominated city, and first in the Westin William Penn, people expected a hard-line women's libber, and then realized quickly that I am not," she recalls. Marasco's responsibilities included overseeing the engineering and maintenance of two hotels—one that was just opening and one that was seventy-five-plus years old. "Faced with the typical 'females don't know/understand' attitude by older engineering personnel, I met frequently with the staff and physically walked the properties to learn the hows and whys of vital operating equipment. I also listened to staff's concerns and suggestions, thereby winning their confidence."

And in 1993, when Bernadette Locke-Mattox was hired as an assistant basketball coach at the University of Kentucky, she became the first woman ever named to the coaching staff of a major men's basketball team. Not surprisingly, the announcement was greeted with skepticism. Rick Pitino, head coach of the Wildcats, told *People* magazine that his assistants "marched into my office, adamantly against it." But once they saw the effect Locke-Mattox had on recruits—and particularly the way she was able to charm recruits' mothers—"that turned it around," says Pitino. And according to Pitino, "The only thing she was lacking when she came here was an aggressive demeanor, a necessity in men's basketball. [But] Locke-Mattox has since grown. Now if something goes wrong, she will get right in the player's face. She's an outstanding teacher."

Interestingly enough, token men face the same obstacles. A study of male nurses who worked in female-dominated work groups, for example, concluded that they, too, had to work harder to prove their worth.

Powell adds, however, that tokens can do much to build their power. "Establish yourself as indispensable to the group in some way, and you're more likely to receive attention due to competence than due to token status," he suggests. "You may also build a power base through your ability to demonstrate self-confidence, take risks, and verbally advance your causes."

Another problem token female managers face is that some employees—particularly men—are still uncomfortable working for a female boss. Why? Some simply don't know how to treat you. In his book *One-on-One with Andy Grove: How to Manage Your Boss, Yourself, and Your Co-workers*, Intel chief Andrew S. Grove acknowledges, "When women first appear in a new line of work, they are greeted with a cautious, awkward attitude by the men around them. We simply don't know how to act, we don't know what we can and can't say; suddenly we become self-conscious."

As a result, many male colleagues may try to stereotype you—as a bitch, a feminist, as too nice, not serious enough, or not capable. Others may doubt your abilities and continuously test you.

How can you pass their tests? Use your female skills to your advantage and bond with your employees. Talk to them. Ask questions. Listen to their answers and, when appropriate, take their advice.

When Jane Evans was named president of Butterick/Vogue in 1974, all seven male vice presidents of the division decided to resign in protest. Once American Can, the parent company, heard about the mutiny, they immediately called Evans to say, "Jane, we may have to rethink this." In response, Evans cracked up. "I burst out laughing," she says, "then I assured them I could handle the situation." Evans, then thirty, called the men together and said, "I understand that you're not too happy about having me here. I hasten to remind you that I am president of this company, and as such, you have more to prove to me than I have to prove to you." Then she challenged them with a bet. "I bet each one of them $10 that in a year, they would be saying I was the best president they ever worked for," she says. "And they took me up on it."

Evans more or less forgot about the wager, but exactly one year later, upon returning home from a European trip, she was met at the airport by a chauffeur bearing a dozen long-stemmed yellow roses and a check.

If you're dealing primarily with male colleagues and/or subordinates, Evans suggests that aside from being very proficient at what you do, you need to make men feel comfortable. And the best way to do that, she says, is to learn to speak their language. "Learn everything you can about the NFL, NBA, etc., and be prepared on Monday morning to talk about the games that went on over the weekend. Learn to make small talk about the latest stories in *Fortune* and *Business Week*. Get to the point where within twenty minutes they no longer notice you're a woman."

Also, use light, but appropriate, humor. "Unfortunately, a lot of men in their fifties or older still think of women in terms of stereotypes—just because they have never worked for a woman, or had a woman work for them," adds Evans, who views humor as "the great equalizer. It's another great way to make men feel comfortable in your presence."

But don't patronize them. Don't flirt with them. And don't assume the role of a helpless female to win them over. Neither should you try to be a male clone, because if you come across as too macho, you risk rejection from subordinates and colleagues—both male *and* female.

Learn to communicate with clout, both verbally and nonverbally (see "Communicating with Clout" below). And work hard! Stereotypes are associated with anonymity, and once everyone sees how competent you really are, you will win their respect and admiration.

Communicating with Clout

Speech Patterns That Say "Don't Take Me Seriously"	Mannerisms That Can Make You a Lightweight
• **Excessive Apologies.** If you've wronged someone, an apology is appropriate, but there's no need to apologize for your thoughts, feelings, or a situation over which you have no control. When you do, it not only takes the punch out	• **Smiling Too Much at Inappropriate Times.** Studies reveal that women smile more than men do. On the plus side, a smile can be an asset. It projects warmth, conveys confidence, and is a valuable tool for establishing

of your statements, it detracts from your credibility.

• **Hedging or Use of Qualifiers.** Words like *well, y'know, kinda,* and *sorta* and phrases such as *I think, I guess, I suppose, You may not agree with me, but . . .* or *I'm not 100 percent sure, but . . .* make you sound weak, uncertain, and uncommitted to what you are saying.

• **Excessive Chitchat.** A number of studies have found that women disclose more personal information in their speech patterns than men do. While sharing personal details has its positive aspects—makes you appear friendly and encourages others to open up—too much self-disclosure in the workplace can turn people off.

• **Empty Adjectives/Adverbs.** Some adverbs tend to have a fluffing effect on our messages, particularly when they are used to emphasize our feelings: *such, just, awfully,* and *terribly.* Certain adjectives—like *sweet, precious,* and *tiny*—also lack clout and substance because they are frilly words typically associated with women. More powerful—and genderless—descriptive words

rapport. However, smiling at inappropriate times—especially when it conflicts with your tone of voice or the words being spoken—can work against you by sending a mixed message. Some women also have a habit of laughing at inappropriate times— when they are nervous, when they are introduced to someone and aren't sure what to say, or when they end their statements. But, like smiling, giggling can make you appear silly and girlish.

• **Tilting or Nodding the Head.** Tilting your head to one side can make you appear submissive. Many women do this without even realizing it; yet it reinforces the cute little girl look—particularly when done while talking to men. And when accompanied by a tag question, the head tilt says you're indecisive. Head bobbing, usually done when listening, is another distracting habit. It can be particularly dangerous, since it indicates that you agree with what someone is saying—even when you may not!

• **Submissive Body Posture.** Good posture conveys a sense of personal power, and research reveals that the most effective power stance for men and women include: *absolutely, remarkably,* and *incredibly* (adverbs) and *excellent, outstanding,* and *terrific* (adjectives).

● **Tag Questions.** A tag takes a firm and decisive statement and turns it into an unnecessary question. *(This idea will work, don't you agree?)* Women typically use tags to avoid confrontation, to try and please everyone, or to get others to buy into their agenda. But overuse of them can make you appear wishy-washy and incapable of making decisions.

● **Disclaimers.** Introductory expressions that excuse, explain, or request understanding *(You may not like this, but . . . , I suppose we could . . . , Maybe this is okay . . .)* not only strip you of power, they invite listeners to disagree.

● **Lengthy Requests.** Generally, the shorter a request the more it conveys, so know what you want to say, and say it concisely and precisely.

● **Superpolite Speech.** Because women are reared on polite language, we emerge experts at using euphemisms and at saying *please* and *thank you* excessively. We also tend to use fewer

is almost military: spine and head erect and straight, feet slightly spread, arms at sides with fingers slightly cupped. Avoid slouching and hugging your chest with your arms. Also avoid standing with one or both hands on your hips. This is a power stance for men but a nonpower stance for women. When talking to a man who is taller than you are, resist the urge to bend your head back or tilt it to one side. Instead, casually take a few steps backward until your gaze is level with his. When you are sitting, refrain from clasping your hands tightly together, leaning forward, and looking down. Gestures like these can make you look nervous or submissive. Instead, place your elbows loosely on the arms of your chair, and occasionally lean to one side in a relaxed manner.

● **Distracting Hand Gestures.** When you are trying to make a point and you twirl your hair, fiddle with an earring or bracelet, tap your pencil, cover your face, or pick at your cuticles, you send out the message that you are tense or uncertain. Instead, focus on using gestures to express confidence. Point. Punch the air with your fist. Steeple your hands, or rub them contractions and to be overly cautious about using slang words. Yet instead of building respect and status, superpolite speech can give us an uptight image. Furthermore, when we focus too much on sounding grammatically correct, the point we're trying to make often gets lost.

● *Self-effacing Remarks.* Women have a tendency to put themselves down—particularly when they are put on the spot. We are also reluctant to boast about our achievements for fear people won't like us if we do. Yet when women do not blow their own horns, they risk being underestimated by their superiors.

● *Fillers.* We're all guilty of using fillers—*um, ah, like, well, uh, er, y'know, kinda,* and *sorta*— especially when caught in situations where we can't think of anything to say. But studies show that women use them in much higher proportions than men do— particularly when we address men and usually out of fear of coming on too strong. Fillers, however, signal uncertainty and lack of preparation. They also open the door to interruption.

● *Asking Too Many Questions.* Studies have shown that women

together briefly. These are power gestures. Also keep in mind that gestures must match and confirm your words, not distract or contradict them, and that excessive or random gestures can diminish the strength of your delivery.

● *Avoiding Eye Contact.* Good eye contact is perhaps the most important gesture a woman can master if she wants to be taken seriously. When you avoid establishing eye contact with someone, you not only signal submissiveness, you also invite interruption. The rules for effective eye contact are simple. Never look down. Instead, maintain frequent eye contact whether you are talking or listening, but don't stare. Too much eye contact can signal anger, challenge, or sexual attraction. So, keep your gaze on the speaker steady and firm, but give (and get) some relief by looking away every few seconds.

● *Allowing the Invasion of Personal Space.* Personal space—or the distance that is usually maintained between two people when they are sitting, standing, or talking, is highly significant in the business world. Studies show that powerful people ask about three times as many questions as men. Asking questions is fine. It shows we're interested in details and want a thorough understanding of a situation. It also enables us to make better decisions. But if we're so busy asking questions, we're not likely to get our own opinions out. Women are also more likely to open a conversation with a question *(Does everyone know why I called this meeting today?* Rather than *I called this meeting to discuss our new benefits package.)*, a speech pattern that signals uncertainty and a desire for attention.

● ***Powerless Voice.*** A whispery voice lacks power, invites interruption, and implies lack of confidence. The same goes for a mumbling voice. A mousy squeak can signal helplessness and sound like a carryover from your childhood days. A monotone not only puts people to sleep, it makes you sound totally uninterested in what you are saying. Since each of us has a range from high to low, practice until you find a pitch that is relatively low (but still comfortable) and sounds forceful.

take up more space and have fewer reservations about invading the space of others. In contrast, less powerful people tend to back off and yield space to others who are more powerful. We strongly advise against invading anyone else's personal space. While such behavior may make a man appear more powerful, it can make a woman appear overly aggressive. The best rule of thumb to keep in mind is to stay in the comfort zone by always maintaining an arm's length between you and the other person. And if someone tries to invade your personal space? You can hold your ground by not moving out of the way. However, if the proximity makes you uncomfortable, taking a few short steps backward may increase your comfort level and help you maintain control. Or suggest that the two of you sit down to continue your conversation. That way you can choose a seating arrangement that will put you in a position of power or equality.

Excerpted from Connie Brown Glaser and Barbara Steinberg Smalley, *More Power to You! How Women Can Communicate Their Way to Success.* (New York: Warner Books, 1992).

How Female Subordinates View You

What do female subordinates think of women bosses? *Working Woman* magazine posed this question in a recent readers' poll and found that the majority did *not* view female bosses as more manipulative, wishy-washy, domineering, or unqualified than male bosses. However, most *did* expect female bosses to be caring and sharing—and many reported feeling disappointed.

Commenting on the survey's results, Judy Rosener, a management professor at the University of California at Irvine, said, "For a lot of women there is jealousy involved." She also theorized, "There are still deep-seated beliefs that to be professional is to be male. Often, women who say they would rather work for a man unconsciously associate men with power."

When Your Appointment Is Controversial

If your appointment is surrounded by controversy, don't expect a red-carpet welcome. Maybe everyone's peeved because they were hoping one of *them* would be promoted. Maybe your subordinates had the opportunity to interview all of the candidates for the position, and you were *not* their first choice. Maybe you've been hired in the midst of restructuring and/or massive layoffs—or worse, been hired to orchestrate reorganization and determine who should be laid off. The details of the controversy are not important. What matters more is that you avoid feeling guilty, that you resist the urge to defer to your new subordinates, and that you don't apologize for your success. Instead, focus on selling yourself to them. After all, their primary concern will be "Where do I fit in?" And if you can make them feel needed and important, you've won half the battle.

"I assumed management of a group of employees at an extremely difficult period," says Laura Martin of Westin Hotels and Resorts. "Across the three departments reorganized to report to me, 25 percent of the employees had just been laid off, including all the managers of each department." To foster each employee's sense of belonging and ownership on this new team, Martin sought immediate feedback. "I asked all employees to identify the obstacles that they personally saw as impeding both their own success and the success of our newly organized group. This 'obstacle list' became the vehicle that enabled us to communicate and to develop a plan on how we would cope, as a group, with the reorganization."

After a difficult reorganization, which Martin says left the remaining employees feeling "dumped on," this process allowed for some constructive venting of frustrations as well. "It also helped me to assume leadership immediately and to demonstrate that, as a team, we had the ability to improve the situation."

Avoiding the Perfectionist Trap

New jobs—particularly when they are the result of a promotion—can be overwhelming and often cause women to doubt their abilities to perform well. "So many new faces to memorize. So much to learn. Maybe I made the wrong decision," we often lament. "The person in a new position may interpret her lack of knowledge about the role to mean that she isn't qualified to perform it," acknowledges Joan Harvey, Ph.D., in her book *If I'm So Successful, Why Do I Feel Like a Fake?* "She might even begin to believe she has misled her employer about her abilities. These feelings of being incompetent cause the person to try to be perfectionist. She doesn't want to make one little mistake because she thinks that will be people's clue to her tragic flaw."

The best way to avoid the perfectionist trap? *Expect* to make mistakes and forgive yourself when you do. Also, don't be afraid or reluctant—as women often are—to ask for help or advice. "When you move into a new position, seek advice from two types of people: those who have many years' experience in a job like the one you will be taking, and those who have recently made the transition," recommends Donna Hansen, Police Chief of Fort Myers, Florida. "The best advice I got came from a police chief who told me, 'Go with your own style.' No one can really tell you to do this or that—you have to be true to yourself and do things at your own speed. Moreover, it's important *not* to model behaviors you don't like or that don't feel right, because that's what ultimately ends up giving us ulcers, heart attacks, etc."

Life in a Fishbowl

Linda Hill, who followed the progress of female managers during their first year on the job, believes that a new boss's first thirty days are especially critical. "Subordinates spend that time making judgments—trying to decide if you deserve their respect and trust," she explains. "They're not so worried if you can do the job, but are looking for clues that you are out for yourself."

Start off on the right foot, and you won't have to waste precious time and energy backtracking to correct your mistakes and undoing bad first impressions. Remember the psychology of change and people's natural resistance to it, then find ways to work around it. Don't expect too much too soon—either of yourself or your subordinates. Take time to take charge. Get to know the people you'll be working with. Establish your priorities and share them with everyone. Be tough and caring. Stay visible and accessible. Don't pretend to know all the answers. And think "corporation first, my needs second."

Above all, be yourself. Nobody can really tell you how to succeed as the new boss. Only you know the answer to that.

CHAPTER FOUR

Attracting, Hiring, and Keeping Good Employees

PROFILE

SHERRY MOSLEY

MANAGER, HUMAN RESOURCE SYSTEMS DEVELOPMENT
CORNING INCORPORATED
CORNING, NEW YORK

"I set very high expectations for myself and expect a lot from my staff. But I also understand that everybody is different, and I really do care for my people. I want them to grow, and I want them to go. I see my responsibility as helping people to stretch and grow and move on."

W hat I do is develop processes and systems," says Sherry Mosley, Manager of Human Resource Systems Development at Corning Incorporated, a Fortune 200 company with some 28,000 employees worldwide. But we're not talking high-tech systems and processes here. Rather, what Mosley shines at is creating processes and systems that enable people to communicate more effectively with one another.

Armed with an undergraduate degree in business administration, Mosley began her career at Corning twenty-seven years ago as a secretary specializing in planning and forecasting. These days, however, Mosley focuses on developing innovative programs in employee, supervisor, and career development. When clients from various departments call on her for training, her main objective, she says, is to help them pinpoint and analyze their needs. "Basically, I sit down with them and find out what's going on in their area, then ask pointed questions like, 'What are we trying to do here? What are some other things that we already have in place in this organization that may feed into this, so you're not reinventing the wheel?' Next I encourage them to look ahead by asking, 'If we're successful in meeting this objective, what is success going to look like? What are people going to be saying in the halls six months from now?' Then I build whatever they need around their answers to these questions. A lot of times what they need is a process or, they may need some training."

When Mosley hires new employees, she specifically looks for people who know how to build relationships, "because what we do is go out and partner with in-house clients." Mosley prefers calculated risk-takers as well, and people who don't use the words "I can't do this." Moreover, because she doesn't consider herself to be a very outgoing person, she tries to surround herself with people who *are* outgoing.

Flexibility, she adds, is also a must, as is the ability to operate independently. "One of my basic philosophies is: You hire good people, let them do their job, and get involved when they need you. But don't look over their shoulder all the time."

To test for the qualities she's looking for in job candidates, Mosley asks very specific questions during the interview process: "Talk to me about a project you've been involved in. . . . Tell me the most difficult thing you've ever had to do in your career, what you think you learned from it, and how you would do it differently." She finds it helpful, as well, to challenge candidates with real-life scenarios they may encounter on the job.

For Mosley, the hiring process begins with a thorough job description—but one that she says has a lot of exceptions built into it. "I basically look at the task that needs to be done, get input and recommendations from the person who has been working in that particular position, then tell the candidate what my expectations are." How her employees meet those expectations, however, doesn't matter nearly as much to her as the end result. "I tell new recruits what the core task is, but stress that it's theirs to accomplish however they see fit. And I do this because I firmly believe that we all need to put our mark on something."

When making hiring decisions, Mosley confesses that she often relies on intuition. "What I've learned over time is that if my gut tells me it isn't right, and I don't listen to it, I always get in trouble," she reveals. And if a new hire will be working with a team, Mosley always allows the rest of the team to interview candidates. "But I make the final decision. Occasionally I've had people say to me, 'Well, if so-and-so worked here, I'd have a problem with that.' And I tell them, 'Well, we'll have to work through that if and when it happens.'"

Every new recruit at Corning goes through an extensive orientation program, which can last from nine to eighteen months and contains nine modules. "You learn about everything from financing to performance management. They also teach you a lot about the community."

Corning also has what they call a Smart Process, which is a self-managed training program, and Mosley has put together her own miniature version of this innovative program for people she brings into the organization. "It's like going on a treasure hunt," she says. "I give new employees a list of people in the company and tell them, 'Meet with these folks and learn a little bit about their backgrounds. Ask each of them how the two of you might be interacting over the next twelve months, and what both of you can do to make that an effective relationship.' The idea here is not only to get new recruits to find answers to important questions on their own, but to learn about different areas of the company, and to start building meaningful relationships up front with those they will be working with."

The whole idea behind the Smart Program, she adds, is that while it allows for independence, it also forces new employees to integrate themselves within the company. "That way, you're not sitting around six months into your new job saying, 'I've talked to this person fifteen times on the phone, but I don't have a clue about who he is.'"

New hires at Corning receive one-on-one training as well—from supervisors and/or other employees. "It all depends on who will do the best job for that particular employee."

Corning is also well known for offering innovative programs designed to keep good employees. "We offer a lot of seminars and workshops on such topics as cultural diversity and gender differences." In fact, by offering these kinds of programs, the company cut its number of departing women managers from 16.2 percent in 1987 to 5.4 percent in 1992. It also saved at least $2 million in recruitment and training costs.

Career development is a high priority at Corning as well. "Our ongoing training programs are based on skills employees need in order to carry our business forward," Mosley says. "Most of these are individualized according to where each person's gaps are. We also work with employees one-on-one to help them figure out where they want to go in the company and what it's going to take to get them there."

Not to say that every employee at Corning is expected to climb the corporate ladder, although most who work for Mosley do. "A few years ago, the turnover rate in my department was very high and someone said to me, 'What's wrong with you, Sherry? You can't keep anybody.' My response was that I don't hire people for life.

"I am a perfectionist of sorts," she admits. "I set very high expectations for myself and expect a lot from my staff. But I also understand that everybody is different, and I really do care for my people. I want them to grow, and I want them to go. I see my responsibility as helping people to stretch and grow and move on." In fact, most of the people Mosley has lost over the years have been promoted. "Of course, if someone wants to stay here, that's fine, too," she adds. "But it's not okay to stagnate. I tell everyone who comes to work for me, 'You have to continue to expand your knowledge base and learn new things. If you can't do that, you really can't work here.' "

And if someone who works for Mosley doesn't meet her expectations? "I confront them," she says. "I sit them down and say, 'We've got a problem here. How are we going to correct it, and what do you need to make that happen?' I also realize that when somebody's performance is not up to par, there could be all kinds of reasons for that other than being incompetent. So the solution may involve getting counseling, taking a leave of absence, or whatever. Basically, I see my job as caring about people and wanting to see them grow and stretch. But I also think that it's important to hold them accountable for what the two of us agreed they would do. After all, *my* job is making sure that what *they* do is a quality job."

• • •

Behind nearly every successful manager is a carefully chosen team of employees. A team that clicks. A team that is supportive of its manager (and vice versa). And a team that can be relied upon to get the job done.

How does a manager assemble such a team? Savvy managers will tell you that hiring the right people begins long before you screen or interview any applicants. In fact, recruiting the best candidates is an ongoing process—and one that should remain a priority even when you have no current openings.

Recruiting First-Rate Talent

Hooking the employee of your dreams begins with attracting an applicant pool that represents the cream of the crop. There are a number of sources you can tap to ensure a continuous supply of top-notch candidates, but first you must be able to describe the *kind* of people you are looking for.

We're not talking about a job description here—that information will vary according to specific jobs you are filling—but a summary of character traits and basic skills you seek in *all* employees. This preliminary screening step keeps you from wasting others' (recruiters, potential applicants) time as well as your own. It also reduces the risk of being forced to hire the "best of the worst" candidates when you have openings that need to be filled quickly.

Grace Pastiak, Director of New Business Development at Tellabs, says, "I look for people who have shown a willingness to invest in themselves, whether it's through education, outside interests, or extracurricular activities. If they've invested in themselves, it's more likely that they'll invest in the company." Pastiak also believes that people who invest in themselves are always willing to learn—and to grow. "Part of the tag line of learning new things is that you have to learn that the old ways may not be right—which is difficult for many people, who will never grow."

On the other hand, Cynthia Danaher, General Manager of Imaging Systems at Hewlett-Packard, looks for strong communication skills, leadership ability, and competency in subject matter. But most important, she says, is the ability to work well with the rest of the group. "I've found many people with great communication skills and promising leadership abilities who do not get along well with their peers. And that's a recipe for disaster at Hewlett-Packard." Consequently, when making hiring decisions that involve a team, Danaher always lets team members interview candidates and have a say in the decision-making process.

Your best source for new team players? Your existing team! Let your staff know that you're always interested in their recommendations for future employees. Better yet, offer compensation to current employees when a new hire is someone they have referred to the company. Scios Nova, a Mountain View, California, biotech firm, for example, boasts an employee referral program that pays workers a $1,000 bonus for every prospective employee referred and subsequently hired.

Also, scout the competition. Karyn Marasco, General Manager of the Westin William Penn, makes it her business to find out where the good employees are, then goes after them. "I recently 'stole' a sales manager from the competition as a result of conversations I had with several top clients," she confesses. "In fact, I'm always on the lookout for good employees. The way I see it, the server at my table in another restaurant could very well be my next 'Employee of the Month.'" And when hiring travel agents, Cindy Bender, CEO of Meridian Travel, a corporate travel agency based in Cleveland, makes it a point not to hire anyone with less than eight years' experience. She, too, prefers to cherry-pick the best agents from her competitors.

Screening Applicants

You've gotten the word out about the types of employees you're looking for and have received a stack of résumes. Now what? Should you try to interview every applicant? No—that would be a waste of time. Instead, refer to your blueprint of the ideal team player, and use these guidelines to screen potential candidates.

As you're weeding out applicants, remember to focus on the big picture—the *person* as well as his educational background and work experience (see "How to Read Between the Lines of a Résumé"). The tendency among managers is to choose people who have done the job—or a similar one—before. And their rationale is valid. Training experienced employees requires fewer hours and resources, plus it costs less. But keep in mind that a person's behavior, attitude, and personality can be just as important as her educational background and technical skills. Besides, candidates with less experience can always gain the necessary skills through training, but you're not likely to have the power to alter their psychological makeup.

How to Read Between the Lines of a Résumé

This composite résumé, along with the explanation that follows, should help you sharpen your résumé-reading skills and enable you to ask good questions in an interview situation.

❶ EDWARD ("TEDDY") BAINS THOMAS III

230 Pine Mountain Rd. ❷   Tel.: (714) 369-1431
San Diego, CA 30906   ❸ Present Salary: $27,950

OBJECTIVE: ❹   Seek challenging position with well-established and growing company with opportunities for advancement and good fringe benefits.

EDUCATION: ❺   Woodlawn High School, Houston, TX
Graduated 1970

- Member, Beta Club
- Officer, ROTC
- Secretary, Key Club
- President, 4-H Club
- Graduated with honors
- Captain, Soccer team

University of Florida, Gainesville, FL, Graduated 1974 with a 3.6 GPA B.S. degree in Computer Science; Minor in Sociology

University of South Carolina, Columbia, S.C., Graduated 1976 M.B.A. Degree

1980 to present: Have taken several continuing education courses in sociology, psychology, art, creative writing, and photography.

WORK
EXPERIENCE ❻

3/94–Present: Director of Customer Service, Computers Plus, San Diego, CA
Responsible for supervising a department and handling customer complaints,
Produce weekly corporate accounting statements for vice-president,
directors, and CEO. Managing Editor, company newsletter.

12/92–1/94: Assistant Manager, DataSystems, Inc., San Francisco, CA
Sold software in busy retail establishment. Trained customers on how to use new hardware and software.

5/91–7/92: Consultant, Wayne Lord & Associates Insurance, San Francisco, CA
Automated manual tasks to increase productivity. Trained supervisors and staff to use new software.

9/86–5/91: Thomas Microsystems, San Diego, CA
Owned and operated a successful retail business. Handled bookkeeping, taxes, sales, and customer service. Managed three employees.

6/78–8/86:	Instructor, Phelps Community College, Houston, TX Taught introductory courses in Computer Science to college freshmen.
6/76–5/75:	Assistant Manager, Wendy's Old Fashioned Hamburgers, Waco, TX Assisted with and supervised staff on night shift and weekends. Responsible for developing and implementing cost-saving measures.
Summers 1970–1976:	Counselor at 4-H Camps and Boy Scout Camps in North Carolina
EXTRACURRICULAR ACTIVITIES: ❼	Volunteer for United Way, Cancer Society, and American Heart Association Board of Directors, First Methodist Church Troop Leader, Boy Scouts of America Member, Chamber of Commerce
HOBBIES: ❽	Hang-gliding, Karate, Painting, Creative Writing, Computer Programming, Chess, Photography
REFERENCES: ❾	John Hudson Director of Personnel Wayne Lord & Associates Insurance 3201 Bay St. San Francisco, CA 91705 (415) 736-3900
	Emily Howell Director of Volunteers American Cancer Society 1061 W. Park Place San Francisco, CA 91726 (415) 736-2943
	Dr. Ronald Lewis Pastor First United Methodist Church 6924 Elm Avenue San Diego, CA 30616 (714) 369-2695

(1) When candidates list nicknames alongside their more formal first names, this usually means that they want to be called by the less-formal name. It's also probably safe to assume that they are informal, down-to-earth types whose more formal names don't suit their personalities. Yet the fact that they also include their formal names on their résumés implies that they have a serious, businesslike side to them as well.

(2) If offered a position in your company, how far would the employee have to drive? If his one-way commute exceeds thirty miles, and he must fight a lot of rush-hour traffic, use caution. He may always be on the lookout for a position closer to home.

(3) Listing one's present salary is unusual and may be a sign of desperation, particularly if the salary seems low in comparison to the candidate's age and experience. If you can come close to matching or manage to slightly increase the candidate's salary—and he seems worth talking to—call him in for an interview. If his present salary is greater than 20 percent more than you can offer, hire with caution. Candidates who take large pay cuts are likely to continue looking for other jobs even after accepting yours.

(4) This job objective is vague and generic—which probably means that countless other managers in your line of work have received identical copies. The fact that the candidate didn't take the time to tailor his résumé to your company or the position you advertised demonstrates poor judgment and a lack of focus. Moreover, his objective states that he is looking for opportunities for advancement and good fringe benefits. This statement also reflects poor judgment. The time to ask about opportunities for advancement and fringe benefits is at the close of an interview or once an offer has been made—not on a résumé.

(5) Despite the fact that this candidate has an MBA degree and graduated from high school twenty-five years ago, he insists on listing several honors and achievements from his high school years but very few from his college career. Obviously, he's trying to puff up his credentials. Nonetheless, his high school activities do suggest that he was a good student (Beta Club, graduated with honors), well rounded (4-H Club, Key Club, soccer team), and probably self-disciplined (ROTC officer), but keep in mind that this was twenty-five years ago.

A candidate's course of study can often clue you in as to whether he or she is more task-oriented or people-oriented. With this candidate's background in computer science and business, he appears to be task-oriented. However, with a minor in sociology, he may also possess adequate people skills.

Notice, too, that he has taken continuing education courses for a number of years and primarily in the social sciences and creative fields. This may indicate that he is sensitive as well as analytical. Continuing education is usually a positive sign, reflecting a keen sense of learning and healthy work ethic.

(6) This candidate has gone overboard by listing every job he's ever held. From 1986 to 1991, he owned and operated his own "successful retail business," which makes you wonder why, if it was so successful, he gave it up. Perhaps he sold it for a profit. From that point on, he hasn't stayed at a job for more than fourteen months. In general, frequent job-hopping indicates a lack of commitment, proficiency, and loyalty—unless the candidate can demonstrate that he has merely used every opportunity presented to him to get ahead and/or increase his income. This candidate's job-hopping pattern suggests that after working for himself for five years, he has had difficulty working for others. On the other hand, it could be that he bores easily, is ambitious, or has an insatiable capacity for learning.

Some of this candidate's language under his past job descriptions is vague. "Responsible for supervising a department," for example, probably means a very small department. Otherwise, he'd say, "Supervised a staff of 56 employees."

Always check résumés for an overabundance of qualifiers. Phrases like "have a working knowledge of . . ." or "assisted with . . ." are usually a sign that the applicant hasn't had a lot of hands-on experience in that area.

Also watch for spelling and grammatical errors. Sloppy work is usually a sign that the candidate doesn't pay much attention to details.

(7) Candidates' outside interests are usually good indicators of their personality. Active involvement in community projects, charities, and churches or synagogues is usually a sign that the person is generous and willing to help others.

(8) Be wary of lengthy personal sections. This candidate has listed a slew of hobbies. On the plus side, this demonstrates that he is active and energetic. The downside is, a manager can't help but wonder how he can spare the time or enthusiasm for work.

When candidates include a list of outside interests, you can gain valuable insights into their personalities by studying their list. If it includes sports, for example, are they competitive sports or are they individual sports? If the list includes hobbies, do they require patience? Creativity?

(9) When a candidate volunteers references (instead of writing "References Available Upon Request)" carefully examine the ones he has chosen. In this composite, the candidate hasn't listed a single supervisor. Instead, he has listed a director of personnel (may be a friend of his), a charity volunteer coordinator (what could she know about his on-the-job work habits?), and his pastor (always a safe choice).

"I'm far more concerned with candidates' moral and business ethics than I am with their experience on a specific job," says Lynn Richardson, Work Group Leader for Customer Service Training at Xerox in Houston. "I've always felt that I could teach people to do a specific job." To pinpoint these intangible characteristics, Richardson always makes it a point to listen carefully to candidates' responses to questions, "so that I can pick up signals about their ethics. If, for example, they worked their way through college, or worked during high school to save money, it shows me something about their sense of responsibility and moral fiber."

Julie Culwell, Manager of Editorial Services for the Atlanta Committee for the Olympic Games, agrees. "When hiring, I look for talent in writing and photography, but I also look for integrity, loyalty, and honesty. I want someone who believes in teamwork and is not out for personal gain," she says.

While managing editorial services at Coca-Cola, Culwell once hired a writer after learning that the candidate had given up a scholarship to her first-choice college. "She made that sacrifice so that she could remain close to home and help care for her mother, who had cancer," Culwell reports. In another instance, when a vacancy at Coca-Cola attracted several hundred applicants, all but one candidate sent in a thick portfolio. "This particular person had very little experience—and she knew it," Culwell recalls. "So instead of trying to pad her portfolio, she wrote me a letter explaining why she felt she deserved the job. It was such a warm and touching letter—like one you would receive from a good friend—and so unlike the other applicants' more formal cover letters, that I hired her. I knew she would be a good team player. In fact, she turned out to be an outstanding employee."

In other words, you shouldn't necessarily toss out an applicant who doesn't fit your "mold." Sometimes, bringing in someone different—who's likely to bring with her new ideas, concepts, styles, and possibly new clients—makes sense. If, for example, sales or productivity levels are down in your department, or your staff appears bored or too comfortable with their jobs, bringing in someone new and different may give them the jump start they need to feel challenged or to become more productive.

"At MTV Networks, we've always valued a sense of humor in job applicants," says Nicole Browning, Senior Vice President of Regional Operations, Affiliate Sales and Marketing. "Yet not long ago we found ourselves steering away from people who were more serious in their interviews. And that's not a good thing for a company. It's a mistake to disqualify people because their approach or demeanor may be different from yours. I've gotten better at this with experience, because I've seen people who have blossomed in the organization whom I might not have connected with during an interview."

When it comes to hiring new staff, one of the most common mistakes managers make is using vague language to define job requirements. Frequently, they'll list duties and responsibilities instead of tangible and measurable performance expectations—which often leaves new employees feeling unclear about what's expected of them. Consequently, in the first six months or so of the job, employees tend to waste far too much time trying to figure out what their bosses want.

Suppose you have an opening for someone to supervise your sales staff. Instead of listing in your job description, "must have proven track record in sales and ability to motivate employees," write, "will be expected to increase sales by at least 10 percent during the next twelve months." This is specific and measurable. Moreover, the individual you hire knows exactly what is expected of him during his first year on the job.

Using specific language in job descriptions will also help you to fairly evaluate employees later. If you've told your sales staff supervisor that he is expected to increase sales by 10 percent within twelve months, you can use this criterion to discuss his performance at the end of his first year.

When composing a job description, you'll also need to think ahead. How might this job change in the next year, in three years, or in five years? What additional skills and training might be needed down the line? If, for example, your company is looking at restructuring a year from now, how would this position be affected? Since employee turnover can be expensive, looking ahead can prevent you from making costly mistakes.

Finally, include a summary of your corporate culture in your job description. This statement might include a description of your management philosophy, your company's policy about promoting from within, opportunities for training and development, attitudes toward women, and other important issues. Be honest and straightforward. That way you don't risk selling an applicant a "bill of goods."

Fine-Tuning Your Interview Skills

Managers' interviewing styles usually differ according to their gender. "Women tend to be chatty, folksy even, because they want to put people at ease," notes Aileen Jacobson in *Women in Charge: Dilemmas of Women in Authority.* Men, on the other hand, tend to "cut to the chase and be more direct."

Both styles have drawbacks. In an effort to make candidates feel comfortable, women often become so focused on playing the good hostess that they fail at getting the information they need about the applicant. In contrast, men who are abrupt and overly direct can paralyze applicants to the point that they blow the interview. Or candidates may be so offended by the manager's style that they withdraw their application.

Many managers waste precious interview time describing—and selling—the job, themselves, and the organization instead of delving into the candidate's background. Remember, it's the *applicant* who should be doing the selling—at least initially. Besides, you jump the gun when you open an interview with an elaborate description of the job and the kind of person you're looking for. Because later when you ask questions, the savvy candidate will know exactly what to say to give you the answers you're hoping to hear. So save your detailed job description and sales pitch until the end of the interview.

Some 80 percent of interviews are completely unstructured according to Therese Hoff Macan, an assistant professor of psychology at the University of Missouri at St. Louis, who specializes in employment interview research. The result? When the interview process is over, and you're faced with a decision, everything—and everyone—is a blur.

A simple scoring system can help you avoid this problem. Macan recommends that you take a look at your job description—before the first interview—and devise a chart of behaviors and skills you are seeking. Next, list each of these criteria in order of importance. Then, once you begin interviewing, you can rate candidates on a scale of 1 to 10 in each category.

Leave space next to each category for notes as well. Studies suggest that when interviewers don't take notes, they tend to remember—and are influenced by—only what happened at the beginning of each interview. But don't take such extensive notes that you interrupt the flow of the interview process or miss candidates' nonverbal behaviors. "If you're worried about missing something by taking notes during the interview, don't do it. But at the very least, make notes at the end of the session," Macan advises.

Always go into an interview with a prepared list of questions. (These should correlate with the criteria on your scoring sheet.) And, to be fair, ask everyone the same basic list of questions. "It's like giving a test to your students," says Macan. "If you gave everyone a different test, what would an A and B mean? How can you compare people if you don't use the same common measure?"

Many managers make the mistake of asking interviewees stock questions. "What are your strengths?" "Your weaknesses?" "Where do you see yourself five years from now?" These are questions that virtually every one of today's job applicants are prepared—and often coached—to answer. Some managers also have a tendency to ask an abundance of questions that elicit little more than a yes or no response. ("Did you have a good rapport with your boss at your last job?" rather than "What kind of relationship did you have with your boss at your last job?") The purpose of an interview is to pinpoint real job skills and to evaluate a candidate's potential. But if you ask general and simple questions, you'll only get general and simple answers.

Twenty Questions

(Open-ended questions that prompt revealing answers
in an interview situation)

General Questions (Icebreakers)

(1) What circumstances in your life led you to choose your profession?

(2) Share with me your description of the ideal job. The ideal boss.

(3) Tell me about your working style. Would you describe yourself as a leader or a follower? As people-oriented or task-oriented? Do you prefer working alone or as part of a team?

Questions Dealing with Candidate's Employment History

(4) How do you typically handle conflict or working with difficult people? Give me some specific examples along with strategies you've used successfully.

(5) What approach do you generally take to solve problems? Give me some specific examples.

(6) Tell me about an instance where your efforts at problem-solving failed—and steps you took to bounce back.

(7) Give me an example of a work situation in which you were criticized. How did you handle it?

(8) Have you ever saved an employer money? If so, give me some figures and tell me how you did it.

(9) Consider your job history and tell me about the jobs you've enjoyed most—and least—then explain why they were your favorites/least favorites.

(10) Give me some examples of instances where you have worked under pressure. How did you handle it?

(11) Tell me about the toughest work-related decision you've ever had to make. What were the strategies you used to reach your decision?

Questions Dealing with Candidate's Present (or Most Recent) Job

(12) Describe your present boss's management style and tell me how it meshes—as well as how it conflicts—with yours.

(13) Review the things you like best about your present job, then tell me about some of your pet peeves.

(14) What do you consider to be your greatest achievement in your present job? How did you achieve it?

(15) Describe a typical day at your present job. Tell me about a bad day. A great day.

Questions About the Current Opening

(16) Tell me what led you to apply for this position. What attracted you to this particular company?

(17) What can this company offer you that is lacking in your present position?

(18) What do you think your references will tell me about you?

Wrap-up Questions

(19) From our discussions so far, how do you see this position?

(20) Here are the goals I'd like the person in this position to achieve in the first year. What steps would you take to fulfill my expectations?

A better approach? Ask open-ended questions that encourage candidates to talk about themselves. (See "Twenty Questions") Place them in scenarios related to the position for which they are applying. Posing "What would you do if . . ." questions can help you quickly zero in on an applicant's strengths and weaknesses. Moreover, what you see is usually what you get. Studies show that what people say they would do in hypothetical situations closely correlates with what they will *actually* do in similar real-life situations.

Another way to get candidates to talk openly and candidly is to ask for examples of how they have handled specific situations in the past (dealt with an angry client, a hostile co-worker, or a demanding boss, for example). Then follow up their responses with more probing questions, like "How did you manage to do that?" or "What made you do it that way?" Or ask them to pinpoint their greatest accomplishment in their last position, then probe for details on how they did it.

Try to avoid "why" questions, as these can make you sound abrupt and demanding. (Example: "Why did you spend less than a year at Acme Corporation?") Instead, use words and phrases like "Explain," "Tell me more about . . ." "Review," and "Describe." (Example: "Tell me more about your decision to transfer from Acme Corporation to Barrett Industries after less than a year.")

It's always a good idea to narrow your applicant pool down to a half dozen or so top candidates and bring these in for a second round of interviews. If the prospect will be part of a team, it's an even better idea to allow her fellow team members to interview her.

"Because a new person will become an integral part of our team, I prefer to have each member of the department interview the candidate," says Kim E. McCaulou, Manager of Marketing Programs at Westin Hotels and Resorts. "In situations where this isn't practical, I ask each job group to nominate an interviewer to represent them. This accomplishes two primary goals. First, the prospective employee gets a full view of the position from many different viewpoints. Second, the department has a greater interest in the new employee's success, because we all selected the candidate."

An alternative to having your team interview candidates is to invite the finalists to spend a half-day on the job. This takes them out of the interview setting and enables you to observe them in the real working environment. (Do they seem interested in your operation? Do they ask good questions? Do they interact well with others?) It also gives your team an opportunity to size up each candidate.

Or try this idea from Xerox's Lynn Richardson. "I interview the top candidates, then narrow the pool down to four or five individuals. My team then makes the final decision." But Richardson's team doesn't interview the candidates per se. Instead, she gives each of the top applicants a role-playing situation to act out in front of her team. "These situations always involve teaching my staff how to do something specific—like how to balance a checkbook," Richardson explains. "Every candidate receives the same instructions and is allowed fifteen minutes for his or her presentation. Each team member then ranks the candidates on a scale of 1 to 5 in several different areas, including professionalism, ability to think on their feet, and so forth."

The first time Richardson tried this approach, she was concerned that everyone on her team would come up with a different candidate as their top choice for the position. "Instead, their decisions have always been unanimous. In fact, it's usually obvious to the entire group as to who has done the best job," she reports. "Moreover, because everyone has been involved in making the decision, each team member feels a vested interest in seeing the new person succeed. As a result, everyone does whatever is necessary to help the new hire fit in, learn the ropes, and succeed on the job."

Allowing Personal Chemistry to Cloud Your Judgment

During an interview, women sometimes feel so comfortable with a particular candidate that they tend to be swayed more by the applicant's personality than his or her job qualifications. "It's very easy to hire someone who is a reflection of who you are, were, or what you might be . . . 'That's me ten years ago, let's hire her,' " says Nicole Browning, a senior vice president for MTV Networks. "There's also a certain comfort level in hiring someone you know you are going to be able to relate to. For instance, if someone has the same sense of humor that you do, you can immediately click on that." But allowing personal chemistry to cloud your judgment can also be dangerous, in that you may choose a person you like, but who doesn't possess the skills or capabilities to do the job well. Besides, you don't want a team of clones. A diversity of personalities and skills is what will ultimately make your team work.

Relying Too Much Upon—
or Totally Ignoring—Intuition

You've narrowed your search to one candidate. She's bright, articulate, and seems extremely capable. Her track record is impressive, and her references have checked out. Yet something about her—call it instinct or a gut feeling—doesn't seem quite right. But you can't put your finger on what's causing your reservations. Do you disregard intuition and hire her anyway? That depends.

On the one hand, intuition—particularly for women—is often more logical than we think. Because women tend to excel at reading body language, we often pick up on nonverbal cues that makes us feel uneasy about certain job applicants. A candidate's failure to look us in the eye, for example, doesn't jibe with her self-description as a "real people person." Or, the candidate who taps his foot whenever we ask questions about one of his former positions, makes us suspect that he's hiding something.

On the other hand, relying solely on gut feelings, of course, is not an objective way to make sound hiring decisions. So, as a rule of thumb, trust your instincts—but not completely. And before making any candidate a job offer, take the time to dig a little deeper. Check a few more of their references. Bring them back for a second interview and see if you can pinpoint what's bothering you. Also, have your team members meet with candidates and see what they think. That way, the final decision is based on more than your observations.

"I have learned to rely on my instincts 99 percent of the time," reports Lynn Richardson of Xerox. "However, I feel strongly about not being the only one to make the final decision. In fact, when I bring my team in on the decision-making process, I don't see it as abdicating responsibility, but rather as effectively delegating an important decision."

Adds Morene Seldes-Marcus, Director of Human Resources for Hi-Fi Buys, an audio-video retail chain headquartered in Atlanta,

"My gut feeling plays a major role in my decision-making. But what I really force myself to do—and others who I help in the hiring process—is to stick with the list of criteria or the behaviors and key experiences that someone needs to be successful in that job. Then I try to ask questions of every candidate that relate to those key elements."

For example, Seldes-Marcus was recently involved with eight others in the hiring of a company chief financial officer. The job requirements included experience in operations and systems, along with a solid financial background. "I knew that inevitably there would be personalities we preferred," she says. "But I tried to get the group of interviewers to help me come up with a profile of the person who would fit best into the position and our organization. I did this by posing questions like, 'What are the key experiences this individual should have in order to help our company move forward?' and by pointing out that we needed someone who had more experience in specific areas than the last person who had held the position."

After interviewing the top four candidates, the selection committee got together and listed skills, behaviors, and key experiences needed for the job, then rated the candidates against that criteria. "But just as I had predicted, the conversation soon turned to the personalities of the candidates, and the gut feelings of everyone involved were to hire someone who lacked the key elements we were looking for," Seldes-Marcus reports. "However, I managed to steer the group back to the profile of the ideal CFO, and in the end we hired the best-*qualified* person."

In an effort to fill vacant positions quickly, many managers make hasty decisions, only to regret them within a few months' time. Rush now, pay later. Some, for example, hire out of desperation. Faced with a dismal applicant pool, they hire the "best of the worst." Or they reluctantly lower their standards, make an offer, and hope for the best. Some choose candidates with strong technical skills but weak interpersonal skills in hopes that the new hire will change. Others get blown away by an overqualified candidate, make an offer, and then wonder why the person quits in less than a year.

Remember, your goal is not to compare candidates so much as it is to match the candidate to the position. And if after interviewing everyone, there's not a good fit, instead of acting out of desperation, consider some alternatives.

Look internally. Can a promising employee be promoted from within? Can you make a lateral transfer, moving another employee into the position—one whose job, once vacant, may be easier to fill? Can you restructure and eliminate the vacant position altogether?

If not, reopen the position and consider hiring temporary staff to fill the gap. The temporary employment industry is burgeoning—$30 billion and growing steadily every year. And while once primarily used as a source of clerical workers, the industry now offers short-term technical and professional staff in many fields.

Or do as Linda Pacotti, Manager of State and Community Affairs for Schering-Plough, does. "Ten years ago, I began taking college student interns—usually one a year—into my office," she says. Students who intern with Pacotti start in January, then are usually persuaded to stay on as summer employees—"so I get seven or eight months out of them," she says. But Pacotti cautions not to make the mistake, as many managers do, of thinking of interns as little more than gofers. "That never happens with one of my interns. As a prerequisite to signing on, the interns must commit to working with me half-days, five days a week. For several months at the start, my interns go everywhere I go and do everything I do. Then they're given corporate projects with real-world responsibilities for researching, launching, implementing, and evaluating. A more accurate word for the experience would be *apprenticeship*."

Keeping Good Employees

One of three new hires you've brought on board within the last year has just handed you her resignation. Another good employee bites the dust, and you'll have to foot the bill for another search, another round of interviews, and another six months of on-the-job training. Ouch.

A recent survey conducted by the Professional Employment Research Council found that eight out of ten workers at all levels would consider making a job change if the right opportunity presented itself. What's happened to company loyalty? According to a recent poll by *Industry Week* Magazine, gone are the days when company loyalty was a given. In fact, while nearly 96 percent of those surveyed said loyalty was important, a whopping 87.3 percent felt that there was far less loyalty between companies and their employees as compared to five years earlier.

In other words, these days a company must *earn* its employees' loyalty. And the best place to start earning it? With new employees. Here's how:

• **If you don't have an orientation program set up for new employees, establish one immediately and make it mandatory for every new recruit.** Orientation sessions should last a minimum of four to eight hours. They should be devoted entirely to making new hires feel welcome and helping them become acclimated to your company. Devote a substantial portion of your orientation program to telling new recruits about your company's history and who's who in your organization, reviewing company benefits and policies and procedures, and providing them with a brief overview of your industry. Allow plenty of time for participants to ask questions. Above all, seize the opportunity to share your company's mission and goals—what makes your operation unique— as well as *your* visions. Paint for them the big picture, then show them where they fit in.

At Baptist Hospital of Miami, for instance, employees are encouraged to think of patients as "guests." Adds Vice President Charlotte Dison, "We also define a 'guest' as anyone whom we come in contact with, not only the visitors or vendors, but patients' families, physicians, co-workers, and volunteers." New employees at Baptist Hospital are issued wallet-sized cards that list guidelines for how to treat a guest. Some are also sent to nearby Naples for an overnight stay at the Ritz to see how guests are treated at a five-star hotel. "Because that's the standard we're trying to achieve," reports Dison.

All new employees at Baptist Hospital also attend a four-hour GREAT—Guest Relations Education And Training—session during their two-day orientation. And on their one-year employment anniversary, new hires attend a two-and-a-half-hour refresher course, called "Still GREAT." Graduates of both courses receive a pineapple lapel pin. "The pineapple is the symbol of hospitality," Dison explains.

• Go out of your way to make new employees feel welcome. Consider assigning a "work buddy" to all new hires—someone they can turn to for immediate answers to questions, someone to introduce them to other staff members, and someone who will join them for lunch (or at least make sure they're not eating alone) during the first few weeks on the job. When Vernon Valentine was hired as a writer/consultant in the New Jersey office of Hewitt Associates, he was delighted with his "red carpet" welcome. "The secretary had ordered all the supplies I would need—not just paper and pens, but schedule books and a wall calendar. One of the more experienced writers left a 'welcome' note on my desk, along with a 'survival kit' (with a candy bar and nerf ball) . . . and *everybody* came by my office to personally welcome me to the 'team,'" Valentine told the authors of *The 100 Best Companies to Work for in America*. "For the first two weeks or so, somebody made a point to stop by and ask me to lunch—every day. Perhaps the most surprising, my name had been automatically added to the office softball roster—the folks who interviewed me had really listened."

• Break bread with new employees by hosting a monthly breakfast or luncheon that they are encouraged to attend during their first six months. This gives everyone a chance to ask questions, relax, laugh, and just get to know one another better. Use this time to learn about new hire's spouses and children. Showing an interest in them as people—instead of just workers—induces company loyalty. At Great Plains Software in Fargo, North Dakota, for example, every new hire has lunch with the firm's President, Doug Burgum.

• **Consider scheduling weekly performance reviews with all new hires for their first six months.** Keep these brief, low-key, and informal, but use them as opportunities to provide constant feedback. Tell new employees what they're doing well and in what areas they need to improve. Communicate your commitment to helping them succeed.

If this strategy sounds too time-consuming, Carolyn Thompson, President of CBT Training Systems, a Frankfort, Illinois, specialist in employee retention and recruitment, suggests, "Have people who are teaching the new employee fill out a performance checklist every week. Then you as manager can say, 'You're really up to speed on this, a little behind on that.' Your performance appraisal process starts right away."

• **Provide adequate on-the-job training.** A survey conducted by *Training* magazine reported that while 69 percent of organizations with over fifty people on the payroll provided training for their middle managers, and 70 percent trained their executives, only 25 percent trained production people, 30 percent trained salespeople, and 34 percent trained customer service representatives. In essence, the very people who had the most contact with clients were receiving the least amount of training!

Expect a new employee to learn by trial and error, and you set him up to feel like a failure. Moreover, left to sink or swim, he's more likely to quit even before his probationary period is over, and *you'll* have to shell out the bucks to recruit and hire his replacement. Keep in mind, too, that mistakes made by new employees have a way of trickling down to your customers, which can affect your company's bottom line. Besides, training pays. Studies reveal that employees who receive adequate training are more confident, independent, and enjoy higher self-esteem. They also have better attendance records, are more reluctant to steal from the company, take greater pride in their jobs, and are more productive.

At American Express Personal Financial Planning, new financial planners are introduced to the business through a mentoring program, which pairs rookie financial planners with seasoned ones. Mary Pierce, District Manager at the company's Salt Lake City office, says, "We found that we were spending tons of money bringing people into the business and losing far too many of them. And while our retention rate was one of the highest in the industry, we wanted to boost those numbers." Currently, eight veteran planners team-coach all new hires. "Under the old system, new recruits were coached by a single veteran planner," Pierce reports. "Now, with eight coaches, the new planner can tap into the resources of the team. That way, he or she is exposed to a variety of strengths and styles. The team of coaches benefits as well, since everyone has an interest in seeing the new people succeed. It's a much more holistic approach to training."

Training new hires is also a top priority at Southwest Airlines. "Humor is considered a real asset here, but it's a difficult thing to teach," explains Colleen Barrett, Executive Vice President–Customers. "You have to be comfortable with humor. It has to be you, and you have to be real." During orientation sessions, whenever the subject of humor came up, new recruits were always pressing Barrett, "Give me a list . . . Tell me steps," and she couldn't do that. "What I *could* do was *show* them what I meant," she says, "so I had our culture committee put together a twenty-six-minute videotape that showcased different employees whom we got complimentary letters about all the time. But I didn't show it so much hoping that new employees would imitate others' styles and shticks. It was simply something that couldn't be put on paper."

• **Don't limit training to new staffers.** Candy Obourn, Vice President and Director of Information Systems and Business Processes at Kodak, has installed a number of programs to hold on to her good employees. "I frequently hold 'town meetings' to discuss the organization's plans, strategies, and status with everyone on my team," she says. Kodak also boasts focus groups designed to provide input to managers on employee issues, a reskilling plan to keep employees current with new technologies, and a career development program.

Hallmark Cards brings in some thirty visiting artists and writers a year for ongoing training and development to inspire their staff of seven hundred artists, writers, and designers. Guests have included sociologist and author Betty Friedan and *New Yorker* cartoonist Gahan Wilson.

At Lotus Development Corporation, software writers regularly spend time with customers to gain *their* outlook on the company's products. "That way, they come to understand the larger purpose of their work without a manager having to *tell* them," says June Rockoff, Senior Vice President of Software Development.

And to make sure that everyone was familiar with the myriad of services offered at Phelps County Bank in Rolla, Missouri, CEO Emma Lou Brent recently designed a year-long, in-house training program in which each department prepared a session for the others. The program culminated in a mock *Jeopardy* game with six employee teams competing and an electric scoreboard tallying the answers.

"Of course, you can have the best training in the world and still get complaints," notes Southwest Airlines's Colleen Barrett. "So I also let employees watch videotapes of customers who have complained to us. Whenever we show this tape, you can hear a pin drop. It's fascinating to see the faces of employees while they are watching. When they realize the customer is talking about *them*, it's pretty chilling. That has far more impact than anything I can say."

Susan Lang, Manager of Technical Support at Aldus Corporation, adds that letters of praise, as well as constructive feedback letters received from customers, can also serve as a perfect vehicle for the ongoing training of employees. "We use a unique and effective communication system for our technicians called 'BRIGHT & SHINING' or 'GREEN & GROWING,' " she reports. "Thank-you letters, which we fondly refer to as 'Bravo' letters, are printed on bright yellow paper carrying a sunshine logo, and are distributed to all members of technical support as well as our sales force. 'Opportunities for Growth' letters, or those in which our customers share suggestions for improvement, carry a wilted flower logo and are printed on bright green paper with the same distribution. Of course, we remove the name of the customer and technician. This allows us all to learn from potential mistakes without embarrassing the offender."

Another good way to retain good employees is to promote from within. Mary Black, co-founder and Vice President of Super Wash, which sells, builds, equips, and services car washes, says that when vacancies occur at corporate headquarters she rarely hires from the outside. "I prefer to train promising employees and promote from within." The company, based in Morrison, Illinois, has a minimal turnover rate.

Above all, don't ever be reluctant to hire someone who seems too good to be true out of fear that they may have an eye for *your* position. If you do, you may be harming yourself. As Claire Coyle, Group Director of Marketing Services at SmithKline Beecham, puts it, "When I hire, I *look* for my replacement. I want a couple of acceptable replacements in the wings should anyone say to me, 'Hey Claire, I want to make you president of the company.' When you have a strong team you can pass responsibilities on to, *you* get promoted."

CHAPTER FIVE

From Staff to Team: The Dolphin As Coach

PROFILE

SUZANNE JENNICHES

GENERAL MANAGER, IMAGING AND DATA SYSTEMS DIVISION
WESTINGHOUSE ELECTRIC
LINTHICUM, MARYLAND

"I don't like yes men, and I don't like everyone marching in step and saluting together. Of course, ultimately the team must arrive at a common goal or approach, but we arrive at a better one by coming at it from different angles."

The ideal coach, according to Suzanne Jenniches, is someone who is a giver rather than a taker, someone with strong leadership skills, and above all, a person who has the ability to inspire others to see beyond what they would normally and naturally see.

Interesting that she would emphasize the concept of inspiration, since Jenniches herself personifies the word.

In 1971, Jenniches was a high school biology teacher who thoroughly enjoyed her job. "Growing up, I had always been very technically oriented, and because all of my role models in the technical fields were teachers, it seemed the natural thing to do," she says. Then an ad on the back cover of a teachers' association magazine caught her eye. "It described master's degree programs offered in the evenings at Johns Hopkins University," she recalls, "and one of the choices was environmental engineering."

Ecology was a hot topic in the early 1970s and one Jenniches was keenly interested in, having recently celebrated the first Earth Day with her students. Thinking that environmental engineering was ecology-oriented, Jenniches tore off the ad's reply form and sent it in on a whim. "Lo and behold, I got a letter back from Johns Hopkins requesting my college transcripts," she reports, "and a few months later I was accepted as a master's degree candidate in environmental engineering."

Having never taken an engineering course in her life, Jenniches began her master's program sixty undergraduate credits behind. She also soon discovered that environmental engineering wasn't biology- or ecology-oriented at all. "But once I got involved, I discovered that I loved engineering."

At Johns Hopkins, several of Jenniches's classmates were pursuing master's degrees in engineering during the evening while holding down full-time day jobs at Westinghouse. Hearing them speak so highly of the company convinced Jenniches to spend her Christmas break from the classroom working at Westinghouse. "It was a two-week trial, and I didn't get paid for it," she recalls. "I wanted to get a feel for the company, and they wanted to check me out, too."

The two clicked, and Jenniches soon gave up her teaching career to accept an entry-level position at the company. "I was the lowliest of the low," she says, "but I did whatever it took to get the job done." As a result, Jenniches eventually worked her way up the ladder from associate test engineer to operations manager. Then, in 1990, when Westinghouse formed its Imaging and Data Systems Division, Jenniches was tapped to direct it. Today she directly supervises eighty individuals and indirectly oversees several hundred other engineers.

Jenniches reports that her insight into the importance of teamwork stems from her humble beginnings within Westinghouse. "I learned early on that there was nothing too insignificant that it shouldn't be done well, and that you should feel just as free to roll up your sleeves and tackle a job as the next person," she says. In fact, Jenniches admits that she struggled, initially, with becoming a team player. "In my early days as an engineer, I firmly believed that *I* needed to get credit for the good work I'd done. But through experience and with the help of mentors, I've realized that the success of the *team* is most important. When your team is successful, you share in that success."

These days, Jenniches puts together her own teams and has learned through experience how to pick the best players. "I don't see teams as static," she says. "I think that very often people within your organization can and should be members of many teams and sometimes two or three teams at once. Consequently, because I never know from one quarter to the next exactly which team a person will be on, I look for individual characteristics—people who are flexible, creative, and who possess 'can-do' attitudes."

Jenniches also looks for what she calls "big picture" people— "those who are able to appreciate the full spectrum of what we're trying to accomplish," she explains. "But I don't want them just to be 'advisors' or to have too global a perspective. They also have to be willing to work on some nitty-gritty, because that is how team members value one another. In essence, the people I hire must have what I call 'zoom lens' skills, meaning that they can move in and out, they can see the big picture, and they can go way down to the very fine details."

When putting together a particular team, Jenniches looks for complementary skills. "I like to have a hardware person and a software person, an administrative person and a quality person, a marketing specialist and a finance person, plus someone for reliability. That way, we create, as much as possible, a team of equals."

Diversity is also important to Jenniches. "I believe in the strength of diversity," she says. "It's a passion of mine. I value diverse opinions, diverse skills, and diverse personalities, all working in harmony as a team. Diverse people bring their special skills as well as the ability to see a problem from a different angle, and that's important to the success of a project." As a result, when recruiting team players, Jenniches tries to mix people from different social and academic backgrounds and combine quiet people with talkative people. "This makes for a tremendously energizing and often chaotic atmosphere."

Jenniches adds that she also treasures a little controversy and conflict. "But I like the conflict to be objective—not personality-oriented," she explains. "I don't like yes men, and I don't like everyone marching in step and saluting together. Of course, ultimately the team must arrive at a common goal or approach, but we arrive at a better one by coming at it from different angles."

At Westinghouse, not all work is performed by teams; yet, even with individual assignments Jenniches likes to see her subordinates rely on others. "There's hardly anything in this world you can do by yourself," she believes. "So even though a person may have an individual assignment, because we work in a team environment it's not unusual for that person to discuss his project with others and even to elicit the support and assistance of his peers. In fact to me, people who can turn an individual assignment into a team assignment without creating jealousies or friction—because it looks as if they're off-loading their work—are natural leaders and managers."

When choosing team leaders, Jenniches believes that to be effective the person must have the respect of the other players. Otherwise, she says, selecting a leader is often obvious because the project at hand is dominated by a particular task. In other instances, where it's not as obvious, Jenniches will rotate leaders. "Lots of times I try people out. I say to them, 'Look, I'm asking you to lead this particular project, even though I know it's not exactly your area of expertise. But I'd like to see you stretch a little bit. I'd like to see you grow.' "

Oftentimes, she adds, team leaders emerge on their own. "And when that happens consistently with an individual, then you know that that person is destined to go up much further in the organization."

As for the qualities of a good coach, Jenniches believes that if you pick the right players, a manager doesn't have to do a lot of coaching per se. "What *is* important in making a team successful, though, is defining what your expected results are. You don't necessarily tell them *how* to achieve them—or even how to split up the workload—but you've got to tell them what you expect." Moreover, Jenniches believes that a manager's expectations should be concrete and explicit. "If you're too nebulous up front, you get a team that works really hard and has a lot of activity, but you're never sure if they're moving forward, backward, or going around in circles. In essence, you need to say, 'We need this product, built by this date, for this cost, and with no quality problems.' "

When working in teams, conflict is inevitable, but Jenniches keeps conflict among her team members to a minimum by stressing constant and open communication. "Usually the biggest conflicts arise when something unexpected occurs," she says. "But if you keep an open dialogue, where there is always an opportunity for discussion, there are few surprises. In fact, what often happens instead is that people soon begin to see that while one day you agree with someone and the next you disagree, it's an issue-oriented conflict, not a personality-oriented one. In other words, not everyone approaches the job the same way. Different people have different strengths, different weaknesses, and different hot buttons. But once you've worked together for a while and have been successful at accomplishing things, people learn to value these differences. In fact, they no longer see them as strengths and weaknesses but as, 'Each of us has a role to play, and this is what I bring to the party.' And once teams recognize this, they get comfortable and start to jell."

But Jenniches doesn't like her teams to get *too* comfortable and every so often will add a new member—"just to keep things stirred up." Her philosophy? "I think you always need to be slightly uncomfortable and reaching a little beyond what you think you can do."

• • •

Over the last decade or so, the concept of teamwork has swept across corporate America, dramatically altering the roles of both subordinates and their managers. Under this new mind-set, tasks once reserved exclusively for management—like decision-making, innovation, problem-solving, and quality control—have become *everyone's* business. Moreover, corporations that have embraced this all-for-one, one-for-all philosophy are prospering.

And no wonder! Employees who work as teams are highly motivated and tend to take more initiative than do employees who are simply issued orders. Team players are also more productive. Given the freedom to decide when and how the work gets done, they no longer must sit around waiting for management's instructions.

Because they have a voice in company decisions, team players often feel a sense of obligation—even responsibility—for the organization's success. Consequently, they are always on the lookout for ways to cut costs, better serve the needs of their customers, increase productivity, and boost the company's bottom line.

According to Grace Pastiak of Tellabs, teams can be great problem-solvers. "I'll give you an example," she says. "One of my teams once said, 'You know this press that's been broken all these years, but our supervisors have been too busy to bother with it? Why don't *we* fix it?' In fact, what I've found, at least in manufacturing, was that there *were* no million-dollar problems. There were a million $5 problems, which our teams were great at solving."

Employees who are part of a team are also generally more content with their jobs. Most find it extremely rewarding and satisfying to see a project through from start to finish. As a result, they also tend to take greater pride in their work. In other words, employee involvement is good for morale, and what's good for morale is good for the bottom line.

"At Ford Motor Company, roughly two years after our Employee Involvement (EI) program began, the company and the United Auto Workers asked 748 hourly workers how they felt about working at Ford," reports Donald E. Petersen, former President and CEO of Ford and co-author of *A Better Idea: Redefining the Way Americans Work*. "About 82 percent said they were satisfied, whereas only 58 percent had said that before employee involvement got off the ground." Many of these workers, he adds, gave up their lunch hours, stayed late, and changed shifts around so that they could stay and be part of the team.

Managers enjoy benefits from the teamwork concept as well. For starters, the pressure is off to be—or act like—experts at *everything*, because managers can supplement their teams with people who are strong and knowledgeable in areas where they are not. Working with teams also enables managers to tap the skills and expertise of those who actually *do* the work, which in turn increases the flow of ideas.

Susan S. Elliott, President and founder of Systems Service Enterprises (SSE), a St. Louis information services firm, says, "I can't come up with a plan and ask those who manage the accounts to give me their reactions. *They're* the ones who really know the accounts. They have the information I don't have. Without their input, I'd be operating in an ivory tower."

Managers who take the time to listen to workers' ideas also gain new insights into problem-solving, and as a result tend to make smarter decisions. Moreover, while managers may still have the final say, employees are more apt to buy in to their boss's decisions when they have played a part in the decision-making process.

Finally, in effective teams players rally around common goals and objectives—all pushing and pulling in the same direction. And when this happens, managers have fewer internal power struggles to contend with.

In fact, the primary role of the manager as coach is to provide a positive and nurturing environment. And that is something dolphins excel at.

Building a Team

Assembling a group of workers and calling them a team, however, doesn't ensure great performance. When teams click, it is usually because the chemistry among the players is just right. Granted, few managers have the luxury of starting with a clean slate and handpicking an entire team from scratch. But as you put together new teams and add additional players to existing ones, here are some tips on what to look for and what to avoid:

• **Mix and match personalities and backgrounds.** Fill your team with introverts and extroverts, seasoned employees and new recruits, creative people and analytical people, players who are detail-oriented as well as those who are task-oriented, and employees with different social, academic, and ethnic backgrounds and heritages. Diversity guarantees a variety of perspectives, which will not only energize the group, but will enable its members to approach goals and problems from different angles.

"At Holiday Inn Worldwide, management's philosophy is top-down, bottom-up, everybody gets a say—then we make a decision and go for it," reports Mylle Bell, Executive Vice President of Strategic Management. Bell says when hiring new team members, she looks for bright, creative self-starters who boast great leadership skills as well as strong interpersonal skills. She also strives for diversity. "Because my teams have to interface and work with all areas of the company, I have to build an eclectic skill base," she says. "But I would do so anyway, because it makes for a much more interesting experience."

Dr. Virginia Weldon, Senior Vice President at Monsanto Company, agrees. "Bottom line, diversity is an asset we've been hiding from ourselves—a neglected resource we have not used," she believes. "Diversity can breathe something vital, something important, something critical, and something desperately needed into our institutions."

However, Tellabs's Grace Pastiak cautions, "There are some people who are so diverse in personality, style, etc. that unless they have a lot to contribute, you're better off keeping them as single contributors rather than team members."

• **Open-mindedness is a must.** On effective teams, members complement one another, but they need not always get along. However, they must trust and respect each other and feel free to express their individual opinions and ideas without fear of being ridiculed or criticized.

• **Beware of "Lone Rangers."** Granted, sometimes players must work alone, but teams work best when workers are dependent upon one another for such things as resources, information, and support. "Sometimes you end up with someone who is a 'Lone Ranger'—more of an individual. The trick here is to respect that person's individuality while working hard to try to integrate that person into the team," says Nicole Browning, of MTV Networks. "Keep in mind, though, that these individuals are often the very ones who bring diversity to the team. If we don't embrace these people in our organizations, we're not going to be very successful moving into the future."

• **Surround yourself with the best people you can find.** Women are sometimes reluctant to choose players who know more than they do. But savvy managers make it their business to pinpoint their weaknesses, then go out of their way to look for team members they can learn from. Another reason to pick the cream of the crop: They'll do a better job, which in turn makes *you* look good!

• **Look for team players, not quarterbacks.** For teams to succeed, everyone must share a collective agenda. Quarterbacks tend to have their own private agendas and are only happy when they're calling the shots. How to handle quarterbacks? Victoria Ogden, President and Publisher of Cape Cod Community Newspapers, offers, "Ultimately, you have to do the fifty-fifty test. If you're giving eighty, and they're only giving twenty, they've got to go. It's got to be fifty-fifty minimum."

• **Match people to projects.** One of Gwendolyn Baker's first jobs was directing the Minority and Women's Research Program for the National Institute of Education in Washington, D.C., during the Carter administration. "Our primary mission involved awarding funds to programs and organizations across the country that fostered the development of women and minorities on college and university campuses," she explains. "All of these awards were based on the needs of the organizations and needs of women and minorities. The problem was, I noticed right away that the evaluation of proposals had always been conducted by traditional groups—composed of 90 to 95 percent white males, and a few white females, but very, very few minorities."

During her first year on the job, Baker had some $3 million to disburse. She decided that 80 percent of the people who would analyze the proposals would be those who had previously been excluded . . . the *very* people who would be most knowledgeable about the needs of the organizations requesting funds—namely, women and minorities.

When Baker told the existing evaluating team of her plans, everyone argued, "But these people don't have any experience." To which Baker matter-of-factly replied, "The only way they're going to get the experience is to give it to them."

"I knew a lot of people around the country to recruit for that 80 percent," she adds. "And I made sure that the other 20 percent were people who *did* have experience evaluating proposals. That way they could train the newcomers." As a result of matching the right people to this project, Baker claims, "I was there for three years, and my team never had a major controversy over who got what."

• **Don't disqualify people you don't like or those you fear you can't control.** This is something women tend to do. "We prefer to have people we like on our project teams, but they aren't always the best choices," writes Dorothy Leeds in *Smart Questions: A New Strategy for Successful Managers*. "You're in managerial trouble if you automatically choose people you can control."

Victoria Ogden agrees. "I like strong people, and they are especially important in this business. The last thing I want is a bunch of docile reporters or timid advertising representatives. All my career, I've had people working for me whom I have not personally liked. But so long as they were doing a good job and sharing in the goals of the company, I *grew* to like them *because* they were contributing to the operation."

Adds MTV Networks's Nicole Browning, "Sometimes there's an individual who has the potential to make a contribution to the team, but they're kind of a 'loose cannon.' Very often, this can be channeled. At MTV Networks, for example, we've invested a lot of money in experts who have come in to work with a particular group that may be having problems, or with an individual who needs one-on-one training. Sometimes it's pivotal to let people have a sense about how they are perceived among their peers, superiors, and subordinates. In fact, this often helps them to become less of a loose cannon and better integrated into the group."

On the flip side, however, Browning adds that there will be instances when someone just isn't a good fit. "They're not happy, and neither are you," she says. "In which case, you may have to let them go."

Making Teamwork Work: The Manager's Role As Coach

Once upon a time, a corporate manager's job was simple and clear-cut. As boss, the manager assumed responsibility for defining goals, planning strategies, solving problems, and issuing orders. As for subordinates, they were simply required to do as they were told. But the teamwork concept has changed all of that. Now, *teams of subordinates* define goals, plan strategies, and look for ways to solve problems. And management's role is to make it as easy as possible for them to do so.

In other words, in corporations that endorse participatory management and organize employees into teams, the boss has now become coach, advisor, monitor, guidance counselor, and remover of bureaucratic red tape. If these are your responsibilities, here are some tips from the trenches on how to make teamwork work:

• **Understand your—and your team's—responsibilities, be absolutely committed to your team's success, and make it your business to demonstrate that commitment,** offers M. Colleen Mullens, a marketing executive for AT&T Business Communications Services in Bedminster, New Jersey. "In approaching an assignment, no matter how untraditional, this philosophy has served me very well," she says. "If it's clear to those you work with that you are personally committed with every fiber of your being to making the team succeed, and that you understand your job and its contribution to that goal, that eliminates many problems."

• **Your role as coach is to help keep your team focused on its goals and, if necessary, assist in fine-tuning members' ideas.** Effective coaches are good listeners and make it a point never to discredit or veto *anyone's* contributions to group discussions. Nor do they permit team members to shoot down other members' ideas. Recognizing that some of the most bizarre pitches often lead to workable—even profitable—ideas, effective coaches encourage *all* players to hear one another out and, if they must disagree, to do so in positive ways.

• **Successful coaches are articulate.** "My primary role is to make sure that the team's objectives are clear. People must understand what their boundaries are and where they need to end up. And when they do, it's a lot easier to get there than to have a 'group grope,' " says Mylle Bell of Holiday Inn Worldwide. "It's also important for a coach to then monitor a team's progress—although monitor is too strong a word. I do what I call an 'up-periscope' by consistently asking, 'Where are we at meeting our objectives? Where might we be off, and how can we get back on track?' It takes a lot of listening."

• **Make sure that every player knows that the team's highest priority is to focus on achieving the *group's* goals—not those of individuals.** For teams to be effective, there is no room for private agendas. As coach, it is your responsibility to make it clear to everyone from the start that power struggles and individual players intent on pursuing their own personal goals—particularly at the expense of the team's—will not be tolerated.

• **Team members must also have a thorough understanding of individuals' responsibilities.** As Diane Tracy notes in *10 Steps to*

Empowerment, "This is important not just to the effective working of the individuals, but to the effective working of the team. If the team is to have any power as a group, it must know who's on first, who's on second, etc."

• **To operate at full capacity, team members need sufficient training to do their jobs and to play their roles—both as individuals and as a group.** Five years ago, Carole Kitchens was one of four managers tapped to launch Sunette, an entrepreneurial start-up division of Hoechst Celanese Corporation. "If you're rapidly trying to develop a business, you can really accelerate that learning curve and smooth a lot of the lumps and thorns if you take a little time to train your people," she believes. When launching the new division, Kitchens and her three managerial colleagues decided to use the team approach to market their product, a high-intensity artificial sweetener. "In retrospect, if we did anything wrong, it was that we were perhaps too impulsive and tried to move too fast. We didn't take the time to train everyone on the team concept and to get everybody to buy into the idea, as well as understand how things would work. And that was a serious mistake."

Sometimes it's easier to demonstrate—rather than preach—this information. At Kodak, for example, Candy Obourn often brings in external consultants to engage her troops in team-building exercises.

• **Team members must also be privy to how their company operates and where it stands in relation to its competitors.** Unfortunately, far too many managers have grown accustomed to sharing company information on a "need to know" basis. For teams to succeed, *everyone* needs to know. You want your players to think like owners, because when this happens, they become focused on responding to the company's needs, boosting sales, and finding ways to cut costs and save money. But to reach that point, they must have the knowledge to make intelligent decisions. And to do that, they must understand the big picture.

At Southwest Airlines, for example, financial information is circulated to every employee on a regular basis. In addition, the company offers a profit-sharing plan, giving employees an opportunity to invest all or part of their profit-sharing funds in Southwest stock. As a result, employees at Southwest think like owners and act accordingly. Which may very well explain why Southwest continues to grow, while the majority of its competitors operate in the red.

• **Effective coaches deliberately keep a low profile.** Their role is not to show and tell what they think, but to observe, to ask questions, and to provide support and resources so that players form their *own* opinions and find their own solutions. And when team players come to them with gripes or problems about the team, tough and caring coaches refuse to discuss the issues one-on-one. Instead, they insist that all problems *with* the team be handled *by* the team. The same holds true for suggestions to improve the team. These, too, should always be discussed as a group.

"The first thing you do to build a team is to clarify roles and responsibilities and eliminate overlapping or unclear things," believes Claire Coyle of SmithKline Beecham. "Next, you empower the people to do their own jobs. And then you absolutely mandate that they resolve problems among themselves and not come to you. Make them deal with their own conflict."

• **Empowering your teams, however, does not mean abandoning them.** As coach, you still need to make sure that people understand what's expected of them, watch performance, and give feedback. Grace Pastiak of Tellabs is a firm believer in creating teams that ultimately direct themselves. "The real secret is to work yourself out of a job," she says. "My experience in life is that the harder I work at doing that, the better things run—and the more I get promoted, although that's really a consequence. To me, self-directed teams are the real secret to getting the best out of everybody, because team members are treated like and act like adults rather than children. This check-your-brain-at-the-front-door routine just doesn't work—regardless of the business you're in."

• **Effective team-building often boils down to managing personalities.** So keep in mind that just because you're dealing with a team, it doesn't mean you should discount or ignore individual needs. In managing her employees, who represent a tremendous diversity of age groups, backgrounds, and ethnicity, AT&T's M. Colleen Mullens believes, "Personality, background, and needs are different for every individual. My job as a manager is to understand those people and their needs. They are all different, and I have found that I am most effective if I look at each individual that way. I focus on their needs, the value they can bring to their assignments, and how I can support the personal career path they have chosen."

• **Sometimes it's necessary for a manager to disapprove a team's ideas and decisions.** How to say no without turning players off to the entire team concept? Always tell them *why*. Granted, not everyone will be happy with your decision, but at least they will understand your rationale. Before you veto a team's ideas or decisions, however, be sure your reasons for doing so are valid. The worst thing a manager can do is turn down a suggestion with no discussion, because then your people will never share their ideas again.

"If you have to veto an idea, let the person or team who raised the suggestion talk about it," suggests Victoria Ogden of Cape Cod Community Newspapers. "Then raise issues about the idea that concern you, and let them address those, too. I think that if you talk things through with people, they'll see the problems. And if they don't, *you're* probably wrong. In other words, if you can't get them to come around to your way of thinking, you'd better start to rethink *your* thinking."

Nicole Browning of MTV Networks agrees and adds, "There have been times when my team has come up with a decision that I didn't necessarily think was a good one. But I've learned an important lesson. Until recently, I had a habit of ostensibly conceding and accepting their decision, but throughout the discussion, I would go back in and try to resell them on my point of view. Now they will actually hold up their hands and say, 'Wait a minute.

This is the decision, and we want to do it this way. You agreed. Now back off, and don't try to resell us.' And they are right.

"I've also learned that the people I have in the field are top-notch professionals and are much closer to the customer than I am," Browning adds. "So when they come together with some really solid idea, they are generally right. For example, they may spend a lot of time, as a team, collaboratively deciding on a model they want to use to approach an account. I may not think their approach is the best approach, but I'm starting to back off. I figure that if this is really going to succeed, they've got to have an opportunity to make decisions—right or wrong—and see the results themselves."

• **Underscore the importance of teamwork in your company by finding innovative ways to reward team players instead of individuals.** At Tellabs, for example, teams compete for an annual corporate team award. The winners are honored at a company dinner and also receive jackets. And at Hewlett-Packard, the company sponsors a program in which managers can reward team members with gift certificates. "The company also gives out the Falcon Award to teams who complete quality work," reports Cynthia Danaher. "And I always make it a point when people do things they think I don't know about, to just walk up to their desk and say thanks."

Another idea: Look for ways to praise your team publicly. Better yet, tie teamwork efforts into performance evaluations and promotion decisions.

• **Help set the stage for team productivity.** In *Thriving on Chaos: Handbook for a Management Revolution*, Tom Peters suggests providing a well-equipped room—much like a corporate board room—where teams can meet for brainstorming and problem-solving sessions. Gestures like this send the message that *you're* serious about teamwork; consequently, team members will be more apt to take their roles seriously.

• **Change the pace occasionally.** At Kodak, Candy Obourn sometimes conducts team meetings at her home in the country. She also actively participates in and encourages "dress-down" days and makes it a point to schedule occasional fun events like "Beat the Blahs" day. "One of our favorites is 'Let's Go Mad' day, in which team members dress up in different costumes, and we have fun and games," she says. "All of this is aimed at getting our folks to let their hair down and interact with one another in new and different ways."

At Phelps County Bank, team players often get together after work for takeout food and to watch videos in the employee break room. And to combat stress, employees play charades every Thursday morning for half an hour while Bill Marshall, the company's senior vice president in charge of loans, plays receptionist.

• **Effective coaches also encourage their team to celebrate its successes.** Teams at Land O'Lakes, for example, often enjoy pizza parties. And celebrations at Hewlett-Packard run the gamut from going out together for meals to division-wide beer busts.

From Dictatorship to Democracy

If your company is just now adopting a teamwork approach, keep in mind that orchestrating a changeover is no easy task. To ensure a successful transition, you'll first need to lay out a master plan. Next, you'll need to thoroughly explain the process—including why you're converting to teams, who it will involve, how long it will take, and the results you'll be looking for—to *all* employees.

When doing this, exude enthusiasm. Get your players pumped up by telling them what's in it for them. Share success stories from other companies who have successfully converted to teams. Also tell them the reasons why teams sometimes fail and how to avoid common trouble spots. Make sure that *every* player truly understands what you're trying to achieve, and don't stop talking, showing, and demonstrating until they do.

Orchestrating a successful transition also requires extreme patience. Remember, most employees are accustomed to being supervised in a top-down management environment. Many have no inkling of how to become self-directed. Some—usually those who feel uncomfortable being handed a lot of responsibility—actually *prefer* being told what to do. Others may respond to you with blank stares or looks of total confusion—even disbelief—when asked for their input. Let's face it: Old habits die hard. "We're in the middle of a paradigm shift between two models of management," explains Warren Bennis, author of *On Becoming a Leader.* "It takes a while for participatory management to catch on throughout any organization."

When teams are first forming, chaos will be rampant, as players scurry in a hundred different directions, trying to figure out what is expected of them. Two things will see them through: permission to learn by trial and error and your constant and positive reinforcement. If your people are slow to catch on to the teamwork concept, you will undoubtedly feel discouraged. But hang in there. As management guru Peter Drucker says, "Get a third of your people to buy in, and the rest will follow."

MTV Networks's Nicole Browning says, "When we began operating in teams, I had one subordinate who completely transformed his management style. Originally, he was the perfect example of a shark. He was dominant, he had a habit of lashing out at people during staff meetings, and he set up rigid and unreasonable rules simply to show that *he* was in control—like not allowing a $60,000 employee to make a $20 decision. These kinds of behaviors were brought to his attention during a performance review, where he was told that he needed to change his management style. Then we began training him to be a coach versus a dictator. Over a year, a miraculous transformation occurred. This came about not only as a result of direct training in a new management style, but because we allowed him to see how he could be effective in a very different way. In the process, he discovered, 'Hey, I'd *rather* be this way.' The next year, he had an outstanding performance review, and we celebrated by sending him a plant for his office and a bottle of champagne."

Initially team members may come up with a few ideas, make a limited number of decisions, and attempt to solve a handful of problems—and *only* because you've directed them to do so. But before you know it, things will begin to click, and the floodgates will open to reveal a myriad of ideas. Your team will begin to set its own goals—and ones that may even be loftier than those *you* would have set for them. Above all, your employees will *understand* the process and begin to enjoy its many benefits. They will also likely be motivated, committed, and feel good about their jobs and their contributions to the company, as well as about themselves.

As coach, you, too, will feel invigorated—about the team itself, and the role you have had the opportunity to play. "What I like most about management is the opportunity to provide an environment in which people of very different backgrounds come together to pursue a goal—the individuals rallying behind something they believe in, that they helped shape—and drive them to success," says AT&T's M. Colleen Mullens.

Granted, you, too, may have to adjust to your new role, which may not be easy initially. "It's a whole different approach to management and decision-making, and it's often hard," acknowledges Nicole Browning. "It's especially difficult for managers not to butt in. You're supposedly in your position because you're more experienced, and it's hard to back off from saying, 'I know how to do it' or 'This is the way it should be done.' But when you allow your team to call the shots themselves, you get a much more motivated staff. You also get workers who are dedicated and loyal to the company because they're happy, they're challenged, and they feel like they are learning."

When It's Not a Team

There are, of course, exceptions. Not every company handles a conversion to teamwork so well—and for a number of reasons. For example, when the idea to make a changeover isn't supported from the top, it simply will not work. And unfortunately, some

CEOs will order a conversion as a quick fix, then back out when positive results are not instantly noticeable.

Management represents another obstacle. Some have grown accustomed to being commanding officers and resent giving up their authority. Others fear that sharing responsibilities—and worse, credit—with subordinates may jeopardize their chances of climbing the corporate ladder.

Refuse to be one of those who merely pays lip service to the ideas of teamwork and participatory management. And forget about looking out for number one. Otherwise, you may very well sabotage *your* future, as Joan S. Gilbert, Manager of Community Relations for Texaco in White Plains, New York, points out in an article for *Executive Female*: "The woman most likely to succeed in the '90s will be a team player who places business goals ahead of her private agenda for recognition. The leaner corporation of the next decade will reward those who are able to look beyond the external trappings of personal success to value the contribution they can make to the company's success. In short, empire building is out; helping your company is in."

Carole Kitchens at Hoechst Celanese Corporation agrees. "It's hard sometimes to put your ego aside. In a start-up venture, in particular, all the turf is lying around for the grabbing, and it's very tempting to take your eye off what you're trying to accomplish long term and think, 'Well, how can I feather *my* nest?' I think it takes a strong person—someone who is building for the future—to say, 'Hey, this may feel good at the moment, but in the long run it's not going to get us where we need to go.' "

Many of the managers we interviewed agreed that when it comes to coaching, women are naturals. After all, we've been raised to be nurturing and supportive. But teamwork may not come so easily to women who are highly competitive and hesitant to share power and glory. "Even though they talk a good game, women often sabotage themselves by competing jealously with one another, when they could, instead, be supportive colleagues and mentors," adds Texaco's Joan Gilbert. "The lesson for the 1990s is that a successful team garners glory enough for all its players."

Teamwork Works

Like it or not, concepts like participatory management and team-work are emerging as the *only* ways to succeed and prosper in the 1990s—and beyond. And on this, companies and managers who have been on both sides of the equation agree. "My experiences at Ford Motor Company convinced me that all U.S. companies—and for that matter, all organizations—can make tremendous quality improvements by tapping the power of teamwork," writes Donald Petersen in *A Better Idea*. When Petersen took the helm at Ford, the company's future looked bleak from an economic standpoint, and both employees and customers were disenchanted with Ford's products. To fix these problems, Petersen looked in-ternally, and credits concepts like employee involvement and teamwork with saving the company. "If Ford's managers had not developed a better relationship with people inside the organiza-tion, our company would have had a difficult time competing in the 1980s," he says. "We would not have outearned General Mo-tors for two consecutive years, and we would not have moved from last to first place in quality among the Big Three automakers."

The biggest payoff to putting employees in charge of quality, he adds, is a first-rate service or product. Case in point: the phe-nomenally popular Ford Taurus, which, Petersen says, evolved as employees combined their suggestions and expertise while focus-ing on customers' needs. "Taurus was the first real test of em-ployee involvement and teamwork."

Indeed, what usually occurs once companies, managers, and employees get a real taste of teamwork and its myriad of benefits to *all* involved, is that everyone gets hooked. And at that point, there's simply no turning back.

CHAPTER SIX

Sharing the Workload

PROFILE

CYNTHIA DANAHER

GENERAL MANAGER, IMAGING SERVICES SYSTEMS
HEWLETT-PACKARD
ANDOVER, MASSACHUSETTS

*"When I delegate, I end up with better-developed employees.
I also think that people not only like working for me, but
that we get good team results—such that if one piece falls
out, the whole thing doesn't collapse."*

Cynthia Danaher confesses that she was never much of a delegator until she became a mother. "Going on maternity leave, you think everything is going to fall apart while you're gone," she says. "Then you come back and realize, 'Wow!' It makes you wish that every *male* could go on maternity leave!"

Maternity leave also prompted Danaher to recognize that the role of Superwoman was not one she cared to take on. "I came back to work and realized that there was no way I could accomplish my goals and still do what I was doing before," she says. "So I had to break the mold and rework it. I also realized that if you have very good people working for you, you can give them whole chunks and let them run, which I quickly started to do—and with very good results."

Today, this mother of three and graduate of Harvard Business School delegates "a tremendous amount" and sees benefits to both herself and her subordinates whenever she shares the workload.

"For starters, I think that when I delegate, I end up with better-developed employees," she says. "I also think that people not only like working for me, but that we get good team results—such that if one piece falls out, the whole thing doesn't collapse. Because I delegate a lot of tasks, my life remains far more balanced than that of other managers. And delegating gives me more free time to accomplish other things."

As for benefits to her subordinates, Danaher believes that delegating makes employees feel challenged. "They understand how they can get things accomplished in a way that they didn't understand before. In essence, they grow their management skills."

Danaher believes that women sometimes have a tougher time delegating tasks than men do, particularly at home. "And in some ways, that gets carried into the workplace," she says. "But I think you have to understand that people may not necessarily do things the way *you* might do them. Consequently, the first few times it's probably a good idea to delegate something that's fairly safe—so that if it does get totally screwed up, it's fairly low-impact. Then you start to understand that different methods bring equal or better results."

New managers, Danaher adds, often have a particularly hard time delegating. "As a new manager, you feel like everything must be done by you, and if it's not, it won't be done well. You're nervous because your reputation is on the line, and everyone is judging not only what you do, but everything your group does. At the same time, you're not yet objective about your team's strengths and weaknesses, and neither are you holding your people accountable yet."

To get comfortable with delegating tasks, Danaher recommends giving a lot of guidance at first. "The thing I do is really examine the issue and ask myself up front, 'Am I going to be upset if someone comes out with something completely different than I would?' If the answer to that is yes, then I give a lot of guidance early on."

But guidance, to Danaher, does *not* mean telling someone *how* to do a task—just letting them know what she wants the end result to be. "At Hewlett-Packard, sometimes the lines of authority are fuzzy, though, and a big part of getting things done is influencing the right people. So if I see that the person I've delegated something to needs help influencing others, I will tell them, 'This is what has worked for me in the past. Maybe you can think about that.'"

Rather than look over her subordinates' shoulders after delegating tasks, Danaher tells them up front how she plans to monitor their progress. "Usually I'll say something like, 'These are the checkpoints where I think we should communicate.'"

It is the lack of this kind of communication, Danaher feels, that causes the delegation process to fail. Another obstacle to successful delegation occurs when managers fail to back the person to whom they have delegated a task. "Oftentimes, I'll tell people in other departments, 'I want this person to handle that,' and they'll come back at me saying, 'Well, we want *you*.' Sometimes you just have to be firm and say something like, 'I trust this person, and she has my full backing,' and you might have to say it over and over again. But what often happens instead is that managers end up getting flattered into taking *back* a task, and in doing so they completely undo the delegating exercise."

Danaher admits to being tough when she doesn't get the results she wants. "I sit people down and tell them I'm not happy," she says. "I don't wait to do it, and I'm very honest about how I feel." In fact, Danaher has been criticized for being *too* honest, but she has no intention of changing. "I think Hewlett-Packard has an environment where everyone tends to be so nice to each other, that when someone says, 'I'm not happy with what you're doing, and here's what I want you to do,' it's a shock to people. But then afterward, I think they learn to appreciate it."

There are very few tasks Danaher never delegates—like "extremely difficult customer situations. And the reason I don't delegate these is because by the time they get to the point that I'm finding out about them, I feel they need my attention. Besides, I think that with a dissatisfied customer, you learn so much about their view of the organization, and I like that learning experience."

Yet even when Danaher doesn't delegate, she makes it a point to share her learning experiences with all of her subordinates.

As a recent guest speaker at Harvard Business School, where she got her MBA, Danaher says the students at her alma mater were anxious to hear about what she had learned in the "real world." And Danaher's number one answer? "How much you have to rely on others to get things done."

• • •

"If I want something done right, I'd better do it myself." "If my team screws this up, how's that going to make *me* look?" "I should get my assistant to proofread this report, but he's been so busy lately that I feel guilty asking him." Women have a cornucopia of excuses they use to justify not delegating tasks. Or they delegate, then suffocate. Yet delegating is one of the best ways to instill pride in employees, because it gives them a sense of ownership and empowerment.

Delegating benefits managers as well. "My delegation strategy is to give away everything I can," reports Claire Coyle, Group Director of Marketing Services at SmithKline Beecham. "And I do that because I need to have a strong team behind me to free me to do special assignments, interesting projects . . . and to grow."

Excuses, Excuses:
The Most Common Obstacles to Delegating

The problem is, female managers are often reluctant to delegate tasks—and for a variety of reasons:

• **Fear** causes many to resist sharing the workload. Threatened by the competence of others, these managers fear being one-upped by their subordinates. Consequently, they figure that if they don't delegate tasks to their employees, they won't be outshined by them.

• **Guilt** also prevents managers from delegating tasks. Typically, these managers refrain from delegating because they mistakenly confuse delegating with *imposing* on others. They also worry that if they delegate they'll be perceived as palming their work off on others, and then what would everyone—particularly the boss—think?

• **Perfectionists** don't delegate because they firmly believe that no one else could possibly do the job as well as they could. Perfectionists also prefer having control over everyone and everything. Moreover, because they tend to lack confidence in their subordinates, delegating just seems too risky.

Debbi Fields, founder of Mrs. Fields Cookies, says she learned this lesson the hard way. In fact, it's only recently that Fields began turning many of the company's day-to-day operations over to her middle managers—and living with their decisions. "In the past, I used to ask managers what they needed, and then I did it for them. 'Your ice machine is broken? Your milk delivery is off? I'll take care of it.' If I saw something I didn't like, I fixed it myself right then and there," Fields recently told *Working Woman* magazine.

But those days are over, she adds, partly because her business nearly failed in the 1980s thanks to her micromanagement style. Also, the company is moving forward with several new ventures that require her attention.

Still, Fields admits that letting go has been hard. "Sometimes it's awful. I've agreed to do things up front knowing full well I didn't like them. You have to let people make decisions in spite of what your gut tells you, as long as they're not betting the farm."

• **Superwomen** feel uncomfortable and inadequate when asking for help. "I *should* be able to do it all myself," they rationalize— and many burn out in the process of trying to prove themselves.

• **High achievers** are fiercely independent and take great pride in appearing self-reliant. "I worked hard to get to where I am today," one high-ranking manager in her early sixties told us, "and I'm proud to say that I got where I am without help from anyone." To this manager—and others like her—delegating is a sign of weakness. It reveals a dependence on others and makes them feel like fakes or frauds.

• **Rationalizers** refrain from delegating by convincing themselves, "By the time I explain how to do this to someone else, I could have done it just as easily myself." Morene Seldes-Marcus, Director of Human Resources for Hi-Fi Buys, acknowledges, "Many female managers have grown too accustomed to doing things themselves. We're constantly juggling twenty balls in the air at the same time—and I've fallen into this trap myself. The mentality is: 'It's just one more thing to do . . . I'll just do it.' Men, on the other hand, are more accustomed to having someone to hand things to . . . to take care of the little details for them."

• **Martyrs** don't delegate because they *want* people to notice how hard they are working. Adopting a woe-is-me attitude, their aim is to gain others' sympathy. But many also have an ulterior motive: to be noticed and promoted in the process.

• **Low self-esteem** prevents managers from delegating as well. Because they have an insatiable "need to be needed," such insecure managers fear that giving up tasks will leave them feeling useless and unimportant.

Sound familiar? Truth is, *all* of these excuses can backfire. In other words, you don't *have* to do it all to be an effective manager. Moreover, when you *insist* on doing everything, burnout is inevitable, which not only can lead to costly mistakes, but can also undermine your career. "Women have a tendency to hang on to every bit of an assignment, even though it may be overwhelming," acknowledge Johanna and Phillip Hunsaker in their book *Strategies and Skills for Managerial Women*. "They check and recheck every detail, making sure that everything is done perfectly. The net result is that they are too busy or overwhelmed to take on bigger and better challenges."

When you refuse to delegate, you also risk losing the respect and cooperation of your employees. Worse, your superiors will neither view you as a team player nor as promotable. Consequently, refusing to delegate can actually *sabotage* your chances of climbing the corporate ladder. As Dorothy Leeds points out in *Smart Questions*, "If you've rendered your staff helpless without you, your boss won't be able to promote you—he'll know that chaos will result. So while you may have preserved your sense of control, you've also likely forfeited your chances for advancement."

Granted, it's true that when you delegate a task, it may not be done the *same* way you would have done it. But chances are, the end result *will* be the same. Besides, when you delegate, you free up time to take on assignments and projects that are not only more challenging, but will give you the opportunity to get noticed—and possibly promoted.

In fact, the ability to delegate tasks is viewed by subordinates and superiors alike as a sign of managerial *strength*, not weakness. It helps you to increase your productivity and effectiveness as well, and offers a slew of benefits to both your employees *and* your organization.

Sharing the Workload: Benefits to Employees and the Company

"Delegation not only builds flexibility into an organization; it also builds job satisfaction. People become excited about working for you," writes Beth Milwid, Ph.D., in *Working with Men: Professional Women Talk About Power, Sexuality and Ethics*. Delegating tasks and responsibilities offers other benefits as well:

• **When you delegate tasks to employees, you send the message "I trust you."** This not only increases their self-confidence, it makes them feel better about themselves *and* the jobs they are doing. For example, at Nordstrom, one of the country's largest upscale clothing retailers, the company's number one goal is to provide outstanding customer service, and sales assistants are empowered to do whatever is necessary to achieve that goal. In fact, the company's policy manual contains just one rule: "Use your good judgment in all situations."

As a result of this trust, Nordstrom sales assistants are extremely motivated and excel at pampering their clientele. Case in point: A customer in Portland, Oregon, once needed some alterations to two suits he had bought, and the house rule is to have alterations ready the next day. When the customer arrived to pick up his suits before going on a business trip, the sales assistant reported that they were not ready. The customer left, but by the time he arrived in Dallas for his meeting, a package was waiting for him at his hotel. Inside were his two suits, an apology from the sales assistant, and three silk ties—a gift from the store. The Nordstrom staffer had called the customer's home to find out his itinerary and spent $98 sending him the suits via Federal Express.

Despite the high cost of pleasing this particular customer, Nordstrom's sales continue to soar—$3.6 billion in 1993, up from $225 million a decade earlier—with this kind of personalized service.

• **Delegating enhances subordinates' understanding of your organization as a whole.** It encourages them to see the big picture and motivates them to do all they can to make sure that the organization is successful in fulfilling its mission and reaching its goals.

• **Delegating increases job satisfaction and instills a sense of pride in employees.** This, in turn, increases subordinates' loyalty and commitment to the company. When employees are given responsibility for achieving a task, they also feel a sense of ownership. And because delegating empowers them, it also makes them more productive. Researchers at the University of Michigan's Institute for Social Research, for example, have found that the more power employees feel, the more efficient they will be. In other words, delegating has a way of *inspiring* employees to prove that your confidence in them is well founded. And this in turn spurs their willingness to take risks.

"At Federal Express, we delegate a lot. As a result, our employees are never afraid to try new things," says Debbie Newport, Manager of Ground Operations in Memphis. "Not too long ago, I challenged my team to come up with ideas for increasing productivity on the sort line in the morning, and they came up with a plan. We realigned all the vans, and they did about a 20 percent productivity increase overnight, just by sitting together in a small group and talking about it."

You Gotta Have Faith: The How-tos of Delegating

Successful delegating entails assigning a task to someone, then giving that person the necessary tools, time, and space to complete the task—which, of course, is often easier said than done. It also involves trusting someone else to get the job done—but not necessarily in the same way *you* would have done it. But in fact, managers who have mastered the art of delegating have also learned the importance of being receptive to others' ideas *and* ways of doing things. They recognize that sometimes their people will make mistakes, and as managers they must grit their teeth and try again. Because the overall goal of delegating is to encourage employees to function on their own. That way, everyone wins.

Sometimes delegation fails, however, and for one of several reasons. Here are the most common ones, along with tips on how to prevent them from occurring:

• **Delegating without clarifying.** Before you delegate a task, *you* need to understand exactly what it involves, what you want to be accomplished, and why. To do this, ask yourself, "Is this task specific and measurable?" If *your* goals are fuzzy, it would be a disservice to delegate the task to a subordinate.

• **Delegating without specifying your expectations.** "In most instances, if people know what's expected of them, they will meet your expectations," believes Hi-Fi Buys's Morene Seldes-Marcus. "If you don't clearly establish those expectations, you're going to end up saying, 'She failed at this. I asked her to handle this project, and I haven't seen anything.' But if you didn't *ask* her to show you her progress at certain intervals, then *she* didn't fail—*you* did. Delegating is a partnership. You don't just hand an assignment to someone and walk away. Structure, support, and direction along the way are critical to successful delegation."

• **Delegating how, not why.** Savvy managers have learned to delegate by explaining what has to be done and why, then letting their subordinates determine *how* the task gets done. This approach tends to spur creativity and innovation, and who knows—they may end up doing a better job at the task than you could have! "Sometimes you need to step in and coach someone on how to do something," points out Victoria Ogden, of Cape Cod Community Newspapers. "But I have a fairly large ego, so I have to be careful. There's always that tendency to think you can do something better than someone else. But you don't teach people anything when you take over for them. You've got to step back, and often that's hard to do."

• **Delegating, then abandoning.** Sometimes managers dump tasks on employees, then more or less disappear, leaving subordinates to sink or swim. Effective delegating means holding an employee accountable. It involves clearly communicating the end result you're seeking, stating the deadline by which you expect the task to be completed, explaining to subordinates how they will be monitored, and telling them how and at what stages you'd like to receive feedback on their progress. It also means letting subordinates know that you are available should they run into obstacles or have questions along the way.

"When you hand someone a project, it's important to say, 'This is what I'd like done, but let me know halfway through how you're doing. That way, if there are any changes to be made, we don't have to handle them at the end. Instead, we can correct as we go," says Morene Seldes-Marcus.

• **Delegating, then suffocating.** At the opposite extreme, managers often delegate a task, then breathe down the subordinate's back waiting for the task to be accomplished. James Autry provides a typical scenario of this bad habit in *Love and Profit.* " 'Joe, I want to delegate this matter entirely to you. Please get it done by September 1st, and let me know how you're doing every Monday morning between now and then. And by all means, if you have questions, or ever need help, let me know.' Then we stop by his office or call him a few days later and say something like, 'Joe, how are you coming on that project?' Translation: 'I delegated that assignment to you, Joe, but of course, I don't really trust you to do it, so I'm going to check on it every time I see you.' "

• **Delegating only the grunt work.** When managers limit delegating to tasks *they* loathe handling—and ones that subordinates are bound to dread tackling as well—employees naturally end up feeling resentful. Sharing the grunt work is often a necessary evil, but try to spread it out among subordinates. Also, be sure to always balance it with tasks your staff will find challenging and motivating.

• **Delegating a task without giving the authority and resources to accomplish it.** Giving subordinates responsibilities without the necessary authority and resources to carry them out automatically sets them up for failure. It is also destructive and self-defeating. "It's difficult sometimes to delegate because you have to give someone the responsibility to ultimately be accountable for that work," acknowledges Morene Seldes-Marcus. "You have to give them the authority to find resources and sometimes to spend a little money. You also have to hand over some decision-making power. Otherwise, they have the responsibility, but they are paralyzed because they can't make decisions. And that's not delegating, that's *control.*

Personally, I don't like control. If I'm going to delegate a task to someone, I want them to grow with it. So I give them the authority or autonomy to do the job, and then I get out of the way."

What to do when delegating ends up spelling disaster? Women's tendencies are to snatch the work back and fix it. But the savvy manager will *also* delegate responsibility for solving the problems that have emerged. That way employees not only learn from their mistakes, but how to handle future responsibilities.

The "Nevers" of Delegating

Of course, there are certain tasks and responsibilities you should never delegate. These include tasks you don't understand and responsibilities you don't feel comfortable with. Neither should employees be expected to take on key aspects of *your* job—like planning departmental or divisional budgets, settling conflicts among other employees, administering performance evaluations, and overseeing tasks that could place the company at considerable risk. After all, the purpose of delegating is *not* to pass the buck, but to get the job done effectively and to provide a growth experience for your employees.

"I hold on to tasks that require my investigating or needs analysis abilities," says Morene Seldes-Marcus. "Say I'm looking at managing a conflict or dealing with a performance issue within the organization. Even though it may be time-consuming to gather all the details, that's a task I wouldn't delegate because, ultimately, I need to make sure that company standards and compliance to laws are handled properly."

Another valid reason Seldes-Marcus doesn't delegate conflict and performance issues is that she feels the need to observe an individual's body language or hear someone's side of the story firsthand. "I don't want to rely on anyone else to bring me that information," she says. "I feel the need to do my own assessment, use my own perceptions, and to probe for understanding until I feel I have enough information to make a decision. My instincts tell me when I've gotten to that point."

Personalized Delegation

Skill in delegating develops over time and with practice. Once you get the hang of it, strive to personalize it by looking for opportunities to help each of your employees stretch and grow. In other words, take time to scratch the surface, and who knows what treasures you may find hidden inside your individual employees.

Dorothy Smiley, Manager of Staffing Systems and Diversity of Westin Resorts and Hotels, for example, says, "I always try to pinpoint the individual needs and strengths of my employees so that I am able to delegate responsibilities accordingly. Recently, as I was getting to know one of my newest employees, I learned of her specific interests and strengths and subsequently delegated a managerial task to her on a permanent basis." This particular employee, Smiley adds, had previously worked elsewhere in the company and was viewed by others as having very limited potential. Smiley's strategy of giving the employee more responsibility, however, worked wonders. "As a result, she began to look forward to coming to work each day, and her morale completely turned around. Moreover, she quickly developed into a very strong contributor to the organization."

Adds Morene Seldes-Marcus, "While I was working as Director of Executive Training and Development at Upton's, a national clothing store chain, I was asked to develop a sophisticated management training program for employee certification. I opted to delegate the task to my training manager, who had never designed a project like that before. I knew that the interaction between us—from the planning stages to implementation—would be critical. But I constantly let her know, 'This is your project. What I want to do is teach you all I know about how to do it. Then you take that information and create beyond that.' Knowing this subordinate's level of ability, I didn't need to give her a lot of details—just the concept. And she *loved* taking the ball and running with it."

Not all employees are like that, Seldes-Marcus acknowledges.

"But if you know your subordinates' skill sets and what turns them on, you can use it. Believing in this particular employee and delegating such an important task to her was the greatest carrot I could dangle in front of her. She was extremely motivated, and because of that, did a terrific job on the task."

Another success story worth noting: Dee Thomas, Vice President of Ewing and Thomas, a Florida-based chain of physical therapy clinics, once delegated the job of purchasing supplies to one of her technicians. The technician, in turn, took it upon herself to make numerous telephone calls to check and compare prices on different items in the area. She also constantly watched for sales on materials the company regularly purchased, and would drive across town on her own time to take advantage of these price cuts. At the end of one year, her efforts surfaced in the company's bottom line. She had saved the company $40,000!

CHAPTER SEVEN

Good Employees Are Made, Not Born

PROFILE

MAGGIE ELLIOTT

SENIOR VICE PRESIDENT, CREATIVE ADMINISTRATION
WALT DISNEY IMAGINEERING
GLENDALE, CALIFORNIA

"What I've found to be most effective—and it's really very simple—is getting to know our talent on an individual level. If I can pinpoint and understand each individual's talent, then I can find out from them *what works and what doesn't in terms of motivation."*

Many managers groan at the mere thought of having to supervise and motivate "creative" types. After all, since artists, writers, and designers typically march to the beat of a different drummer, they are notorious for being fiercely independent, difficult to work with, and often eccentric.

Not according to Maggie Elliott, Senior Vice President of Creative Administration at Walt Disney Imagineering. "What I've found is that creativity comes in all forms," she says. "And whether it's an artist or an accountant, if you respect an individual's creativity, that immediately helps you to work through what the myths regarding creative types are all about."

At Walt Disney Imagineering, Elliott oversees a division of three hundred individuals: concept designers, show writers, illustrators, artists, model makers, production designers, and show producers. "These are the people who come up with all of the ideas that surface at our theme parks. They also help to insure that the integrity of these ideas is maintained as they move through all the disciplines—architecture, engineering, etc."

Anyone who has ever visited Disneyland, Walt Disney World, EPCOT Center, or Disney-MGM Studios can't help but marvel at the end results of this group's work. So how does Elliott keep the members of this think tank motivated?

"What I've found to be most effective—and it's really very simple—is getting to know our talent on an individual level," she says. "If I can pinpoint and understand each individual's talent, then I can find out from *them* what works and what doesn't in terms of motivation. For example, something as simple as movie passes may be as meaningful to one person as an assured parking space is to another."

Of course, motivation also requires communication on the same wavelength, so much of Elliott's time is spent listening to and learning what she calls different "languages." "By that, I mean discovering how each individual communicates and processes information," she explains. "I'll give you an example. Recently, I was having problems communicating with one of my managers. When I brought in an outside facilitator to work with my entire management team, this particular manager and I volunteered to participate in one of the exercises. Each of us was asked to write down our definitions of the word 'formal.' The images that popped into my mind were vivid, colorful, and very picture-oriented: sparkly dresses, black tie, the Academy Awards. In contrast, the definition my manager came up with was very black and white and heavily word-oriented: authority and discipline. You couldn't even put pictures to his definition."

What this demonstrated to Elliott and her manager was that they had very different ways of communicating and processing information. In essence, they could be using the same words, but saying—and hearing—completely different things, which was causing a complete communication breakdown.

According to Elliott, most artists don't think in terms of words. "They think in terms of pictures. So you have to talk differently to them. Of course, all of this takes a tremendous amount of time and patience, but the end results are well worth the effort."

Another tactic Elliott uses to keep her staff's creative juices flowing involves making sure that everyone has the opportunity to express their ideas without fear of being ridiculed or shot down. "Sometimes the craziest ideas contain the seed of something that is incredibly dynamic."

To spur this free flow of ideas, Elliott encourages her staff to participate in such activities as hallway conversations among subordinates. "Many managers' first and normal reaction might be to wonder why their employees aren't at their boards working," she says. "But if you begin to understand your talent in a creative environment, then you realize that they are creating and inventing even when the conversation they're having is about something unrelated to their jobs. In fact, artists often need a break from the boards, because it puts distance between them and their work. Then they are able to return to the task at hand with a fresher perspective."

Training—both on and off the job—is a motivational tool Elliott often uses as well. "We have life drawing classes and sculptural classes. We offer a lot of illustration courses as well, where we bring in outside illustrators who are tops in their fields. We also offer a series of presentation classes that cover the nuts and bolts of formatting a presentation as well as analyzing your audience and how to slant your presentation accordingly—whether you're giving a lecture to your college or pitching an idea to CEO Michael Eisner."

These in-house classes are offered free of charge during lunch hours and before and after work. In addition, employees who take night classes at local colleges and universities are eligible for 100 percent reimbursement if the course is job-related and they earn a passing grade.

Making sure employees feel in on things is another priority at Walt Disney Imagineering. The company hosts a Wednesday morning breakfast at least three times a month on company time.

"Everyone is invited, and these meetings revolve around a specific topic," Elliott reports. "The topic might be trends in the entertainment business or the effects Las Vegas is having on the Southern California marketplace." In addition, an in-house newsletter, published weekly, updates employees on projects different teams are working on.

As for incentives, some employees at Walt Disney Imagineering are eligible for a discretionary year-end bonus, where a cash award is given. "There are also a tremendous number of psyche benefits around here—like the handwritten thank-you notes that senior executives take the time to write," Elliott says. "Other benefits include special employee screenings of Disney films and an annual Employee Forum, where the current project status is shared along with a question-and-answer session. We also send our employees to trade shows, seminars, and conferences."

Elliott also motivates her staff by constantly looking for ways to challenge them. "You don't pigeonhole talent. That's really key."

Elliott should know, as she is an artistic and creative individual herself—thanks, in part, to talented genes. "When Walt Disney decided to create Disneyland, he launched WED Enterprises. To staff it, he pulled together a group of individuals from his movie studio, and my father, a motion picture art director, was one of those people." Later, when Disney passed away, Elliott's father took the helm at WED Enterprises—now known as Walt Disney Imagineering. "So I was raised in the world of art and Disney," adds Elliott, whose childhood memories include climbing the gates of Frontierland during construction.

After graduating from high school, where she majored in theater arts, Elliott landed a summer job at WED. "My first assignment was to feather tiki birds for Walt Disney World," she recalls. And while she planned to go to college and had dreams of becoming a fashion designer or doing something in the theater, Elliott couldn't bring herself to leave WED. Instead, she stayed on at the model shop and helped the company get EPCOT Center off the ground.

"In those days, there was constant turmoil in the model shop. All of us were working well into the night as well as weekends, and it was taking its toll. Finally, one day someone said, 'Wouldn't it be nice if we had someone to coordinate this work—to get the information to us ahead of time, so that we knew what to anticipate and wouldn't have to kill ourselves meeting these deadlines?' " Elliott took it upon herself to put together a proposal and was subsequently asked to fill the new position.

"I had never considered management as a career," she says. But after much soul-searching, she accepted the challenge. She also enrolled in college and took as many night classes in business as she could handle and still perform well at her new job.

Her track record since then has been impressive. In the mid-1980s—despite a takeover threat and a reduction in the WED workforce from well over one thousand to under five hundred—she was promoted to director. And in the early 1990s, she was promoted to senior vice president.

"The way I describe what I do, is that I'm the business partner to the creative executives. I run the administrative, operational, and business side, and they are the inventors and creative visionaries for the product that we produce. My job is to keep the information flowing to the creative people, so that they are free to do what they do best. In other words, I'm a behind-the-scenes stage manager, and they are on stage."

Maggie Elliott may not be in the spotlight, but considering how well she manages to motivate such a diversity of people, she, too, deserves to take a bow.

• • •

Tough economic times have led to mega-mergers, rampant downsizing, and massive layoffs, leaving many of today's workers with little or no job security. As a result, the days of blind allegiance are gone, and company loyalty can no longer be commanded. Today's workers need a reason to feel committed to the companies they work for, and it's up to their managers to provide those incentives.

How? Managers must first have a clear understanding of what

today's workers want and need. Next, they must find ways to fulfill those needs and desires.

In survey after survey, two of employees' biggest gripes are not feeling in on things and lack of recognition for a job well done. Today's workers also say that they want jobs that are challenging and interesting.

Successful managers know that motivation to do a good job is not something that they can instill in their employees; rather, it must come from within an individual. But these managers also recognize that what they *can* do is spur self-motivation by giving workers what they need and want most. Here's how they do it—and how you can, too.

Need: Making Employees Feel in on Things

One of the most common complaints heard from employees is that they are constantly kept in the dark. Few rarely feel as if they truly know what's going on in the companies they work for. Even when dealing with managers, many employees say they have no idea where they stand, or how they are doing on the job. Yet feeling in on things is critical to self-motivation, because it gives employees a sense of control, a sense of ownership, and a sense of importance. This in turn increases their productivity, commitment, and loyalty to the company.

There are a number of ways you can help employees feel in on things . . .

• **Communicate with your staff on a regular basis**—and don't feel as if *you* have to do all of the talking. *Listening* to employees' ideas and concerns can be equally—if not more—motivating. Holding regular staff meetings, for example, is a good way to keep the lines of communication with your subordinates open. But since these meetings are typically reserved to discuss and settle specific issues, they are rarely motivating. Consequently, to really communicate with your staff, you need other forums.

Karyn Marasco, General Manager for the Westin William Penn

in Pittsburgh, for example, meets monthly with representatives from all areas of her hotel just to talk. At Kodak, Candy Obourn regularly schedules what she calls "Chats with Candy." "I invite employees from all levels of my division to have breakfast with me. We have no agenda, and I encourage everyone to talk about what's on their minds. It works very well, and more often than not, I get more information than I give."

At Odetics, a West Coast high-tech firm that makes robots and data recorders for the space shuttle, town hall meetings are held whenever the company is planning to institute an important new policy or procedure. The company also holds what it calls "C-cube" meetings (C-cube stands for "control change through communication") over lunch. A random group of employees is invited to these meetings and asked for their feedback on new ideas management is pondering.

Other managers hold semiannual or annual retreats at off-site locations, devoted both to raising issues that concern everyone and to brainstorming solutions to common problems. Still others, like Grace Pastiak, communicate through daily visits with their staff and by remaining accessible throughout the workday.

• **Keep your subordinates abreast of what's going on in your company**—from its financial status to what the competition is up to. Share customer feedback—both positive and negative—with every employee as well. Very often, if employees are simply made aware of the company's standings, they will be motivated to find ways to maintain—or increase—its status.

For example, at A.G. Edwards employees are glued to their speaker phones on the last Friday of every month, when Chairman Ben Edwards delivers a brief report on how things are going in the company, then opens the line to questions.

At Preston Trucking, based in Preston, Maryland, drivers who must miss meetings are sent audiocassette tapes filled with company news and interviews. And at Wal-Mart, one of the country's most profitable discount department stores, the closing price of company stock is broadcast daily over the intercom in stores and in warehouses. Workers here are also kept up-to-date on their own store's weekly sales and profits.

Keep employees posted on pending changes in the company as well, because if you don't, the rumor mill will operate in overdrive. As Nancy Singer, President and CEO of First of America Bank–Northeast, Illinois, points out, "When people don't know what's coming, they invariably assume the worst. I tell everyone as quickly as possible exactly what I plan to do and what their role will be when there is change. If you keep your people informed, they have more of a sense of ownership, and they work that much harder. They also keep you informed—so you find out about problems before things get out of control."

• **Acknowledge employees' suggestions and ideas.** Once employees are privy to what's going on in the company and where it stands, many will come up with ideas for improving your operations. Your job is to listen to and show appreciation for *every* suggestion. Even if you don't use employees' ideas, it's important to thank them for their contributions. Otherwise, you can bet they'll never give you another one! "It's far too common among managers to take suggestions from employees and never do anything," believes Victoria Ogden. "You have to act on the good ideas. You also have to tell people when you *don't* think their idea is a good one. That way you don't leave them sitting around waiting and wondering."

And if you do end up putting an employee's idea to use? Recognize his or her contribution publicly. Better yet, ask the person to join you at meetings where the idea will be discussed. Also make it a point to show your subordinates tangible results of their ideas once they have been put into action.

• **Establish an employee of the month/quarter/year award**— and let your subordinates choose the recipients. Since 1986, Tellabs has bestowed quarterly Just-In-Time Awards to outstanding employees. "Past recipients of the award are the ones who decide from the nominations who gets the next one," reports Grace Pastiak. "We thought that was important. Since those are the folks who are performing with excellence, then they should be able to judge excellence."

And at Silicon Graphics, every year thirty-five to forty people are nominated by colleagues as employees who represent the spirit of Silicon Graphics. "Our spirit is one of caring, dealing with people in an upfront way, and getting on with the job," explained Edward R. McCracken, Silicon Graphics's CEO, in a recent interview with *Harvard Business Review*. "We announce the finalists of the 'Spirit of Silicon Graphics' and the winner at our Christmas party. Then we take all of them and their significant others to Hawaii not only to celebrate but also to help plan how to keep our spirit growing as we get larger."

• **Don't be afraid to roll up your sleeves.** "The best motivation is to get down and do the work with the employees," believes Karyn Marasco, who often helps in the kitchen and other areas as needed at the Westin William Penn. Working side by side with subordinates on special projects—or where needed—not only motivates, it builds camaraderie and encourages communication.

It can also open managers' eyes to day-to-day problems subordinates face. "Some years ago, I went into the mailroom to help get things organized and was reprimanded by my manager, 'I'm not paying you to clean up the mailroom,' " says Lynn Richardson, now Work Group Leader for Customer Service Training at Xerox in Houston. "But while I was in the mailroom, I had an opportunity to work alongside an employee who was having some job-related problems. We talked and were able to resolve them. So, in many ways, the mailroom served as a great equalizer to me."

Need: Recognition for a Job Well Done

June Rockoff, Senior Vice President of Software Development at Lotus Development Corporation, is a master of motivation. In 1989, when she volunteered to take over management of the team responsible for creating a new version of Lotus 1-2-3 for Windows, she walked into a disaster. The product was six months behind schedule, six managers had come and gone, and the creators felt that Lotus managers could not be trusted. Yet somehow Rockoff managed to step in and not only clean up the technical mess, but boost morale.

A mother with three young children—and an extremely supportive husband—Rockoff worked side by side with software developers seven days a week. Moreover, she made sure that team members were heralded for their dedication and hard work. She presented tailor-made posters to recognize individual achievements. She had a rock video made of the entire team, which was later shown to the entire company. She introduced "guest chef" night on Tuesdays, when testing forced team members to work late. On these nights, Lotus executives—including the CEO—would cook and serve gourmet meals to the seventy to eighty individuals involved in the project. Whenever the team made a breakthrough, she arranged for the company's top brass to drop by and say congratulations. And when the product shipped, Rockoff took out a full page ad in the local newspaper to say thanks to her employees. In addition, she arranged to have champagne bottles popped and broken over the first delivery trucks.

Other managers we spoke to offer cash bonuses as a motivator. For example, whenever a member of her staff brings in a new business lead, Christine Anderson, President of Christine Anderson & Associates, a public relations firm in Los Angeles, offers them a percentage of the monthly retainer for the duration of that account. "This way, I'm not the only one pursuing new business, and motivation stays high because the paychecks keep rising," Anderson says.

Recently, when the Society of Incentive Travel Executives (SITE) Foundation surveyed a cross section of American workers, 95 percent of those polled ranked a cash bonus as a meaningful incentive. But don't make the mistake of equating motivation solely with cash. Showing appreciation for a job well done doesn't have to cost a bundle. In fact, some incentives and awards don't cost a dime—and employees often prefer them. Sixty-three percent of respondents in the SITE survey, for example, mentioned that a simple "pat on the back" could work wonders.

Here's a collection of simple but effective low-budget ideas to help motivate your staff:

• **Use novelty prizes to recognize outstanding work.** These can run the gamut from T-shirts and coffee mugs to bumper stickers and desk accessories. Also, consider having your company and/ or departmental slogan printed on these items to remind everyone of your overall goals.

At Tennant Company, the world's largest maker of industrial floor maintenance equipment, employees who "consistently meet their job standards and display a positive attitude" are eligible to win a koala teddy bear. Employees nominate one another for these prized possessions, and an employee committee chooses the monthly winners. Koala T. Bear Awards, as they are called, are delivered by a committee member, dressed in a bear costume, who arrives unannounced at the winner's workstation.

And while directing Kodak's Corporate Information System Unit, Katherine Hudson, now President and CEO of W.H. Brady Company in Milwaukee, started what she called the "Corporate Crabgrass" project. "I was trying to find a way to show my team that I understood their hassles" she says. "So I encouraged them to find ways to eliminate or simplify procedures, and the winners received a personalized, gold-painted crabgrass cutter. At first, my staff thought it was a little too cute. But then a funny thing happened. The cutters became status symbols, and every one started competing for them. My favorite went to a guy who suggested that the company cut a hole in the fence surrounding our building so employees wouldn't have to walk ten minutes out of their way to the main entrance."

• **In lieu of cash, consider offering employee perks for outstanding work.** Johnna Howell, Corporate Director of Staffing and Development at Westin Hotels and Resorts says, "As I don't have the wherewithal to provide large cash awards to those who excel in their responsibilities, I have consistently sought noncash ways in which to reward my staff. I try to take each person individually and ask myself, 'What turns them on? What motivates them to work harder?' Depending on the person, the answer might be public recognition, comp time, increased responsibilities, leadership roles, task force appointments, challenging work, small personal gifts, or personal time with me such as a private breakfast or lunch."

At Silicon Graphics, a company known for its high morale, employees receive a six-week sabbatical after four years of service. Anheuser-Busch offers its employees two free cases of Anheuser-Busch products every month. And at Fel-Pro Incorporated, the world's largest markers of gaskets for automobiles and industrial use, in addition to a variety of cash bonuses, workers also get special holiday gifts, elder-care consulting and referral, two free changes of work clothes annually, free income tax preparation, group auto insurance rates, and a free eye exam and a new pair of glasses every year. No wonder so many of Fel-Pro's employees are second—even third—generation!

• **Develop in-house rituals of recognition—the sillier the better!** When employees at Christine Anderson & Associates obtain an extraordinary number of media placements for a client in a one-month period, Anderson herself bestows a cardboard "gold crown" on their head at a staff meeting. "The crown, purchased for one of our birthdays a few years back, is in pretty sorry shape," Anderson reports, "but the 'Queen Bee' sentiment works just the same. We also have a gold star stamp that all of us use on progress reports to recognize work well done."

At The Fontayne Group (TFG), a marketing and public relations firm based in Los Angeles, "Megan Bucks" are a hot commodity. These flashy "dollar" bills are made in house and bear the face of Megan Hanlon, the firm's senior vice president responsible for all corporate finance. Every new employee receives an initial supply of Megan Bucks to spend or save. Employees can then earn different denominations of Megan Bucks for such things as coming up with great ideas, working above and beyond the call of duty, helping someone else meet a deadline, and working overtime. But there are penalties, too. Megan Bucks must be forfeited for such actions as showing up tardy for meetings, missing deadlines, and turning in expense reports late.

Ninety Megan Bucks earn employees a free day off. Other ways to spend this currency include purchasing subscriptions that the firm doesn't already have and buying extra office supplies outside one's allotment.

"Great ceremony accompanies the presentation of Megan Bucks," reports Robin Ratcliffe, Vice President of TFG/East in Pittsburgh. "Most employees keep their Megan Bucks tucked in a special spot in their desks, and many proudly display their first-ever Megan Buck on their office bulletin board."

• **Give credit where credit is due**—by *publicly* acknowledging employees' extra efforts. "At Cape Cod Community Newspapers, we have what we call a 'Wall of Fame,' " reports Victoria Ogden. "At weekly meetings, managers nominate good ideas employees have recently come up with or outstanding work people have done. These might run the gamut from an accountant who found an error in the telephone bill or an ad representative who sold a great big ad, to a beautiful color job on a special supplement or a congratulatory letter from a satisfied customer. Employees can also nominate their peers. Winning examples of outstanding work and good ideas are then posted on a bulletin board for everyone to see. Plus, I write little blurbs of explanation and thanks beneath each entry."

Bulletin boards are also used as a tool to recognize good work at the Sunette Division of Hoechst Celanese. "The way our program works is that anyone can fill out a card to say 'Thanks' or 'Great job' to anyone else. They then post their message on the board," says Carole Kitchens. "This effort has turned out to be a real bright spot amidst a lot of turmoil, and I think it has also helped to bridge some gaps."

Other ideas worth considering: Spotlight employees in your company newsletter. Send photos and short write-ups of employees and their achievements to your local newspaper for wider coverage. Compliment subordinates for good work in front of others. Have your CEO call, write, or visit outstanding individuals to add his or her personal thanks for a job well done.

"Motivation is one of my main responsibilities," adds Claire Coyle, of SmithKline Beecham. "I see everything at my disposal as a potential motivating tool—appraisals, promotions, awards, certificates, congratulatory notes, little gifts. But I also champion the department with upper management. That's a big part of a leader's job—to sell the value of your team, particularly when it's a service group."

• **Just say thanks!** "When I received approval to hire a person to work for me—my first managerial role—the general manager of my division told me, 'The Golden Rule is just as relevant in your business life as it was on the playground,'" says Barbara Behrman, former General Manager of Marketing for Heinz U.S.A., now director of Retail New Product Development with Jimmy Dean Foods. "He emphasized that managing requires superior people skills. You must be sensitive to your employees' performance and personal needs and be as considerate to them as you would like them to be to you. Most importantly, though, he showed me that the words 'thank you' can be the basis for a superior manager/employee relationship—something we should all remember."

• **Put it in writing.** In addition to *saying* thanks for a good job, write a note of appreciation to employees who have gone the extra mile—and tell them you are placing a copy of your note in their permanent personnel file. At Tellabs, for example, Grace Pastiak created a special recognition pad to communicate messages of thanks. "It looks like a regular pad of paper, but it has an excerpt on it that reflects the company's mission statement," she reports. "It reads, 'We believe in the skills of all our people and the excellence that they bring to their jobs,' then there's a big blank space for writing in whatever I want. I send these out four to five times a week, up the ladder and down the ladder, inside the company and outside the company."

Adds Nicole Browning, "At MTV Networks, we are E-mail mavens. Management not only sends congratulatory E-mail to subordinates, but shares employees' accomplishments with higher-ups in the organization as well. People love it. All of us like to hear that people are taking note of what we're doing."

• **Encourage celebrations of all kinds.** "Our offices are always decorated with designer balloons and streamers for birthdays, and birthday cakes are essential," says Christine Anderson of Christine Anderson & Associates. "I always try to caption the cakes with a PR slogan or two, lest my employees forget they are at the office. Here's an example: 'For Lisa on her birthday, with the understanding that she will secure a *Newsweek* cover story by next week . . . ' "

Johnson Wax names a "Customer Service Person of the Month," and at the end of every quarter, management takes all the winners—along with the staff—somewhere special. "We might take a cruise on Lake Geneva, for example, or rent out a sports box at the Bradley Center in Milwaukee," reports Project Manager Bridget Shirley.

And at Quad/Graphics in Pewaukee, Wisconsin, management has been putting on musical revues for staff at every company holiday party since 1981. Founder Harry V. "Larry" Quadracci tells his employees, "You perform for us throughout the year. This is our opportunity to perform for you."

Other reasons to celebrate: breakthrough sales, record-breaking months, milestones reached, major projects completed.

• **Reward team efforts as well as individual performances.** When you reward the efforts of a group, you reinforce the concept of teamwork. Recognizing team efforts also enables you to make more people feel like winners, particularly those employees who don't often warrant recognition for their individual contributions.

Ideas for rewarding group efforts might include serving doughnuts and coffee in the morning, ordering pizza for lunch, and sponsoring team parties. At the Westin William Penn, special lunches are often served in the cafeteria to reward the staff for working especially hard. And in some companies, managers open the soda machines on particularly productive days.

Rewarding teams or groups of employees can also encourage camaraderie. Susan Groenwald, President of the Barter Corporation, for example, sponsors an annual banquet where departments enjoy some friendly competition. Each department is responsible for writing and performing an original "fight" song.

Warning: Incentives Can Be Misunderstood

Incentives can be tricky. On the one hand, you want your employees to work hard to gain them. On the other hand, prizes and awards must be attainable enough that employees don't become discouraged trying to win them—which can totally unravel self-motivation. Be certain, then, that the goals you set are reasonable and reachable.

When launching an incentive program, here are some other guidelines to keep in mind.

• **Don't use incentives as a Band-Aid.** "Too often, incentive programs are created in place of regular good programs," points out Donna Brown in an article for *Management Review*. "The best people in the company haven't been getting the best jobs and good raises, so management puts incentive programs in place as a way around that. What management should be doing is building relationships and educating and training employees so they can be better at their jobs. Instead, management is trying to buy love."

• **Incentives must be deserved.** Make sure your incentives are sending the *right* message by bestowing prizes and awards for outstanding performance *only*. If you give a prize or award to a poor performer in hopes that he will be motivated to improve, you send the message that poor performance is acceptable.

• **Competition among employees or teams is fine, so long as prizes are equally obtainable by *everyone*.** If certain individuals or teams have an obvious advantage at winning, you'll be perceived as playing favorites, and discouragement (in contrast to self-motivation) will be the end result.

• **The more prizes, the merrier.** An abundance of small but attractive prizes will usually be more effective than one large one. So instead of blowing your budget on a pair of round-trip tickets and a hotel room for a week's stay in Jamaica, purchase several getaway weekends at a nearby resort. That way, you avoid having one lucky winner surrounded by a bunch of upset and jealous losers—who, incidentally, may have worked equally hard.

• **Immediate recognition has greater impact.** Incentive programs should rarely last more than thirty days. Otherwise, people lose interest. Instead, rewards should be presented as quickly as possible. This reinforces good performance and is also perceived as more sincere.

• **Reward what you want to see more of.** In other words, if you want to build team spirit, avoid pitting individual team members against one another. Instead, have teams compete against other teams for rewards.

Need: Jobs That Are Challenging and Interesting

For some employes, feeling in on things and winning incentive prizes don't mean nearly as much as feeling challenged. How to motivate these employees? Try these tips:

• **Share the workload.** When employees have plateaued, and you have nowhere to promote them, delegate as many challenging tasks to them as possible. Give them more freedom in planning and scheduling their workload, making decisions, and solving problems. Put them in charge of showing new employees the ropes. Use them to demonstrate specific tasks when training other employees. Let them take charge of a special event, project, or meeting.

At 3M (Minnesota Mining and Mfg.), employees are encouraged to devote 15 percent of their work time to projects of their own choosing. "We call it bootlegging," says Dr. Tom Wollner, Staff Vice President, Corporate Research Laboratories. "The 15 Percent Rule was designed to enhance innovation at 3M by encouraging employees to spend time developing their own new product ideas." One 15 Percent Rule success story is the Post-it note, developed by 3M researcher Art Fry, who became frustrated at bookmarks falling out of his choir hymnal.

• **Stir things up.** If feasible, consider having your employees rotate jobs every six to eight weeks or so. Doing this stimulates teamwork, lifts workers out of ruts, and usually results in renewed enthusiasm for the job. Moreover, as workers attempt to learn new jobs, those who have held those jobs prior to the rotation process are encouraged to act as mentors.

• **Help them to grow on the job.** In the SITE survey, 87 percent of the respondents said they viewed special training as a positive incentive, so consider bringing in speakers to the workplace for special training. "I'm a firm believer in in-service training, so from time to time I bring in outside consultants who are specifically involved in the communications area to talk with all of our people within the department," says Karen Himle, Vice President of Corporate Communications at the St. Paul Companies. "Doing this seems to make a big difference just in terms of how people view themselves and their contributions."

Instead of choosing the speakers yourself, however, consider letting a volunteer committee of employees choose them. And while you're at it, let *them* take charge of arranging and setting up the training sessions as well.

Another idea: Determine subordinates' career aspirations, and if these are realistic, let them "apprentice" with someone who holds a position to which they aspire for a few hours a week or month. For example, Viking Freight System in San Jose, California, boasts a mentor program open to hourly nonmanagement employees interested in moving up the ranks.

Under the Associate of the Day Program at Rosenbluth International, *any* associate (as employees are called here) can spend a day with another associate of *any* rank to see what his or her job is like. This helps workers decide if they would like to apply for a job in another department of the company or if they would like to try to become a top officer in the company.

And at Browning Management in Carmel, Indiana, team coaches change monthly. "We have a company breakfast every month that is designed to bring our entire staff up to date on what's going on in the firm," reports Sue Baird, Vice President. There's a theme for each breakfast, and the company makes buttons displaying the theme. As employees arrive at the breakfast, each one picks up a button, and if there's a sticker on the back of someone's button, he or she becomes the team coach for the month. "Our coaches get a supply of stars to hand out during the month for outstanding work," Baird adds. "At the next month's breakfast, the employee on each team who has earned the most stars receives a gift certificate for dinner for two. And coaches for the month receive two cinema tickets each."

• **Help them grow off the job as well.** Preach to your subordinates the importance of continuing education, earning degrees, joining and taking an active part in professional associations, and attending seminars and workshops of interest. Then make every attempt to put your money where your mouth is. At the Fontayne Group, for example, every employee is eligible for up to $250 annually in educational fees for courses geared toward gaining additional professional or personal skills. "The company also underwrites professional memberships for employees, subject to approval of the firm's chief financial officer," says Robin Ratcliffe.

If there are no funds in your budget to support these initiatives, at the very least make it easy for employees to continue their education and training by providing them with a flexible work schedule.

Different Strokes for Different Folks

Motivation is perhaps most effective when it is personalized. And the trick to personalized motivation is to find individuals' hot buttons, then look for ways to push these every chance you get. "I have a personal relationship with all of my employees and know what makes each of them tick," says Lynn Richardson of Xerox."Consequently, I try to reward them according to their needs—be it via public recognition, a note of thanks, a day off, a monetary bonus, or a simple pat on the back."

Employee Ownership: The Ultimate Motivator

At huge corporations like Avis and Procter & Gamble, Employee Stock Ownership Plans (ESOPs) are offered to nearly every employee. But even small companies can arrange for employee ownership. Consider Dee Thomas's story.

In the mid-1980s, Dee Thomas and Betty Ewing, both physical therapists, owned Ewing and Thomas, a successful chain of physical therapy clinics based in New Port Richey, Florida. When a larger company tried to buy them out, Thomas says the two decided instead to "sell the practice to the only people who we felt would treat our employees and patients the right way—our employees themselves." Financially, this made the most sense to the partners, but what Thomas and Ewing didn't realize about their ESOP was that it would also emerge as a great motivational and marketing tool.

Since the ESOP purchase, Ewing and Thomas has been guided by an executive committee made up of employees from all parts of the practice. "Because they are owners, members of the committee are very active in proposing ideas to improve the practice," Thomas reports. Fewer employees are taking sick leave and filing workers' compensation claims. And because they are now self-motivated, nearly every worker is willing to go the extra mile.

Moreover, Thomas says that the plan has helped to increase employee retention, which is critical in her business—where there are roughly five thousand new physical therapists available to fill twenty thousand jobs each year. "Recruiting is a lot easier, too," she adds.

At Phelps County Bank, which is also employee-owned, turnover is virtually zero and motivation is sky-high. "If you're just an employee, you know no matter how hard you beat your head against the wall, you may or may not get a promotion," said one employee. "Here all that gets put aside. Anything that I can do for this bank to improve it, to bring in new customers, to increase the bottom line, I benefit from."

Stock options and profit-sharing can bring about equally positive results—because employees still have a stake in the company's bottom line. In *The 100 Best Companies to Work for in America*, a majority of the companies chosen offer generous profit-sharing plans or stock options. Profit-sharing encourages company loyalty as well. In a survey by Dr. Charles Hanson and D. Wallace Bell of more than 2,500 employees working for twelve different companies in the United Kingdom, 73 percent said that the existence of profit-sharing improved employees' attitudes in a company. In addition, 68 percent thought it changed their view of the company for the better. But 96 percent also agreed with the statement that while profit-sharing is welcomed by the participants, it should *not* be seen as a substitute for an adequate wage or salary.

The Best Motivators in Life Are Often Free

Of course, none of these incentives, prizes, and awards will work unless you've established a good relationship with your staff. In fact, research conducted by Harvard University's Bureau of Vocational Guidance reveals that 80 percent of all job failures are due to poor relationships between employees and supervisors and not to problems with job responsibilities. In other words, when employees feel discouraged, self-motivation is virtually impossible. Consequently, they don't give their best efforts.

So before you even attempt to motivate your subordinates, focus on establishing, improving, and/or maintaining positive relationships with them. Here's how:

• **Know everyone's name.** Call your staff by name whenever you speak to them—whether it's to say good morning or to ask them a question about a project they are working on. Using a person's name makes people feel known and valued.

• **Show your subordinates that they are important to you.** Treat everyone with dignity and respect. Take an interest in their hobbies, personal lives, families, backgrounds, and outside interests. Remember—and recognize—their birthdays or other special events in their lives. Small things and personal touches make people feel important. And when employees feel important, they are more inclined to give their best efforts.

"Whenever time permits, I take coffee breaks with my staff," says Carole Kitchens. "Sometimes I'll bring doughnuts in the morning and say, 'Let's stop for ten minutes and just talk.' I try to rotate taking them to lunch one-on-one, and because I'm terrible at remembering birthdays, I host an annual birthday luncheon for *everyone*. All of these things may sound corny, but they work!"

• **Spend time with your employees.** Drop by their workstations just to say hello or to ask how things are going. Give them plenty of opportunities to share work-related problems and help them find solutions. "You have to walk around, and you have to understand what people are doing. Most of us in management don't do enough of that," believes Victoria Ogden. "The worst thing to do when there are problems is to stay inside your office with the door closed, then shoot out a memo. You've got to do the walk and the talk."

Even more important, Ogden adds, is providing subordinates with a forum to share their problems and concerns. "Just going up to someone and saying, 'Hi, how was your weekend?' is nice. But if they are really angry about something, they're probably not going to tell you that. Consequently, I think you have to set up opportunities for people to talk honestly—and a good way to do that is through work committee meetings, regular staff meetings, and so forth."

• **Take care of the little things that tend to irritate employees.** On page one of Viking Freight System's employee handbook, there's a statement that reads: "Most people spend approximately one-third of their adult life working. Viking was founded on the idea that anything to which a person dedicates that much of his or her life should be enjoyed." And top brass at Viking practice what they preach by making their employees' working environment as comfortable and enjoyable as possible. Trucks are equipped with AM/FM cassette radios and heated mirrors. Drivers and dock workers get free coffee at terminals, and off-duty rooms are stocked with televisions and VCRs.

In an article for *Management Solutions*, R. Bruce McAfee and Myron Glassman add, "A manager's objective must be to reassure employees the organization is responsive to their needs. This can be done by identifying those 'little things' bothering employees and correcting them. For example, employees in one firm were complaining that they were having trouble opening and shutting doors on bookcases. The firm removed the doors, and complaints ceased. In another firm, employees complained that the parking lot was not sufficiently large to accommodate all the cars. The firm painted lines showing where cars were to park, and the problem was solved. In still another firm, employees were bothered by the fact that their telephone was ringing on all incoming calls. The firm changed its system so that all incoming calls rang in only two offices, thereby eliminating the problem. Note that many of these 'little things' are inexpensive to correct. In the above situations, for example, the firms' costs were minimal. Yet the payoff was significant."

• **Clarify company visions, remove obstacles, then set everyone free.** "I think my primary roles are to clarify the vision for the department, remove roadblocks, and provide resources," says Karen Walker, Vice President of Operating Services for Compaq

Computer Corporation. "And I've found that if I do those things well, people stay motivated. As Compaq has grown and changed over the years, people really do see that they control their own destinies here. Ours is an environment where you can pretty much do what you want to do and have the talent to do, so people here are self-motivated. But they have to know where they're going. Consequently, if we can all share a common vision about what it is that we are here to do, then I can just turn everyone loose to do their work. And that's very motivating."

• **Provide constant feedback.** "People have accused me of being honest to a fault," reports Victoria Ogden. "But I don't think that's possible. I think honesty is terrific—even when what you have to say is not positive. If someone is doing a poor job, and nobody tells them, they're completely demotivated. People *want* to know where they stand with you."

Keep in mind, though, that studies show praise has a much more powerful effect on self-motivation and productivity than does criticism. But remember to be *specific* and *descriptive* with your praise. For example, instead of saying, "Good job, Mary!" try, "I was impressed with how you kept your cool with that irate customer, Mary!"

"Don't be afraid to stand up and clap," says Ogden. "I've also been accused of being a cheerleader, but if someone does a terrific job, I think you should scream out, 'Terrific job!' I think what often happens, instead, is that we save things. We say to ourselves, 'I'll tell them about that later,' and later never happens."

Adds Morene Seldes-Marcus, "To me, feedback is the most motivating action a manager can take with a subordinate. Let your staff know about any performance you are pleased with. Tell them how it has impacted the company, how it has contributed to the overall success of the team's project, and so on. Feedback is the fuel that feeds the fire."

• **Use phrases that motivate.** "I always ask my employees for their personal opinions about any moves we make in the business," says Christine Anderson. " 'What do you think?' is possibly the biggest motivator and ego boost of all." Other powerful phrases to include in your vocabulary: "I'm proud of you" and "Thanks."

Motivation Pays

It pays—literally—to have highly motivated employees on your team. Not only are they more productive, they boost morale by setting good examples for their co-workers. Highly motivated employees are absent less and make fewer mistakes than those who are poorly motivated. They also affect your company's bottom line by reducing the costs of rehiring and training new employees and by boosting profits with their can-do attitudes.

CHAPTER EIGHT

The Lighter Side of Managing People

PROFILE

COLLEEN BARRETT

EXECUTIVE VICE PRESIDENT–CUSTOMERS
SOUTHWEST AIRLINES
DALLAS, TEXAS

"If people can laugh at themselves and not take themselves too seriously, they don't come across as stuffy and all wrapped up in themselves. In fact, if they can loosen up a bit, then the atmosphere and work environment are far more pleasant. And it's my personal belief that if your work atmosphere is pleasant, you provide far better customer service, no matter what your business or product is."

Company humor an oxymoron? Think again. At Southwest Airlines, humor is part of the job description. In fact, the airline not only recruits people with a strong sense of humor, it teaches them how to be creative and funny both in the air and on the ground.

At company orientations, for example, a videotape, compiled by Southwest's "Culture Committee," is shown to every new recruit. Entitled "Dwayne's World," this takeoff on the popular "Wayne's World" segment on *Saturday Night Live* shows gate agents cracking jokes with customers, and flight attendants reciting safety regulations in rap. Of course, the training tape also emphasizes that there's nothing wrong with a completely straight PA announcement, so long as it's caring, concise, and articulate. But the company's basic philosophy is that happy employees are productive employees. And a little bit of playfulness appears to translate into big payoffs for Southwest.

Consider these facts. In *The 100 Best Companies to Work for in America*, Southwest Airlines ranks in the top ten. "Everybody here is really upbeat and always happy," one worker told the authors. "They want to come to work. They get here early, and they have smiles on their faces." Southwest employees, including flight attendants and ticket agents, are encouraged to dress comfortably— no suits, high heels, and pantyhose required. Moreover, workers at Southwest are considered "internal customers" and are treated as such. So it comes as no surprise that the company has a waiting list of applicants eager to partake in what the company calls the "Southwest spirit."

While its major competitors operate in the red, Southwest has managed to turn a profit every year since 1972. And in 1993, based on U.S. Transportation Department statistics, Southwest became the first carrier to rank number one in on-time performance, fewest lost bags, and fewest customer complaints—an honor known in the industry as the "triple crown."

"You've got to have a sense of humor to survive in this world," says Colleen Barrett, Executive Vice President–Customers, who began as a secretary with the airline when it first took flight in 1971. "If people can laugh at themselves and not take themselves too seriously, they don't come across as stuffy and all wrapped up in themselves. In fact, if they can loosen up a bit, then the atmosphere and work environment are far more pleasant. And it's my personal belief that if your work atmosphere is pleasant, you provide far better customer service, no matter what your business or product is."

Southwest's unique culture, Barrett reveals, starts at the top. "Our CEO, Herb Kelleher, is single-handedly the one who has really convinced all of our employees that it's okay to have fun at work." Indeed, Southwest's colorful CEO himself has been known to run up and down the aisles of his airplanes dressed as the

Easter Bunny or as a leprechaun, passing out peanuts and drinks to the passengers.

At Southwest, the emphasis has always been on customer service. "We play a lot of games with our customers," Barrett reports, "especially when they face long flight delays on the ground or get stuck circling the airport waiting to land." Some of Southwest's most popular games involve finding out who has the ugliest driver's license photo, or who boasts the biggest hole in their socks. Prizes run the gamut from coffee mugs and pens to luggage tags— "we're sorry" prizes, the airline calls them. "It's amazing what people will do to win a prize," Barrett remarks. "We've had passengers get up and sing on the PA system, share their most embarrassing moments with a planeful of strangers, and even waddle down the aisle like a duck."

In addition to fun and games with their customers, many of Southwest's gate agents and flight attendants prefer to take a zany approach when making required (but usually dull and mundane) safety announcements. For example, there are those who impersonate Elvis Presley, Robin Leach, Mister Rogers, and Arnold Schwarzenegger while reciting boarding instructions at the gate or in-flight safety regulations in the air. Others take the dress-up route, donning outrageous costumes on Halloween or posing as elves and reindeer on Christmas Eve and dancing in the aisles while the captain sings Christmas carols over the PA system.

In addition to contributing to a healthy morale among employees, this license—and freedom—to have fun at work results in fierce loyalty to the company. For example, when oil prices skyrocketed in 1990, employees took the initiative to pitch in and purchase the airline $135,000 worth of jet fuel through payroll deductions.

Southwest's customers also appear to be a loyal bunch. "We get eleven thousand letters a month, and they are nine to one positive," Barrett says. "In fact, at least weekly someone writes, 'I've been flying for over twenty-two years, and I *heard* the safety announcement for the first time on your airline.'" Of course, not all the mail Southwest receives is positive. "Every now and then, we hear from someone who *doesn't* have a good sense of humor," Barrett confirms.

Usually when Barrett gets complaints, she'll reply with a cover letter that says, "I respect your right to feel the way you do, but I'd like to show you another perspective." Then she'll enclose copies of complimentary letters the airline has received. "I figure it's at least a third party—it's not me singing our praises," she says.

Barrett, who has a staff of forty-seven to help her answer Southwest's mail, believes in trying to inject humor into the company's written responses as well. "We once got a letter from a passenger saying, 'I'm not going to fly on Southwest anymore because you put the toilet paper rolls in upside down.' We couldn't tell if it was a joke or a bona fide complaint, but we decided to go out on a limb and have a little fun with it. We wrote back, 'What the hell were you doing upside down in our bathroom?' The passenger thought it was hilarious."

But Barrett is quick to point out that humor is not something that is forced at Southwest. "There are certain standards and rules of job performance that must be met," she says. "And we don't *make* people do something funny or weird. But we don't discourage it either." What Southwest *does* do is caution its employees to use good judgment and to steer clear of inappropriate humor. "We stress never getting into ethnic issues, avoiding jokes that involve religion or politics, and staying away from anything that has sexual implications.

"Another thing you have to be careful about is trying to be funny when you really aren't capable of pulling it off," Barrett adds. But you can be playful and still have a lot of fun without being a comedian, per se. In fact, Barrett describes herself as "fun, but not necessarily funny."

As for her employees, they call Barrett the "backbone of this airline" and say she is extremely organized and meticulous. Which is not surprising, considering that in addition to overseeing the airline's executive office, she manages a slew of departments at Southwest—marketing, public relations, employee communications, human resources, government affairs, to name a few.

Barrett's unusual title, Executive Vice President–Customers, was changed from Vice President of Administration to emphasize the airline's commitment to its customers. "Over the years we have grown from a small, closely knit group—like a family, almost—to over thirteen thousand employees, so we constantly worry about how to preserve our 'Customer Service' culture," she says.

With this goal in mind, Barrett insists that the C in Customer be capitalized in all of the airline's correspondence, and she does not believe in form responses. Instead, all letters to Southwest are answered with a personal letter or telephone call—and always within thirty days.

Barrett is the instigator of Southwest's "Culture Committee" as well, a group she says is composed of a wide range of employees who meet quarterly to brainstorm ways to maintain the airline's special spirit.

Perhaps it is this special spirit that has enabled Barrett to rise through the company ranks from secretary to the airline industry's highest-ranking female executive. Or perhaps her success can be attributed to sheer determination. "I don't see obstacles; I see opportunities," she says. "I'm very persistent, and I mess my nose in everyone else's business. Besides, my mother always told me that I could do anything I wanted to do, and I believed it."

• • •

Can you have fun on the job and still be productive? To write *This Job Should Be Fun: The New Profit-Strategy for Managing People in Tough Times*, author Bob Basso, Ph.D., and co-author Judi Klosek, J.D., interviewed over twelve thousand CEOs, managers, and frontline workers and found the answer to be a "resounding and provable 'yes!'" Yet in a separate survey conducted by *Industry Week*, 63 percent of the respondents claimed that their jobs were no fun at all. Nearly half (48.8 percent) who responded complained that a "dog-eat-dog" climate prevailed in their firms. And 38.6 percent said initiative-stifling bureaucracies killed any opportunity to have fun.

In recent years, stiff global competition and a tight economy have left much of corporate America feeling somber and serious. Yet it is for these very reasons that companies need to lighten up!

Humor's the Ticket

"I get to look at a lot of successful businesses in the U.S., and they all have one thing in common: They care about their people," reports Fran Solomon, a humor consultant and "Vice Empress" of Playfair, a humor consulting firm in Berkeley, California. "The managers of these companies," she adds, "have two things in common: a sense of humor about themselves and a willingness to laugh at things."

Indeed, a dash of fun and frivolity in the workplace can work wonders. Consider these benefits of humor . . .

• **Spurs creativity and aids in problem-solving.** In a set of studies conducted by psychologist Alice M. Isen, subjects who watched a humorous film of "bloopers and practical jokes" were better able to find creative solutions to puzzling problems than were those who saw an exercise film or a film about mathematics. "Feeling good can enhance creativity," Isen told *Glamour* magazine. "We know that to be creative, it's beneficial for people to feel good about themselves. Humor seems to tap those same feelings."

• **Promotes a sense of teamwork.** In the workplace, laughter is the glue that bonds. "Humor builds solidarity," reports Barbara Mackoff, a Seattle-based, Harvard-trained psychologist who has conducted research on humor for the past eight years. "The creation of inside jokes is a means of bonding; shared history is what teamwork is all about."

At Browning Management every other Friday is "Casual Day," and employees can wear whatever they want. Teamwork on those days, the company reports, is noticeably more effective and productive.

And in his book *Making Humor Work: Take Your Job Seriously and Yourself Lightly*, Terry L. Paulson, Ph.D., tells of a company that started a "TGIF joke network" to end the week on a humorous note: "Every Friday at 4:45, a person starts the chain with a joke, and the others call their chain partner with the week's joke."

• **Energizes the workforce.** Humor boosts morale, which in turn boosts productivity. In *Peak Performers: The New Heroes of American Business*, Charles Garfield, Ph.D., reports that he observes humor to be one of the elements present in all peak performers.

"At A.G. Edwards, instead of putting profits in our corporate objectives, we put in having fun," Chairman Ben Edwards told the authors of *The 100 Best Companies to Work for in America*. "We concluded that you really couldn't enjoy what you were doing unless you like the people you worked with. And the bottom line was that you couldn't like people unless you trusted them and respected them. I think material rewards and happiness are similar in that you don't find either when you seek them. They come as by-products of doing something well, of caring for other people." In fact, Edwards adds that once the company stopped focusing on the almighty dollar, profit margins widened.

• **Reduces stress/prevents burnout.** Ongoing studies of medical students by Joan Loggin, M.D., a cardiologist at Loma Linda University School of Medicine in Loma Linda, California, reveal that laughter leads to both relaxation and reduction of stress. Physiologically speaking, laughter initially *raises* our blood pressure and heart rate, Loggin says, then it *decreases* both. Simultaneously, it increases our sensory perceptiveness and allows us to perform tasks better. Moreover, because of its tranquilizing effect, laughter often provides that emotional distance we so desperately need when feeling overwhelmed and stressed out.

Lisa Rosenberg, Ph.D., R.N., Assistant Chair of the Department of Psychiatric Nursing at Chicago's Rush-Presbyterian St. Luke's Medical Center, adds, "The act of producing humor, of making a joke, gives us a mental break and increases our objectivity in the face of overwhelming stress." This is particularly true, she says, for people in jobs that require the ability to think quickly and make snap—but accurate—decisions, like the medical emergency fields. In these arenas, humor—particularly black humor—helps employees to cope more effectively with on-the-job pressures, Rosenberg believes. But the use of "sick" jokes, she adds, isn't limited to the medical emergency fields. "Consider the many jokes told in response to the Lorena Bobbitt incident or about Jeffrey Dahmer," she notes. "When situations make us uncomfortable and anxious, we often make jokes about them. And we do this to help distance ourselves from such catastrophic events. One researcher calls this common coping mechanism 'mental flossing.' "

• Deflects hostility/keeps minor disagreements from escalating into major arguments. Humor allows you to say things—in an acceptable way—that you might not otherwise have the nerve to say. And because it's difficult to be angry with someone when you are laughing, or making someone else laugh, humor can also serve as a powerful weapon to deflect hostility.

In 1993, just weeks after Senator Carol Moseley-Braun's battle with Senator Jesse Helms over the renewal of the United Daughters of the Confederacy insignia, Moseley Braun found herself in an elevator with Helms and his associate, Senator Orrin Hatch. Helms remarked to Hatch, "I'm going to make her cry. I'm going to sing 'Dixie' until she cries." To which Moseley Braun coolly replied, "Senator Helms, your singing would make me cry if you sang 'Rock of Ages.' "

• Alleviates monotony. At Lotus Development Corporation, employees in need of a lift can tap into the company's extensive joke database at any time. And at Ben & Jerry's Homemade in Waterbury, Vermont, the company once celebrated Elvis Day, serving the "King's" favorite food—greasy hamburgers and peanut butter and marshmallow sandwiches.

Adds psychologist and "Joyologist" Steve Wilson in *The Art of Mixing Work and Play*, "When work is highly demanding, boring, or repetitive, there's a natural inclination on the part of workers to seek out balance through fun and humor. If you as boss don't allow it, employees will wait until your back is turned to laugh and have fun. They won't work as hard and often withhold their best ideas."

• **Bridges gaps between managers and subordinates.** Humor is an extremely effective way of enriching relationships between people and making them feel equal in status. As Victor Borge once said, "Laughter is the shortest distance between people."

In essence, *because* it spurs creativity, promotes teamwork, energizes the workforce, reduces stress, alleviates monotony, and bridges gaps, humor can most definitely affect your company's bottom line.

Humor: A Prerequisite to Success

The problem is, many female managers are reluctant to demonstrate a sense of humor in the workplace. Why? Chalk it up to social conditioning. Since childhood, it's been hammered into our heads that girls shouldn't—or can't—tell jokes. Consequently, as adults we tend to suppress our sense of humor, mostly out of fear that others—particularly men—won't find our jokes funny. Or we worry that people will disapprove of our "unladylike" behavior. Many of us also fear that showing our humorous side will make us appear unprofessional or diminish our importance, and as a result we won't be taken seriously. Quite the contrary.

In fact, *not* demonstrating a sense of humor can place you at a disadvantage. In a survey by Robert Half International of vice presidents and personnel directors at one hundred of America's largest corporations, 84 percent said they thought employees with a sense of humor did a better job than those with little or no sense of humor. And in a similar survey—of CEOs—by Hodge-Cronin & Associates, 98 percent stated a preference for job candidates with a good sense of humor.

And when the CEOs polled were asked to list the qualities they felt prevented women from getting ahead, "lack of a sense of humor" was near the top of their list. Mitch Kapor, former CEO of Lotus, (now chairman of ON Tech. Inc.) is a good example. When interviewing candidates for jobs at Lotus, Kapor said he specifically looked for people who could laugh out loud. "People who like to muffle their laughter, that says something about them. This is a big test of mine," he told Robert Levering and Milton Moskowitz, co-authors of *The 100 Best Companies to Work for in America*. Added a Lotus manager, "No manager sits around in this company with a stone face. How you laugh is how you manage."

It appears, then, that a sense of humor is not only an asset in the workplace, it is a prerequisite for promotion. As Regina Barreca puts it in *They Used to Call Me Snow White . . . But I Drifted: Women's Strategic Use of Humor*, "Humor may be tolerated in lower level positions, but it will be demanded in higher ones, because humor appears as evidence of intelligence, personal strength, and quick thinking."

Having a healthy sense of humor works for women in other ways as well. When you take the risk of being funny, you convey self-confidence. Learning to lighten up also puts problems in perspective and lessens your fears of taking risks and making mistakes. Yet another reason women—particularly token women—should harness the power of humor: "It can break boundaries of a group that excludes you," says Barreca. "Quick-witted and amusing talk can help you integrate yourself into another set of peers."

Besides, men consistently use humor to their advantage at work—and therein may lie another reason women are reluctant to be funny on the job. "My male colleagues are always cracking jokes, which I'm not very good at," one manager told us. "But what really bothers me is that their humor is often cruel. They pick on people, and I could never feel comfortable doing that."

Indeed, men's and women's humor is decidedly different, as is their reaction to humor. In an interview with *Mirabella* magazine, Jayne Tear, a gender dynamics consultant, acknowledges, "Men's humor style usually involves kidding and teasing others, whereas women will often tell a funny story about themselves or laugh together about something. Say you've just made a lousy presentation to a group of colleagues. A guy might come up to you afterwards and say something like, 'You look like you've been hit by a truck.' A woman will probably find that remark offensive, and certainly won't find it funny or friendly. Instead, a female colleague might say, 'Want to go out for a cup of coffee?' While a woman might welcome that suggestion, a man might think you were babying him."

A recent article in *Psychology Today* also compared men's and women's humor: Men's humor is competitive and stems from distrust, hostility, envy, and jealousy. It is generally sarcastic, often singles out victims, and is usually negative in tone. While it makes some people feel good, it's usually at the expense of others. It targets the weak, and typically focuses on "what one of us did." It's overall goal: "rhetorical oneupmanship."

Women's humor, on the other hand, is typically cooperative and stems from caring and concern for others. Consequently, it brings people together, it is generally positive, and it makes everyone feel good. It is based on kidding, typically focuses on "what any of us might do," and often targets the powerful. Its overall goal: "spotlighting issues in their lives."

Think about it. Clearly, when it comes to motivating and influencing subordinates and making workers feel important, the female approach offers definite advantages. The trick, then, is to take a chance by tapping your hidden reserves of humor and make them work *for* you.

Unfortunately, however, a falsehood many women buy in to is that displaying a sense of humor means being a comedian. Truth is, humor in business has very little to do with cracking jokes. Rather, as Barbara Mackoff defines it in her book *What Mona Lisa Knew: A Woman's Guide to Getting Ahead in Business by Lightening Up*, humor is "a state of mind, an attitude that can be learned and practiced. Once learned, this attitude can make a remarkable difference in your self-esteem, in setting and approaching goals, handling relationships on the job, and keeping life in the office in manageable perspective."

From her vantage point, Mackoff notes that as women gain confidence in the workplace, they are beginning to recognize that a sense of lightness is essential. Here are some pointers to help *you* enjoy the payoffs of using humor at work:

• **Connect with others through humor.** Share funny things that happen to you with your colleagues, superiors, and subordinates. Look for ways to create inside jokes at the office, as this builds solidarity. For example, while everyone else in America dreads April 15, a group of Philadelphia CPAs celebrates tax day by doing a "Briefcase Brigade" strut and chant at a local nightclub. Maybe you've heard their rap song on the national news: "I don't care what people say. I just want to be a CPA. I don't care for rock 'n' roll. Rather find a tax loophole."

• **Use humor to create an atmosphere of fun and camaraderie.** "Because the group of employees I manage is large and diverse, I make it a point to organize activities that can bring the whole group together," says Laura Martin of Westin Hotels and Resorts. "For example, we often have casual day 'clean-up' parties where the managers and the staff get together to clean up an office space, then share pizza together. Frequent cheap, silly, social get-togethers have also helped foster a sense of belonging."

These kinds of activities create an upbeat atmosphere and make people look forward to coming to work. Bank of America, for example, sponsors joke-telling contests among its employees. And at Intel, where employees view informative videos every quarter at Business Update Meetings (BUMs), on April Fool's Day, the company compiles a videotape that spoofs its regular videos. In one recent presentation, for example, Dick Clark took CEO Andy Grove's spot, explaining that Grove had left the company to become a professional musician. Later, Grove was shown rapping.

• **Spark up your written materials—memos, letters, training guides—with a dash of humor.** Several managers we interviewed make it a habit to paste work-related cartoons to the bottoms of their memos and meeting agendas. And in designing her employee handbook, Cynthia Fontayne, President of the Fontayne Group, a marketing and public relations firm, opted to use a fair number of clever sayings, cartoons, and other humorous materials to emphasize "rules" and attitudes rather than belabor points with a more formal approach. One page in the handbook, for example, urges staffers to back up their computer work. Under a big bold headline that reads, "I can't, I'm wearing magnetic underwear," and offered as "Computer Backup Excuse #685," appears this short message:

Doing computer backup really gets under people's skin.

They'll do anything to get out of doing it, because backing up is so utterly boring.

But not doing it can definitely be a matter of getting your education at the college of hard knocks.

We're reminded of the Ph.D. candidate in biology who did hunger research for his doctoral thesis without backing it up.

He had data from a year's worth of injecting and weighing rats stored on the disk. The computer crashed, the rat data was erased, and he had to do it all over.

Back to the rat race.

So do your backup.

• **Don't get mad, get even . . . with humor.** In the heat of an argument, the unexpected use of humor can defuse a confrontational situation—and may even melt an opponent into an ally. In other words, fight fire with fire, since, as Barbara Mackoff points out, humor is often the best way to reestablish control in a sticky situation.

In her book, *Molly Ivins Can't Say That, Can She?*, syndicated columnist Molly Ivins shares this classic tale about Ann Richards, governor of Texas.

Several years ago, there was a big political do at Scholz Beer Garten in Austin, and everybody who was anybody in political Texas was there. About halfway through the evening, a little group of us got the tired feet and went to lean our butts against a table by the back wall of the Garten. Like birds in a row were perched Bob Bullock, the state comptroller; me;

Charles Miles, a black man who was then head of Bullock's personnel department; and Ann Richards. Bullock, having been in Texas politics for 30-some-odd years, consequently knows every living sorry, no-account SOB who ever held office. A dreadful old racist judge from East Texas came up to him, "Bob, my boy, how are yew?" The two of them commence to clap one another on the back and have big greetin'.

"Judge," said Bullock, "I want you to meet my friends. This is Molly Ivins with *The Texas Observer*."

The judge peered up at me and said, "How yew, little lady?"

"This is Charles Miles, who heads my personnel department."

Charlie stuck out his hand, and the judge got an expression on his face as though he had just stepped into a fresh cowpie. It took him a long minute before he reached out, barely touched Charlie's hand and said, "How yew, *boy*?" Then he turned with great relief to pretty, blue-eyed Ann Richards and said, "And who is this lovely lady?"

Ann beamed and said, "I am *Mrs.* Miles."

Congresswoman Pat Schroeder shares another great story—about her mother—in the book *Women in Power: The Secrets of Leadership* by Dorothy W. Cantor and Toni Bernay, with Jean Stoess. "In one of our campaigns, [my mother] was knocking on doors and someone said, 'I wouldn't vote for Pat Schroeder, and I think she ought to stay home with her kids.' My mother said, 'Well, I was a working mother, and I had two kids.' And the lady said, 'Oh yeah? Well, what happened to 'em?' And my mother replied, 'Well, one's a lawyer, and the other one is Pat Schroeder.' "

• **Use humor to encourage feedback.** Incorporating a sense of humor into your management style makes you appear more relaxed, confident, and approachable, which enables your subordinates to feel more at ease. This, in turn, opens the lines to more effective communication by increasing the amount of feedback you get. For example, instead of using an employee survey, Hal

Rosenbluth, CEO of Rosenbluth International, once sent his associates (as employees are called here) crayons and paper and asked them to express what they felt about the company. Thrilled with the results, the exercise has since become a tradition. "It elicits feelings that aren't going to come out in a survey," Rosenbluth told the authors of *The 100 Best Companies to Work for in America.*

• **Use humor to impress.** One of our favorite stories is the one about Charlotte Beers, Chairman and CEO of the world's largest advertising agency, Ogilvy & Mather Worldwide. In the 1970s, Beers won over an audience of skeptical male clients by dismantling—and reassembling—a complicated drill while explaining a marketing plan. No wonder she has shattered the glass ceiling!

• **Take the lead.** To be effective, fun must be ongoing—not something that happens whenever management is "in the mood." So flaunt your sense of humor and encourage your subordinates to follow suit. Hang funny posters in unexpected places (restroom ceilings, break room cabinets) throughout the company. Hang up a bulletin board designated "Humor Only," and encourage everyone to fill it with cartoons and jokes.

At Ben & Jerry's Homemade, for example, executives have held quarterly meetings at midnight—to accommodate the third shift—where some of the staff came dressed in pajamas. And once, when communication was chosen as the theme of a meeting, every participant received a set of wax lips.

• **Use humor to put problems in perspective.** In *What Mona Lisa Knew*, Barbara Mackoff tells the story of a manager who placed the name Dangerfield over the surnames on her co-workers' nameplates when they complained that their department got no respect. "It didn't solve the problem, but it helped put it in perspective and improved everybody's mood so they could get down to work," Mackoff reports.

And following a year of massive budget cuts and layoffs, one manager we interviewed sent her staff (in lieu of the company's traditional year-end bonuses) a humorous Christmas card. On the front of the card was a sketch of a grumpy-looking Santa Claus along with the words *"Money is scarce, times are hard; here's your damned old Christmas card."* Inside, the poem continued:

Merry Christmas . . .

I'm writing this note to remind you
that inflation has taken away
the things that I hold most essential:
my reindeer, my workshop, my sleigh.
Now I'm making my rounds on a Donkey,
He'd old, he's crippled, he's slow.
So you'll know if I don't see you at Christmas,
that I'm out on my Ass in the snow!

—*Santa Claus*

• **Use humor to cut tension and reduce stress.** At the Quarasan Group in Chicago, Randi S. Brill, President, sets the pace for an offbeat office atmosphere. Her office hat display, for example, includes a brown bag ("for bad hair days"), and she has been known to lighten the tension on a hectic day with one of her on-the-mark celebrity impressions (Mayberry's Barney Fife is a favorite).

At Johnson Wax, Bridget Shirley and her colleagues decorate a Christmas tree with homemade baubles—all bespectacled like Shirley's boss. "It's a way to keep stress levels in check," says Shirley, who cites humor as one of the hallmarks of her management style. And whenever things get too crazy at MECCO in Warrington, Pennsylvania, CEO Lisa Bergson calls a "stress break" and directs everyone outside to play volleyball. "Absolutely no calls during the game!" she insists.

• **Delegate humor.** "Let's face it. I'm not a good joke teller. I'm not a funny person," confesses Johnna Howell at Westin Resorts and Hotels. "So the way I bring humor into the workplace is to delegate it to others. They are also responsible for contributing to the 'lightness' of our meetings and activities. We all laugh a lot."

Many managers appoint committees designed to create humor rituals in the workplace and allow employees to rotate serving on these committees. At Ben & Jerry's, for example, a "Grand Pooh-Bah" oversees an official "Joy Gang." The Gang—with its own annual budget in the thousands—is charged with keeping employees' spirits high. Antics have included renting rollerskates for use in the corporation's hallways, inaugurating a new stairway by staging a model car race down the stairwell, and Clash Dressing Day. The company also participated in National Kazoo Day, handing out kazoos to all its employees.

And at Odetics, which *Industry Week* magazine has dubbed "the wackiest place to work in the U.S.," a "Fun Committee" serves the same purpose. Humor rituals here have run the gamut from "coach potato" contests and 6:00 A.M. sock hops to telephone booth stuffing contests and Hula-Hoop competitions.

• **Use humor to break monotony.** "At Tellabs on Halloween, we all dress up," reports Grace Pastiak. "Once I dressed up as our vice president of engineering, who is six three, and I'm five four. I put on a man's suit, and then on my head I put a cone with a wigged head on top of that. I had little lightning rods and cartoon sayings like 'Earth to Pete' coming out of the head. It was hilarious, and everyone got a real kick out of it."

• **Use humor as a training device.** Six years ago, Anna Rolphe, Vice President of Century Publishing in Coeur d'Alene, Idaho, instituted a humor program to increase her employees' knowledge of the company. "In the early days, we held a lot of contests that encouraged workers to go around the company and ask people lots of questions about what they were doing," she says. These days, the company has a Humor Committee, which is run by the employees themselves. The committee meets at the beginning of each year and brainstorms the entire year's programs, with committee members volunteering to chair individual events. "Doing this teaches organizational and leadership skills, and gives employees pride in ownership," believes Rolphe. To date, the committee has sponsored a myriad of programs, including scavenger hunts and murder mysteries. "We also had our own Academy Awards," adds Rolphe. "We videotape a lot of our activities, so that everyone can keep up with what employees in other areas of the company are doing. So at our awards ceremony, each department presented 3–4 clips, and we handed out awards for Best Actor, Best Actress, etc."

Rolphe credits a recent 10 percent decrease in turnover to the company's humor program. "There has also been a noticeable reduction in workplace accidents at Century Publishing," she adds. Moreover, despite the fact that the company has quadrupled in size over the last decade, Rolphe says its commitment to humor has helped to preserve its special characteristics. "I've always felt like we're part of a family here and feared we might lose that as we grew. But humor has helped to keep those lines of communication open."

• **Liven up your presentations and speeches with humor.** Include cartoons on overheads and slides that relate to the topic or main message of your speech. Pepper your talks with funny stories. "Use humorous personal anecdotes instead of jokes," advises Malcolm Kushner, a San Francisco–based humor consultant and author of *The Light Touch: How to Use Humor for Business Success.* You'll not only tell them better, this personal touch enables you to better connect with your audience.

During the 1992 elections, for example, Maryland Senator Barbara Mikulski, who was running for reelection, spoke at a $100-a-plate power lunch sponsored by the Washington Democratic Senate Campaign Committee that featured eleven female senatorial candidates running for election. "Poking fun at her short stature, she recalled her initial arrival on the Senate scene and having to ask the Senate carpentry shop to make a special box for her to stand on when she addressed her colleagues," reports Ronna A. Freiberg, Director of Government Affairs for Kenetech Windpower in Washington, D.C. "Then, referring to her fellow female candidates, she quipped, 'I've already alerted the shop to be ready to make a lot more boxes!' "

• **Use humor to break the ice.** In another campaign speech, Arizona Senate hopeful Claire Sargent also commented on 1992's breed of female candidates for the House and Senate: "I think it's time we voted for senators with breasts. After all, we've been voting for boobs long enough."

• **Use humor to educate.** Don't be afraid to laugh at yourself when you make a mistake. In fact, make it a point to turn your— and everyone else's—mistakes into learning experiences by sharing them with your subordinates. "To the younger members of our staff, everytime something goes wrong, it has the same degree of tragedy," believes Randi Brill, president of the Quarasan Group. "When you can make light of something, it puts things in perspective."

In *Making Humor Work*, Terry Paulson shares a great story about a manager who appears to have perfected the art of using humor to transform mistakes into learning experiences. "One business owner put a large bill on the conference table and told his staff one of his recent errors and what he'd learned," Paulson writes. "He then gave his challenge: 'Anyone who can top it gets the money.' He had the trust of his staff. Each shared a recent error and that evoked laughter. The 'winning error' earned the money and a lot of laughter. Beyond that, everyone present learned from each error discussed."

• **Convey messages that might be viewed as controversial using humor.** While a vice president at Kodak, Katherine Hudson, now President and CEO of W.H. Brady Company in Milwaukee, excelled at motivating her staff. "The only problem was that the more you motivated people, the more they wanted to interact with you, and it got to the point where people kept jumping in to see me, one after another. This prevented me from giving my undivided attention to anyone. So to make it easier for everyone to drop by and chat without interruption—and to keep the people who managed them from becoming angry that they were meeting with me—I started something I called 'Deli Days,'" she says. "These were held a few days each month. If you wanted to see me, you took a number from a ticket wheel outside my office. Above it was an electronic numbers board, which I controlled with a switch under my desk. The idea was that you took a number and waited until it popped up on the board. While you waited, you could continue working, without hovering outside my office waiting for an opportunity to dart in. Each person had five or six minutes to talk with me about anything he or she wanted. The program turned out to be a hit, and it organized my time, since there were only certain days when these types of meetings could take place."

Hudson reveals that when she first unveiled this idea, it wasn't well received by everyone. "When I first put up the numbers board, I met with a large group of staffers, many of whom were not yet aware of its existence and had complained that they didn't get to see me very much," she reports. When she suggested that they come to the next Deli Day, one employee challenged Hudson by saying, "Yeah, and I bet if I go, I'll get a pound of baloney." Hudson remembers the room getting real quiet as everyone waited to see how she would react. "I just cracked up," she says. "I thought that if I was going to introduce something like an electronic numbers board, I couldn't suddenly become defensive. From that point on, I'd tell people, 'Come to Deli Day. You may think you're going to get a pound of baloney, but then again, you may like what you get.' "

• **Celebrate milestones and achievements with humor.** In *The Art of Mixing Work and Play*, Steve Wilson tells about an office that rings a brass bell every time a sale is made. "This encourages everyone to keep going," says Wilson. And another company, he reports, taped candy bars to the last page of its quarterly stockholders report.

• **Compile a humor first-aid kit for your employees.** Employees at Eastman Kodak have a humor room at their disposal. The room is stocked with Monty Python and *Candid Camera* videos, books by popular comedians, and a variety of toys and props designed to stimulate creative thinking and help employees relax. Other companies furnish employee break rooms with crossword puzzle and word search books as well as board games like Trivial Pursuit.

• **Give your subordinates permission to have fun by setting a good example.** Kim McCaulou, Manager of Marketing Programs at Westin Hotels and Resorts, says, "In my opinion, the only way to encourage a sense of humor is to be the first to laugh. If I as a manager can't laugh at a given situation or at myself, the people who work with me will not laugh either. Laughter and humor are a requirement for team-building, a pleasant work environment, and for stress reduction. Giving your employees permission to have fun, by first leading the pack, and then not stifling the impulse when others lead, is absolutely necessary."

• **Use humor to bridge gaps.** Laura Martin, also at Westin Hotels and Resorts, hosts an annual "Know Your CFO" birthday party for the company's chief financial officer. "All the staff are invited," she says, "and we do this because many of our employees don't have a lot of contact with him."

CAUTION:
Humor Can Be Hazardous at Work

To be effective, humor must be appropriate, and the definition of appropriate depends on your particular corporate culture. So it's probably wise to observe how humor is typically used and received within your company so that you avoid making a fool of yourself.

And let's face it. Some people simply don't have—or appreciate—a good sense of humor, and may be put off by your sense of mirth. "Humor can misfire," Randi Brill acknowledges. "You really have to be aware of each person's sensitivity level, and you have to consider the environment of each situation."

Keep in mind, too, that what is considered appropriate may vary depending on whether you are dealing with superiors or subordinates. "When you have a style like mine, you can't behave like that twenty-four hours a day if you want management to take you seriously," says Katherine Hudson. "And if you're criticized by top management, there's usually something to it. You have to know how to read the signals."

For example, in 1988, when Hudson was Director of Corporate Information Systems at Kodak, she searched for ways to send a message to her employees that if they took full advantage of the new equipment that the company was installing they would "suddenly see more" and, as a result, become more informed. "So I decided to use 'Suddenly Seymour' from the musical *Little Shop of Horrors* as our theme song," she says. "When top management wanted me to present the new strategy, my staffers took bets as to whether I'd actually play it. Well, I did. About a third of the senior managers loved it, a third didn't care, and another third hated it. What I learned was that what makes your staff comfortable does not always make your bosses comfortable."

Joel Goodman, Ed.D., founder and president of The Humor Project in Saratoga, New York, cautions that humor at others' expense will usually cost you as well. "There's a difference between laughing *with* others and laughing *at* others," he says.

You should also avoid sarcasm. *You* may think your comment is hysterical, but someone else might find it negative and derisive. And when you use humor as a means of self-defense, do it nonchalantly via your speech patterns and body language. "It has to appear not to matter to you at all," says Regina Barreca. "Otherwise it won't work."

Before Cheryl Fisher Custer was sworn in as Georgia's first female district attorney in 1991, she had to pass muster with the governor, who told Custer in an interview that she didn't "look tough enough" for the job. Custer, however, managed to win him over when she suggested that he call a few attorneys who would refer to her by a word that begins with B. And once while Custer was serving as assistant district attorney, an out-of-town colleague cornered her during a court recess and waxed on and on about the rigors of law school and the demands of his profession. Assuming she was someone's clerk or secretary, the man finally asked

Custer, "Honey, can you point out the assistant district attorney who will be handling this case?" To which Custer drawled back, "Honey, you've been insulting her for the last ten minutes."

"Jest-in-Time" Management

When encouraging merriment on the job, keep in mind these two rules of thumb: First, participation in fun and games is not something that can be mandated. To realize humor's many benefits, participation must be voluntary. By all means, do all you can to encourage your staff to take their jobs seriously and themselves lightly, but don't demand it. Second, be sure to maintain a proper balance between work and fun. Make it clear to your staff that all aspects of job performance must still be met—regardless of whether the process of achieving those goals is fun or not.

Humor must be balanced against the condition of your business as well. In other words, when profits are down, losses are up, and layoffs are imminent, you need to be careful about the messages you send. Not to say that you should banish humor from the workplace altogether during tough times—that's when you need it most—but certain activities (costly ones in particular) should definitely be curtailed.

Studies show that children laugh an average of four hundred times a day. In contrast, adults laugh an average of fifteen times a day. Pathetic, isn't it? As a manager, *you* can help boost these statistics by lightening up yourself and encouraging those who work for you to work hard at getting more "smileage" out of life. After all, mirth is not only good for the body and soul, but also sparks creativity. And because it zaps the fear out of taking risks, enriches working relationships, downsizes problems, *and* increases productivity, it's also good for the bottom line.

No joke.

CHAPTER NINE

Managing Conflict and Difficult Employees

PROFILE

KAREN JOHNSON
CORPORATE VICE PRESIDENT, CONSUMER AFFAIRS
BORDEN, INC.
COLUMBUS, OHIO

"My philosophy is, 'Let's get it out in the open.
Let's get it resolved. Let's find the best solution we can.' "

An "iron fist in a velvet glove" is how colleagues and subordinates describe Karen Johnson, Corporate Vice President of Consumer Affairs at Borden. "Most of my staff will tell you that the day after I talk to them, they'll sit back and say, 'Hmm . . . I think I got scolded,' " she admits.

Maybe that's because Johnson is so soft-spoken. Or maybe it's because, according to her staff, she also dresses in a very feminine style, is an incredible listener, and a real "people" person. But make no mistake about it. This lady is tough as well as caring.

"I once had to fire my best friend," Johnson says. "And I'll never forget it. It was probably the hardest thing I ever had to do, and I can still recall every minute of that day. But looking back, it was the best thing for her. In fact, she handled it better than I did. She went into another field and became successful at it. But I lost her as a friend."

Managing difficult employees is one of Johnson's many specialties, and a process she believes begins when employees are first hired. "You must be very clear about the job description," she says. "Beyond that, you must also state your expectations. I always go over personality qualities I'm looking for as well—like a sense of humor, integrity, a willingness to take risks, and always meeting deadlines—things that aren't going to be in the job description, but that I expect."

Johnson also assures her people that she will be doing a lot of coaching and teaching—and if they make a mistake, they'll know it right then and there. "Because when I give my first performance review, I don't want anything to be a surprise."

In addition to being honest and direct with her staff up front, Johnson prefers managing conflict by facing it head-on. "My philosophy is, 'Let's get it out in the open. Let's get it resolved. Let's find the best solution we can,' " she reports.

Over the years Johnson says she has dealt with her fair share of difficult employees and discusses the three kinds that bug her the most. "Those who grumble, I tell them, 'Look at the big picture. Let's get focused and find out how to get rid of all this griping and move forward,' " she says. "I have a tough time dealing with disrespectful employees as well," she adds, "particularly because I've had people take advantage of me, and I've learned the hard way not to let it happen again. Typically I'll tell the disrespectful subordinate, 'I work hard to earn your respect. Why don't I have it?' " Then there are the incompetents. "I usually say to them, 'I'll give you six months, and I'll coach you.' The majority of the time they will shore up, but the worst thing to do is to let them go on and on. You're doing such a disservice to them and the rest of the staff."

Johnson manages to keep problems in the workplace to a minimum, however, by creating an open environment, "so that if something is happening, my staff will be obligated to tell me. I tell my staff, 'My door is *always* open. I *don't* want to hear it from someone else. You can make mistakes. Just come tell me.' "

But the real key to dealing with difficult employees is learning how to manage different personalities, Johnson believes. "Early in my career I took a course that covered what's known as the Leadership Grid.* How it works is, you draw four squares on a sheet of paper. In the upper left corner are analytical people, and below that are amiable types. In the top right corner are dominant people, and below that are aggressive types. In my training, I learned not only which type I was (amiable), but how to work with other styles." As a result of this training, Johnson says that she has learned to put people in their "boxes" pretty quickly. "But I've never avoided hiring a certain type, because I think it's a good idea to have a variety of types. If you hire only people who are like you, you're not going to like it. Diversity breeds creativity."

In her eighteen years with Borden, Johnson has had nine bosses—"mostly dominant and aggressive types"—which has not only enabled her to sharpen her skills at working with personality types different from her own, it has also made her extremely flexible. Together, these skills have likely been a major contributing factor to Johnson's career success. After receiving an MS degree in home economics from the University of Wisconsin–Stout, Johnson studied for six weeks at Le Cordon Bleu in Paris. Upon returning to the States in 1962, she accepted an entry-level position working in the test kitchens at Pillsbury. Her goal at the time was to be director of the test kitchen someday, and ten years later she realized that dream.

In her tenure, Johnson was tapped to be on the development team to launch the legendary Pillsbury Doughboy. She says it was a challenge for a home economist to be accepted as part of this creative team. "After all, it was the 1960s, and women were just beginning to enter the workforce in large numbers. But I was determined to make it work."

In fact, Johnson not only made it work, her suggestions led to

---

*For more information on the Leadership Grid, refer to Robert R. Blake and M. A. McCanse, *Leadership Dilemmas: Grid Solutions* (Houston: Gulf, 1991).

a first in food photography—"the use of a snorkel-camera [time lapse photography] technique to explore the cinnamon swirls inside hot-baked Danish rolls," she explains. Involvement in this project also got Johnson noticed, and she began moving up the ranks.

As one of the few women in management at Pillsbury, Johnson learned quickly how to interact with male executives. "Although I've always been a diplomatic person, I learned how to position what I wanted to say. I'd sit back and plan strategy—how will this be perceived?" But Johnson also learned that trying to please everyone would get her nowhere, and in fact when once asked to give face-to-face feedback on the personal strengths of her own division president, Johnson didn't hesitate to dole out constructive criticism. "Successful people may be well liked, but we didn't get that way by trying to please," Johnson says. "As our responsibilities increase, we may have to disappoint, displease—even anger—others."

In 1976, Borden wooed Johnson away from Pillsbury, assigning her to create the company's first consumer affairs department. She entered Borden at the director level, and by 1983 she was elected the company's first female corporate vice president with officer status, making her a member of the CEO's top management group. Today, Johnson remains the only home economist in business to hold this title.

"Karen has made great strides in a company that still has its fair share of old boy networking," one of her employees told us. Indeed, Johnson currently oversees an annual operating budget of $1.5 million, supporting corporate consumer sales of $5.8 billion.

Back in the days when her career aspirations were limited to becoming head of the test kitchen at Pillsbury, Johnson never dreamed that she would end up where she is today. But she admits she *was* always ambitious and has had great mentors along the way. Her first—though Johnson may not have realized it at the time—was in grade school: an uncle who encouraged her to read *The Wall Street Journal*. "He was truly an entrepreneur—ran a barber shop, was the village mayor, ran the local theater, made business loans, and sold Maytag washers and pianos," she recalls. "I watched how he managed his businesses and dealt with people, and that intrigued me."

Another of Johnson's mentors is her mother. "She continues to add a balance-of-life perspective that has kept me contemporary and focused. Each year, we've taken a major foreign trip together and have now been around the world. Diverse cultures teach a great deal and have enriched our lives, personally and professionally. Her young spirit is also a great inspiration for me."

Because of her successful experiences with many mentors, Johnson now sees giving back to young people as one of her obligations. She developed and chairs an advisory board at her alma mater and recently started a scholarship in her name. "I gave my first one last year to a young woman from China. It was very emotional for me as well as for her. But then I think women are very nurturing, and we need to find a way to use that to our advantage." Not surprisingly, in May of 1994 Johnson received an honorary doctorate degree from the college—the first woman to earn this honor.

These days Johnson says she loves her job, but that being the sole woman at the top still has its drawbacks. "I often wish I could get my people more involved," she says. "We're still fighting for the worth of our role and our contributions in some respects. I try to fight for them, but sometimes I run into roadblocks. For example, I have a marketing group that sometimes refuses to recognize us. Nevertheless, I just move on and bide my time, working hard at putting us where we can really be recognized until they come around."

• • •

If you've been in management for a while, chances are you've encountered your fair share of difficult employees—from infuriating know-it-alls who undermine you at every turn, to those who punch the clock at the crack of dawn still inebriated from an all-night drinking binge. Part of you likely wishes you could ignore their annoying and disruptive behavior and that, in time, they would miraculously improve on their own. Or that you could bid them good riddance without having to go through the lengthy— and often futile—process of issuing warnings and documenting poor performance and unacceptable behavior. After all, *your* reputation is on the line.

But while there will always be a handful of difficult employees who can zap the caring right out of you, and who really don't deserve a second chance, many problem employees *are* worth rescuing.

Of course, there is no magic formula for saving these poor souls. Oftentimes, you have to trust your instincts, wing it, and hope for the best. However, there are also a number of specific approaches you can try before throwing in the towel and letting difficult employees go.

Women and Conflict

The problem is, women are often so intimidated by conflict that we go out of our way to ignore it or to avoid it. Others of us take a deep breath and try to handle it as quickly as possible. But should things not go well, and *our* feathers get ruffled in the process, we tend to get angry and hold grudges—which can create even *more* conflict.

Some of us approach conflict much the same way our mothers attempted to stop arguments we had with playmates when we were children—by trying to convince duelers, "Now, now. Say you're sorry, and let's make nice." This tactic, however, can also escalate or create additional conflict. Then there are those of us who steamroll our way right smack into the middle of conflict, making demands, barking orders, and relishing every moment of it because it makes us feel powerful.

Yet neither the Charlie Brown nor the Attila the Hun approach is effective at resolving conflicts. Instead, the manager as referee must strike a balance. In fact, this is where the female advantage factors in. As the first female chief of staff at Detroit Receiving Hospital, Dr. Kathleen McCarroll clearly operates in a male bastion. But she sees her gender as a plus when it comes to managing conflict and handling difficult colleagues and employees.

"I think I am able to facilitate compromise, build consensus, defend the weak, and reprimand the bully in a different way *because* I am a woman," she says. "I am able to get away with more because they perceive me as coming from a position of weakness. If I say, 'C'mon, guys. Let's do it this way,' I'm not seen as a big ego threat. Whereas if another man says something like that, the heels dig in. That's not to say they won't dig in with me, too. But I don't constitute the same kind of threat."

The Upside of Conflict

Conflict doesn't have to be negative and destructive. In fact, when handled effectively, conflict offers many benefits. For starters, it clears the air and gives everyone involved an opportunity to have his or her say. You receive a wide variety of thoughts, ideas, and opinions that ultimately may lead to practical solutions. At the very least, everyone ends up with a greater perspective and understanding of the problem.

Conflict often provides managers a chance to clarify goals and expectations of the team and the organization, and to redirect efforts if need be. It also offers managers a golden opportunity to fine-tune their listening skills. In the heat of battle—whether you are a player or referee—you must be able to listen to ideas and opinions that are not in harmony with your own—and not get upset as a result. Moreover, to find a workable solution, you are forced to open your mind and consider other people's perspectives.

During conflict you must also be strong enough to admit when you're wrong and when other people's ideas are better than your own. That way, conflict can lead to positive change and mutual respect.

Conflict can result in a tremendous learning experience as well. When we master the art of disagreeing without taking things personally, we grow stronger and become better managers of both ourselves and others. Learning to manage conflict also boosts our self-esteem, for when the dust has settled—and we've survived—we feel good about ourselves. And in time, and with practice, many of us begin to view conflict in a whole new light—as something that can be healthy, even exhilarating.

The Dangers of Conflict

But conflict can also be painful and frustrating. It often feels scary, too—particularly to women who have grown up repeatedly being told, "Don't rock the boat." "Don't make waves." Thanks to this kind of social conditioning, many of us were never taught how to handle conflict in socially acceptable ways. As a result many of us run from it. Or we fly off the handle and get overemotional. "Women frequently don't trust themselves to handle conflict with poise and dignity," notes Maria Arapakis in her book *Softpower! How to Speak Up, Set Limits, and Say No Without Losing Your Lover, Your Job, or Your Friends.* "It's not so much someone else's emotional outburst we fear, it's our own. We're scared we might blow up, say something we later regret, or—heaven forbid—break down and cry."

Unresolved conflict can wreak havoc in the workplace as well. It zaps employee morale. It leaves workers feeling confused about who is supposed to be doing what. It permeates the atmosphere with a lack of trust, thus preventing teams from working together.

Conflict also kills motivation, stifles creativity, and produces unnecessary anxiety. Perhaps worst of all, it breeds contempt for managers who fail to have conflicts resolved.

Conflict Management

The trick to handling conflict in a tough and caring way is to walk that fine line between holding people accountable for their job performance and solving problems *for* them. In other words, you *want* a certain degree of conflict to be present; you *want* differences to be aired and discussed. But you *don't* want to be forced into playing den mother/psychologist/judge/baby-sitter.

Here are some tips to help you manage conflict more effectively:

• **Make it a habit to nip conflicts in the bud.** "While my natural inclination is to avoid conflict, it is not a practical reaction in the workplace. Therefore, I attempt to manage the situation immediately, deal with it, and eliminate the source of conflict as soon as possible," says Kim McCaulou of Westin Hotels and Resorts. "By dealing with it quickly, rather than allowing the situation to persist, I find that the issue causes much less pain for all involved."

• **Be willing to confront people and situations head-on.** For many women, this is scary and almost feels sharklike—more like something a male manager would do. But it's the only way to get to the root of conflicts and to find workable solutions. But before you confront, do your homework, and confront in such a way that you show the other person that you have *their* best interests at heart. "I guess my ability to confront people and to be direct could be considered a masculine quality," acknowledges Helen Pastorino, co-founder and president of Alain Pinel Realtors, headquartered in Saratoga, California. "But it's not callous or hurtful or unconcerned. I don't confront out of emotion. My confrontations are well grounded because I *know* the situation and the background. I'm not out to hurt; I'm out to help fix the problem."

Karen Walker, Vice President of Operating Services at Compaq Computer Corporation, adds, "The fact that I have an engineering degree has served me well in this area. It's given me the ability to really look at problems and to dissect them analytically and logically. In fact, I have a good rational and logical pattern for almost everything I do. But I also think that having an emotional or intuitive side, too, is helpful. That way I can play left brain *and* right brain, which helps me to be more effective at resolving conflicts and allows me to get better results."

• **Teach and demonstrate that it's okay to disagree.** Grace Pastiak of Tellabs always ends project meetings by asking, "What did we do right?" "What do we need to do to improve?" Just by asking these two simple questions, Pastiak feels she sends the message to everyone that, "It's okay that we didn't do something right, and that there are areas for improvement, or that you disagree with how we did them." Pastiak also encourages her employees to tell her if they think what she's doing is wrong.

• **Don't beat around the bush.** Be open, honest, and direct in your communications and encourage others to be that way with you and one another. Katherine August, Executive Vice President of First Republic Bancorp, is a firm believer in straight talk. "Sometimes all of us avoid dealing with a conflict directly, and then the relationship becomes strained. Approaching differences of opinion directly usually clears the air."

• **When you're hot.** If someone attacks *you*, or in the process of managing conflict you get upset, put some distance between you and the others involved until you have had a chance to calm down. Once your emotions are in check, then confront whomever you need to calmly and professionally. Otherwise, you *create* problems rather than solve them.

• **Don't take it personally.** According to Katherine August, the best way to manage conflict without hard feelings is to remember that "this is business. This is about working to make the company do as well as possible."

• **When conflicts develop between employees, limit your role to that of an intermediary.** "When I'm called in to resolve an administrative problem between two doctors—typically male—I listen and mediate by saying, 'Well, I can see both sides . . . ' and then work through to get it resolved," says Dr. Kathleen McCarroll of Detroit Receiving Hospital. McCarroll believes that men often have trouble compromising, and that's where female managers can help. "Men come off the football field and go into leadership positions. And generally, they haven't learned to conciliate. They've learned how to put on their pads and go fight."

• But don't solve the problem _for_ them. "A natural reaction of people in conflict is to find an authority figure to resolve things for them. We learned this easy way out as kids," believes James Autry, author of _Love and Profit._ "Sitting in judgment is, in itself, a bit of a power trip, and you shouldn't let employees suck you into the stern judge position."

In other words, you need to remain impartial. Let both sides air their grievances. You want _them_ to own the problem, because that way _they_ find the solution. And when that happens, the solution is more likely to stick.

• If both parties are extremely hostile try meeting with them separately one-on-one first, then bringing them together to listen to each other. Have them take turns speaking, with you paraphrasing and clarifying what each has said before the other one speaks. Point out what you think may be the problem, then ask for suggestions on how to correct it. "Asking if either can suggest a solution that all three of you can live with is always preferable to the solution coming from you," believes Sam Deep, author of _Smart Moves._

• Check to see if conflict itself is the problem or if it's just a _symptom_ of another problem. Very often, conflict results from personality differences or a clash of styles. But sometimes conflict is due to a management problem that requires clearing up policies, writing better job descriptions, and/or clarifying the authority employees have in handling their responsibilities. So always be ready and willing to dig and ask questions to get to the heart of a disagreement.

• Sometimes ultimatums are unavoidable. It's usually preferable to try to manage conflict without resorting to toughness, but some situations require being candid. "When a change is made, someone may not agree with that change and attempt to rally support for his position," reports Katherine August. "When this happens, it is important to discuss the situation honestly, letting the person know he is valued, but that his current attitude is unacceptable."

• **When dealing with conflicts between employees and one is clearly in the wrong, help him find ways to save face.** The ideal resolution for conflict is win-win, or at least it should feel that way to those involved. But when it turns out to be win-lose, it's helpful for managers to be sensitive to those who come out looking like losers. "Create a face-saving measure should one be perceived as the loser," recommends Deep in *Smart Moves*. "It will take the edge off prickly feelings that could hamper the solution or create another problem."

• **Consider using humor to manage conflict.** Not to say that you should attempt to laugh away problems, but using the humorous touch can get rid of anger and any other emotional obstacles that might be standing in the way of problem-solving. In *Making Humor Work*, Terry Paulson tells as an example the story about a manager in search of a way to break the tension at a confrontational meeting. "Just prior to starting the meeting agenda, he took out a target and pinned it to his chest to a chorus of laughter from the others in the room. The humor broke the tension and contributed to early problem-solving."

Criticizing Difficult Employees

Women, who have been raised by the creed "If you can't say anything nice, don't say anything at all," often have a tough time criticizing employees. Therein lies the beauty of *constructive* criticism. It is *designed* to be positive. But delivering constructive criticism is an art. Here are some tips to help you perfect the technique.

• **Don't put off confronting difficult employees simply because criticizing them makes *you* feel uncomfortable.** Wait, and the problem will only get worse. In fact, sometimes employees will even appreciate your concern. "Whenever one of my employees is not performing well, I immediately call a conference and inform the individual of the performance problem, then ask for their input," says Johnna Howell of Westin Hotels and Resorts. "In each case I've had to do this, we've had an open discussion about their performance and what actions needed to be taken to solve the problem. In one case, an employee whose performance later improved told me that that was the first time someone had cared enough to talk with her and really work together to solve the problem."

• **Make criticism specific.** Very often, employees don't have a clue about what they are doing wrong, or about how to improve. Consequently, you have to spell it out for them. Otherwise, the criticism will be neither constructive nor effective, and the employee will be left feeling confused and discouraged. For example, instead of saying something vague like, "You're not pulling your weight around here," try, "Our division can only meet its monthly quota if each worker completes twenty-five units a day, and your average for this week is fifteen per day."

• **Tell them *why* their behavior is a problem.** When employees understand why their behavior is a problem, they are usually more responsive to feedback. Using the above example, you could tell the employees, "If our division fails to meet this month's quota, company sales could drop by 20 percent. And if that happens— with the budget as tight as it is—none of us may get merit raises this year."

When employees can see the consequences of poor performance or problem attitudes, they are more likely to make an effort to shape up. For example, in her nine-year career at the YWCA, Gwendolyn Baker, now President and CEO of the U.S. Committee for UNICEF, says she once had a young white female subordinate whom Baker felt was resisting her leadership because she was black. "I finally sat down with her and said, 'You know, I feel I have a responsibility to you whether you like it or not, because I'm not only your boss, but I am a woman interested in you and your future. And if you continue to go through life with this kind of attitude, you're not going to get where you need to go. You've

got a lot going for you. Why don't you learn to handle your
resistance in a different way so that you don't close the door?' A
couple of conversations with her like that, and she understood
and changed."

• **Avoid the pillow technique.** Terry Paulson describes this in
*They Shoot Managers Don't They? Managing Yourself and Leading
Others in a Changing World* as "giving the guy a goodie, zapping
him, then dishing out another goodie before ending the conversation." An example of this, according to Paulson, might go something like this: "Basically you're doing a fine job, but you blew it
at that meeting yesterday. Don't worry, I'm sure you'll do fine."
The danger of using this sandwich technique is that neither of
your messages will be effective. In other words, not only will your
critical remarks lack punch, but your compliments will come across
as insincere.

Above all, keep in mind that the primary purpose of criticism
is to fix something, to right a wrong—and not to be negative.
"One reason why criticism ruffles feathers and too often fails to
get results is because it's communication with a stick rather than
a carrot, so it's heard as a demand, threat, or order," believes
Hendrie Weisinger, Ph.D., a psychologist who has conducted hun-
dreds of seminars on criticism for Fortune 500 companies. "Most
of us equate criticism with faultfinding," he says in an interview
with *Executive Female* magazine. "And where does that lead? If
what you have to say is just going to be make another person feel
bad, don't say it. Criticism should be an evaluation of both the
merits and demerits of an action or a situation, but most people
omit the positives."

Reprimanding and Disciplining
Difficult Employees

Poor performance and violation of rules, however, cannot be ignored. And if you look the other way, this not only hurts the

company, but if one employee gets away with it, others are likely to notice and follow suit. Moreover, you'll be labeled a pushover.

All managers struggle with appropriate ways to reprimand and discipline subordinates. But women are often blinded by personal feelings and have a tougher time disciplining and reprimanding someone they like. They also worry about what their employees will think. However, if your actions are fair and just, most of your subordinates will be supportive of you. When the Wyatt Company of Chicago surveyed 5,400 employees for its WorkAmerica Study, for example, it found that nearly half of the respondents believed that managers were too tolerant of poor performers.

The Manager As Terminator

Firing difficult employees is a tough decision—particularly for women, who are often paralyzed by compassion. But sometimes it's unavoidable.

There are several ways to terminate employees. Here are some ideas to ponder, but ultimately you must choose the methods that feel most comfortable to you.

• **Do it quickly.** "It should be like taking off a Band-Aid—fast and with as little pain as possible," believes Emily Koltnow, co-author of *Congratulations! You've Been Fired.* "Granted, this may sound heartless, but there are advantages to this approach. By not dragging the process out, you allow the employee to preserve her self-esteem. Doing it quickly also prevents the employee from falling apart emotionally in front of you."

• **Be tough, but caring.** When women fire, they tend to act more as counselors, notes Aileen Jacobson in *Women in Charge.* "Able to empathize, to actively listen, they can ease the transition period. They're more supportive of the person rather than telling them to clean out their desk." Granted, you may not be comfortable rushing through the firing process, but don't drag it out by spurring a discussion that analyzes what the employee might have done differently. This *is* heartless and may lead to false hopes by causing the person to argue with your reasons for firing him, in hopes of changing your mind.

• **Never terminate someone when you're angry.** If you don't have sufficient grounds, you may have to eat your words later. If you're angry, wait until you've had a chance to calm down before confronting the employee. And if you have any doubts whatsoever that the termination won't stick, it's usually wise to suspend subordinates—pending a full investigation of the problems—before firing them. That way you avoid being haunted by a lawsuit.

• **Be prepared to answer questions.** Employees will likely want to know such things as when they must leave, how much vacation time they have left, if there is any severance pay, how long their health insurance benefits will continue and at what cost. They might also want to know if they will be eligible for unemployment, and if so, how to apply.

• **Never delegate the task of firing a subordinate.** This is *your* responsibility and should not be palmed off on someone else. Granted, you may dread it, but it should still come from you. "Firing someone is always difficult," acknowledges Sherry Mosley, Manager of Human Resource Systems Development at Corning. "It should never be easy, and if it is, you shouldn't be supervising people. But I think there is a point when you look in the mirror and ask, 'Have I done everything that I can?' And if the answer to that is yes, you have to let it go—it's for the good of the other person, too."

Terry Paulson agrees in *They Shoot Managers Don't They?* "Don't think of yourself as a monster," he says. "If you informed the employee early and consistently of his shortcomings, he fired himself by not acting responsibly."

Besides, the employee may actually be grateful. Claire Coyle, of SmithKline Beecham, says, "I fire and demote as openly as possible. I don't sugarcoat. I say, 'Hey, this is the situation. This is the expectation. Prove to me you can do it. If you can't, then that's the situation." Coyle, who firmly believes that when a person is in the wrong job, it's not good for the company or the person, adds, "Sometimes a person I've fired from the wrong job acts like they have been let out of jail."

The Aftermath of Termination

After terminating an employee, you need to meet with your staff and tell them what has happened. You need not divulge your specific reasons for firing someone, but you will need to calm others' fears. Keeping the issue under wraps breeds gossip and starts rumors. Besides, many of your remaining employees may be worried that they are next.

You also need to take a few minutes to evaluate both with yourself—and your staff, if appropriate—what went wrong and to determine steps you can take to prevent history from repeating itself. In other words, here lies your silver lining: From firing you learn how to make better *hiring* decisions.

CHAPTER TEN

Win-Win Negotiating

PROFILE

SUSAN PRAVDA
ATTORNEY AND MANAGING PARTNER
EPSTEIN, BECKER & GREEN
BOSTON, MASSACHUSETTS

*"I'm tough in that I take tough positions and try to represent
my clients to the greatest extent of my abilities. But I'm not tough
personally at the table. I don't yell. I don't slam my fists on the table.
That just doesn't work for me, and the one thing I believe about
negotiating is that you have to stick to a style that works for you."*

She has been called ruthless and acknowledges, "I will push as
hard as I can, and particularly as hard as the client wants me to."
She has been called an opportunist. But since she views the term
in a positive sense, attorney Susan Pravda, Managing Partner of
the Boston office of Epstein, Becker & Green, a national law firm
with 220 attorneys, is entirely comfortable with that label as well.
She has also been described as "tough on issues, but soft on people." Indeed, Pravda's clients say that during negotiations she
"goes for the jugular." But they also describe her as "personable,
funny, and very savvy."

In other words, Pravda appears to be the ideal lawyer . . . an opponent's worst nightmare and a client's dream come true. But she also appears to be a victim of the old double standard. "If I were a man, I think people would describe me as tough, but not ruthless," she says. "Men can slam their hands on the table and get away with it. I can't do that."

Yet being a victim of the double standard doesn't concern Pravda much either. "I'm not afraid to roll with the punches. You have to do the best job you can for your client and not worry about whether anyone is going to say you're too tough as a woman doing it, because otherwise you are not serving your client well."

Pravda's thick skin and sense of determination have helped her enormously. Consider her astounding success at the age of thirty-four. In 1983, fresh out of Harvard Law School, she became one of 278 lawyers at a Boston powerhouse firm. By her third year, Pravda, who specializes in mergers and acquisitions, had orchestrated leveraged buyouts, attracted numerous clients, and emerged as one of the firm's top lawyers in terms of billable hours. Yet in her fifth year as an associate, she grew tired of being characterized by some as "too aggressive." Thus, Pravda and Gabor Garai, her mentor at the firm, decided to leave and start up what is now the Boston office of Epstein, Becker & Green. Today the two are equal partners both in the workplace and at home, having tied the knot in 1992. Pravda says her leaving her former law firm was primarily driven by her entrepreneurial spirit. "We wanted to run our own show," she explains.

The Boston office of Epstein, Becker & Green has sixteen lawyers and specializes in representing clients who are buying and selling middle-market companies. "I define middle-market as between $5 million and $150 million," Pravda says. "So my clients can be large corporations who are selling a division or a subsidiary, or who are buying a company. More typically, however, they are entrepreneurs who are in the business of buying and selling companies for a living."

Pravda says that there are probably three major strengths she brings to the negotiating table. "First, I think I am very creative, and that is probably key to solving problems that come up. Second, I'm tough, but in a different way than what is characteristically considered 'male toughness.' I'm tough in that I take tough positions and try to represent my clients to the greatest extent of my abilities. But I'm not tough personally at the table. I don't yell. I don't slam my fists on the table. That just doesn't work for me, and the one thing I believe about negotiating is that you have to stick to a style that works for you."

The third thing Pravda brings to a negotiation, and which she believes is critical to success, is the ability to listen. "I didn't do that as well five years ago," she admits, "but I've learned both from personal experience and from training a lot of young associates when to stop talking and when to start listening."

Successful negotiators, Pravda believes, also have a knack for reading between the lines of a situation. "You have to be able to get your pulse on what is bothering the other side," she explains, "and intuition can often tell you what the other side really wants. I think that one of the mistakes that people often make during negotiations is that they focus too much on the business matters—on the dollars and cents—which is critical. But often it's not as critical as the small stuff." And the power of intuition, she adds, is dependent upon asking the right questions.

Another of Pravda's strengths is "schmoozing" with her opponents. "I think that if you're at an initial stage of negotiating, it's helpful to plan that your 10:00 negotiation is not going to start in earnest until 10:30 or so, because you're going to spend the first half hour getting to know them as people and finding out what's important and of concern to them. Whether it's talking about their new offices, or noticing pictures of their kids in the office and asking questions about that, you need to allocate time for breaking the ice."

Most people try to negotiate on their own turf—or at the very least, in neutral territory. Not Pravda, who prefers going to her opponent's setting—and for a host of reasons. "First of all, I think they are more comfortable there, and I'm not uncomfortable. And if the other side is more comfortable, you're going to get further. Moreover, it's an immediate concession that you can give and that won't cost you a thing."

Case in point: Pravda is currently negotiating a transaction in a small town in Pennsylvania, which is impossible to get to by plane. "The fellow who's selling this company doesn't like to leave his hometown." At our first meeting—held in his lawyer's office in Pittsburgh—there he sat, looking very uncomfortable. So when we began discussing our next meeting, I turned to him and asked, 'Would you like us all to come to your hometown the next time?' And he was so happy. He gave us a tour, took us out to dinner, and clearly enjoyed it."

Pravda, through a little investigating, had also discovered that the man, who ran a manufacturing plant, was accustomed to dressing casually. "So when we went to the meeting, we all showed up in slacks and sweaters, and he was thrilled."

When negotiations take place on her turf, in Boston, Pravda always offers to take the other parties out to dinner the night before—"because that always helps." In fact, Pravda never enters into a negotiation cold. "I always find a way to talk to the principal negotiator on the other side a few times before we meet." What Pravda usually does is throw out what she calls "test issues," little points that shouldn't be controversial, just to get a sense of how her opponent responds to things. "Once I'm able to gauge whether they are very reasonable or take hard-line positions instantly, this helps me to prepare both myself and my client."

Once negotiations begin, if Pravda's opponent won't budge, she usually tries one of two tactics. "One is to let time pass," she says. "If we really get to a stalemate, I try to skip it and go on through the rest of the issue list, then return to it. Because sometimes what happens is that people back themselves into a corner and can't—or won't—get out without saving face. Another tactic is to break into small groups. Take a couple of people out and see if someone can come up with a creative solution—a new approach—that, if it's face-saving, will allow the person to be able to say, 'Well, okay, that was a deal breaker, but this is a *different* issue.' "

Then there are situations where a person really won't budge, at which point Pravda checks with her client to figure out whether there is another approach they should try or if the deal is still viable. "I often put myself in my opponents' shoes and try to figure out whether their position is extreme or unreasonable or whether, in fact, it's a position, that if I were in their shoes, I would probably stick to as well."

When negotiations get tense, Pravda tries to analyze whether the tension is good or bad. "Sometimes the last thing you want to do is *cut* the tension," she believes. "In fact, you want it to *build* because it can force your opponent to confront an issue." But when the tension is on her client's side, Pravda does try to cut it. "I think that almost all clients tend to get carried away then. They lose sight of their objectives or they get too emotional and angry to focus."

Tension can also be risky, she adds, when the other person is feeling "beat up on." In such instances, one of the things Pravda tries to do is suggest something like, " 'Why don't we table this issue for the moment and get back to it at the end.' Then, you can turn it around at the end and say, 'Well, I think we've accomplished five things. Maybe we need to go back and accomplish number two now.' "

Pravda says she also tries to determine whether "there's really an issue here, or whether everyone has just really worked themselves up for nothing." In fact, when things get hot, Pravda often sits back while everyone else is carrying on, and lets her creative juices flow. Then she'll pipe up with, "I just thought of another approach. Do you think this would work?" Purposefully framing her comments in question form, she says, lends a softer approach and more often leads to mutual solutions. "And even if it doesn't work, it breaks the tension and lets everyone focus on something slightly different that might work."

The only time Pravda herself tends to get hot during negotiations is when she feels someone is not acting in good faith. And if that happens, she'll either "call them on the carpet or walk out." For example, once at a closing for a company one of her clients was buying, the family selling the company decided at the last minute not to sign the papers. "I told my client, 'They are playing a game here. They have gotten you all the way down the road and sucked you in, and now they've taken away a point they gave up three weeks ago.' " Pravda then advised her client that the two of them return to the table and say, "Thank you very much, gentlemen. Good-bye." When her client questioned Pravda's strategy, she insisted, " 'Let's just do it. My sense is you will get a phone call.' And sure enough, the lawyer on the other side called first thing the next morning."

It's bold moves like these that have likely led others to describe Pravda as tough and ruthless. But as a female lawyer—and a young one to boot—she has had no choice but to learn how to hold her own. There are times, she admits, when she's been patronized because of her age and gender. "I had one instance where there were two days of negotiations, and after about two hours of snide comments from the negotiator on the other side—who was a fifty-year-old male—I'd had enough," she recalls. "So I took him out of the room—because I didn't want to embarrass him in front of the other people—and I said, 'Look, this has got to stop. I'm just as good at doing this as you are—maybe better—and I'm sorry if you feel insecure. But stop it now, or we're all going to walk out, and my client is going to explain that your client needs to hire a new lawyer.' That was it, and he stopped. But that's only happened to me once. Most of the time, if someone is patronizing, they get the hint pretty quickly when you show them that you know exactly what you're doing."

There are times, in fact, when Pravda believes women have an edge over men at the negotiating table. "We can be more accessible as people, instantly," she says. "We usually have a greater ability to befriend the other side. And quite frankly, I think that some people enjoy the difference. They get a kick out of the fact that it's not 'business as usual.' " But Pravda also believes that women only have an advantage if they use it correctly. "You have to ask yourself, 'Is there something about my status that allows me to use it to my benefit?' I've always taken that view of everything. If you have a great command of French, and you can converse in French, that can also be terrific. My advantage is that, like most women, I schmooze pretty well. So it's easier for me to break the ice and build a better rapport with people. Also, I've found that a lot of men relate differently to men than they do with women, and sometimes they actually find it *easier* to talk to women. And if I can take advantage of that, I do."

Of course, on the flip side, there are disadvantages to being a female negotiator. "Men have an immediate sort of male bonding that can happen," Pravda acknowledges. "They might have the same frame of reference, or they might be used to dealing with men more. And while it's getting easier for women, there are certain misconceptions that still come into play. Like when you take a tough position and everyone assumes, 'Well, she's either inexperienced and taking a tough position, or she feels like she needs to make a point.' But I think it's fairly easy to get over that hurdle simply by demonstrating competency."

Not to say that Pravda hasn't felt excluded. "It used to always bug me when, in the middle of negotiations, someone would call a bathroom break, and there would be twelve men heading off to the men's room, leaving me all alone. And you *knew* that conversations went on in there." For that very reason, Pravda designed the conference area in her new offices with single bathrooms. "When everyone asked, 'Why are you doing that?' I told them I knew *exactly* what I was doing!"

When asked how she thought her opponents would describe her negotiating style, Pravda summed it up in one word: tough. "I'm definitely tough. I get the deal done. I don't get bogged down in the details to the point where I lose the forest for the trees." But Pravda also likes for her opponents to walk away from the table thinking she's fair. "I don't try to make points just to make points," she says. "So on the things that I can concede on, that are fair to concede on, I do. I'm not the kind of person who sends out the first draft of the document that's a killer just for the sake of doing it. I'd rather start out closer to where we're going to end up, because then I think that the impression your opponent has is that you're fair from the beginning. It's always easier to deal with somebody who views you in that light than if they see you as just hostile to begin with.

"But I also think that you can be fair *and* tough," she adds. "I don't think that they are exclusive."

• • •

As women rise through the ranks in corporate America, increasing numbers of them are pulling up a chair at the negotiation table.

And with them, they are bringing a refreshing new style. A style that prefers compromising and building consensus over arguing and making demands. A style that is not black or white, but creative and flexible. A style that is win-win versus win-at-all-costs.

In other words, women appear to approach negotiations in entirely different ways than men do. But it is *precisely* these differences that often give female negotiators an edge.

Advantage: Women?

In fact, according to Deborah Kolb, Ph.D., a Boston psychologist and a professor of management at Simmons College, contrary to what experts believed in the past, women's differences at the negotiating table work to their advantage. How?

For starters, Kolb says that whereas men tend to view negotiations as a contest of wills, women are far more likely to make everyone involved feel like winners. Women tend to focus more on relationships as well. They care about the people they are negotiating with and make an attempt to get to know them as people before facing off with them as opponents. Men, on the other hand, tend to focus more on the task at hand.

Women often consider the history behind the negotiating problem, which Kolb says can help all parties at the table because it broadens their frame of reference. In contrast, men tend to limit their attention to the issues, which can also limit the scope of the negotiations.

Women tend to pay attention to and pick up on subtle clues as to how well the negotiations are proceeding. "And when the relationships are good, women behave in ways that strengthen the table's sense of community and abet further negotiation," Kolb says in an interview with *Psychology Today*.

Marsha Londe, Director of Corporate Accounts for Shadco Advertising Specialties, based in Atlanta, agrees. "I think that because women are generally good listeners, this gives us an advantage in developing rapport with the other side," she says. "Let's face it. Men have as many personal crises in their lives—like dealing with aging parents or difficult children—as women do. But man to man, they don't typically relate or share these stories. If they throw it out in conversation to me, however, I'll pick up on it, remember it, and ask them about it the next time we meet. And they will appreciate my asking. Men *need* to talk about personal situations just as much as women do. But men don't often give other men a chance to do that."

Yet another strength women possess, according to Dr. Virginia Weldon, Senior Vice President at Monsanto Company, is the ability to "change the context" of conflicts during negotiations and in other settings. "In disputes, men will often continue at loggerheads far longer than is necessary or useful, while women will try to find a different way," she notes. "In other words, men often play power; women tend to change the context. And that is a vital and often overlooked strength that women bring to the table—and to the workplace."

In a speech Weldon gave to the American Medical Association in late 1993, she shared an example of what she meant.

A few months ago, the Norwegian foreign minister had the unenviable task of mediating between Israel and the Palestine Liberation Organization. Now every one of us has for years seen pictures of how peace accords take place—in formal meeting halls, with participants seated at a table whose shape they have argued about, with official smiles for the media, and with the arguments saved for the private discussions. A "frank and candid exchange of views" has been a euphemism for a knock-down, drag-out shouting match.

But the Norwegian foreign minister did something different. He and his wife, Marianne Heiberg, invited the Israeli and PLO representatives into their home on the outskirts of Oslo. These talks—which often lasted late into the night—went on in secrecy for eighteen months.

And when discussions would reach an impasse, Marianne Heiberg turned to what must be one of the most unusual tools ever used in diplomatic negotiations—her four-year-old son, Edward. She would have him come into the room and ask the negotiators to play. And they would. These men—hardened toward each other by literally centuries of history and hate—played together with a four-year-old boy—on the floor.

And while playing with a little boy certainly helped break the tension, it also made the point that what was at stake was the future—the children—the Israeli children and the Palestinian children, and that was why a peace accord had to happen. And that's why it did happen.

Marianne Heiberg did something very powerful—and very much like a woman. She changed the context.

Negotiations, however, need not be a battle of the sexes. Bonnie Kasten, who for over a decade has taught thousands of men and women how to negotiate, believes that men and women can learn a great deal from each other. From her years of teaching, Kasten has noted that distinct behaviors emerge in men and women when negotiating. In a chapter for *Not as Far as You Think: The Realities of Working Women* (edited by Lynda Moore) entitled "Separate Strengths: How Women and Men Manage Conflict and Competition," Kasten writes, "Women tend to listen attentively and clarify others' positions, use logic to support their ideas, comment on areas of agreement, and avoid provoking their opponents. Men on the other hand, tend to make firm proposals and demands, make few concessions and hold their positions, use time as their ally, and bargain to get what they want."

Negotiating research, Kasten adds, clearly indicates that successful negotiators use *all eight* of these behaviors. "So if men and women would learn to develop the other sex's strengths, then each gender would have a full complement of skills," she believes.

In other words, successful negotiations call for a style that is both tough *and* caring. Here are some tips to help you develop those skills:

• **Do your homework.** Preparation is power, so know everything about the other side: their needs and goals, their track record, their company history, their corporate style and philosophy. Try to figure out what their bottom line will be, on which points they might be flexible and on which ones they're not likely to bend. When calling on clients, Janice Scott, a resident of Reading, Pennsylvania, and sales representative for Zep Mfg. Co., international manufacturers of industrial maintenance products, is always well prepared. "I find out as much as I possibly can about the facility I'm visiting, the products and service that I will present, and my competitors' products as well," she says. "I know I will be tested, because I'm a woman in a male-dominated field. But I also know that if I can influence them with my technical expertise, I'll get the sale."

Susan Pravda also makes it a point to know as much about the people she'll be negotiating with as well as their companies. "I'll look them up if there's a resource I can do it in. That helps a lot, because you'll invariably find out that somebody graduated a year ahead of you in school, or they wrote an article for the same magazine or journal that you also did." Pravda also picks up the phone and polls colleagues to see if they've run into that firm or organization. "Because people are so different, it's important to find out about the human being. Negotiation is such a style issue. It's not style over substance, but it's as much style as substance."

• **Don't insist on meeting on your turf.** Conventional wisdom says you should always try to negotiate on your turf, because that way you're in control. But, like Susan Pravda, Nicole Schapiro, author of *Negotiating for Your Life: New Success Strategies for Women,* disagrees and believes that agreeing to meet on your opponent's turf offers many advantages. "I get a lot of environmental clues about who they are," she writes in an article for *Executive Female* magazine. "There are countless sources of information: the office building, the foyer, elevators or stairways, hallways, the entrance to the office where I'm going, signs on doors. Are there receptionists, secretaries, assistants? How does my negotiating partner treat them?"

Schapiro adds that she also takes note of how she's received. "Does the person I am to meet come out to get me and walk me into the meeting room? Does he stay behind the desk, as if defending it? Or does he come around to put me at ease?"

Yet another reason to negotiate on the opposing side's turf is that when things get hot, you're more in control. For example,

Schapiro says that when she needs time to gain perspective or regain control—even to think before making an important decision—she likes to walk away from the negotiating table, something that can't easily be done if she's negotiating in her office. Yet when negotiations take place in someone else's office, Schapiro might say, "Well, it looks as if we're bogged down here. Let's both do some more homework and maybe get back together again sometime." Then she'll walk. And what usually happens then is that the opposing side will call her back and offer to continue the discussions.

• **Ask good questions—and at the appropriate times.** You can cut to the chase at the beginning of negotiations, for example, by asking open-ended questions. "What's your position here?" "What are your goals?" "What would like to see happen here today?" Then listen—hard—to their responses, which may often contain valuable information and clues on how you should proceed.

• **Know what *you* want to accomplish.** Map out your best-case scenario, your worst-case scenario, and everything in between. Anticipate potential objections to every one of your requests, and be ready to overcome those objections. And if you're new at negotiations, you might want to practice by having a mentor or colleague play devil's advocate.

Should you go into negotiations with a list of concessions you can make without a great deal of sacrifice? Many negotiators say yes. But Susan Pravda disagrees and says she prefers going in, instead, with a list of what her client's priorities are. "I don't go with a list of concessions because what I think I'm willing to concede and what I think may be important to the other side may not be what's important to them," she explains. "So what I try to do is identify the two or three or four critical points that my client *has* to get, then try to find out the flexibility on everything else. Otherwise, I think you may end up conceding more than you need to. And I don't think you can determine that until you are into the negotiations."

• **Take your time getting to what you want.** "In negotiating anything, there has to be a win for everyone," believes Johnna Howell of Westin Hotels and Resorts. "I always try to determine what it is that the other person wants, and what it is that I really want. This helps me to sort out my interests, needs, and emotions more clearly and to try to put myself in the other person's shoes. One thing that has taken me a long time to learn, however, is how to frame my position with the right words. I tend to want everyone to lay all of their cards on the table, look at them, develop the most appropriate solution, and move on. Seldom does this approach work, because many people do not lay all of their cards on the table (even though they enjoy seeing *yours*). I have learned over the years that being this forthright does not do my position any good. I now take my time with my words and agreements until we are finally able to reach a joint agreement."

• **Determine the other person's negotiating style, and react accordingly.** In her article for *Executive Female*, Nicole Schapiro describes four basic negotiating styles and tips on how to deal with each one. "Steamrollers," for example, are "aggressive, driven negotiators. To deal with them keep your goal in mind, take risks and think fast. Don't get hung up thinking about what a bully this person is." Steamrollers constantly ask "What" questions, as in "What's in it for me?" They don't like to waste time and will often not finish their own sentences or allow you to finish yours. "And if this happens often, it's a sure sign that you're providing too many details," Schapiro warns.

"Datacrats," on the other hand, spend enormous amounts of time mulling over every aspect of a situation before making a decision. "When pressured, they feel unsafe and dig in their heels—they'll procrastinate and withdraw altogether." The best approach to use with datacrats, then, is to get them to trust you. Don't rush. Instead, let *them* set the pace, and try to mirror their voice and gestures.

"Butterflies," according to Schapiro, are expressive, love to socialize, and crave attention. Typically, their fashion and communi-

210 • SWIM WITH THE DOLPHINS

cation styles are flamboyant and dramatic. Basically, butterflies want to *enjoy* the negotiating process, and they don't like a lot of details. "If butterflies are having fun with you, you will close the deal," Schapiro predicts.

Then there are what Schapiro calls "Nice Guys." They smile a lot—even when someone is saying something they disagree with. These people-pleasers' greatest fear? "That they will offend someone and then be excluded from the privilege of helping." And how to score big with them? Schapiro advises giving them lots of choices and lots of time to make their decisions. "By showing them special attention you will gain extra points."

• **When you concede on a point, make a big deal out of it—even if it's not.** In *Smart Questions: A New Strategy for Successful Managers*, Dorothy Leeds suggests, "When you give up something you consider minimal, create the impression that it's a significant compromise on your part. When a negotiator wins a major concession by giving up something insignificant, he gains a tremendous psychological boost. It's like trading a five-dollar bill for a ten-dollar one."

• **Check your emotions at the door.** It's okay to *look* angry, because that way your opponent sees you that have the capacity to get mad. You don't need to bang your fists on the table, throw papers, or scream at your opponent. In fact, this is likely to get you nowhere. But neither should you fade into the woodwork when things get tense. Focus on being assertive. Play hardball with words and body language. This strategy can be equally effective— if not more so—for women.

• **Plan to be tested.** Let's face it. Men are accustomed to negotiating with other men. As a result, many won't have a clue about how to deal with you. Some may automatically think "piece of cake," and you can show them differently. Others will insist on patronizing you. Resist the urge to get defensive and launch a counterattack. That's what they *want* to happen. Besides, if you allow yourself to fly off the handle, you risk losing your concentration on the task at hand.

Instead, try ignoring patronizing remarks. Sometimes a hostile opponent just needs to blow off steam, and if you let him, he'll be less hostile afterward. But if that doesn't work, challenge your opponent verbally by saying something like, "Do you expect me to respond to that?" or "Your childish behavior is wasting precious time. Do we want to work a deal here or not?" If the abuse continues, consider saying to your rude opponent, "I'm willing to work a deal when you're ready to stop attacking me. In the meantime, we have nothing to discuss." Then walk out of the room.

• **Take advantage of men's stereotypes about women.** Laurel Bellows, a Chicago attorney and past president of the Chicago Bar Association, often makes it a point to let her male opponents know that she's a mother. That way, she figures, they will *assume* that she won't put "twenty-four hours a day, seven days a week, into this negotiation." She might also let it drop that she's planning a family vacation, so that her opponents will assume that she'll be eager to wrap up the deal before she leaves. "Then they're going to be very surprised when they find out that that *isn't* what my priorities are, that I've sent my family on without me. And then I'm a whole lot grumpier because of it, and a whole lot less likely to give them what they want," she says.

• **Don't rush in to the negotiating process.** Try to establish a good working relationship with your opponent before you start making demands. In an article for *Inc.* magazine, real estate executive Marjory Williams recalls how making this mistake early in her career taught her a valuable lesson about negotiating. Working as a buyer for a large department store at the time, Williams's boss gave her an assignment. "He told me, 'Marjory, the department is overstocked, and the markdowns are way too high. One of the major problems is such-and-such, a vendor. Go to New York and tell him the inventory levels are too high, the goods aren't performing, and we need $8,000 to help cover our markdowns.'"

Williams went to New York, and upon shaking hands with the vendor, told him exactly what her boss had said. "It was my first experience with the boom-zero effect," she says. "He was insulted and angry. Who was I, brand-new in this area, to say his products weren't good? And who was I to make demands of him? Ignoring his needs, not to mention his feelings, I scored a fat zero."

Within a month, Williams and the vendor were able to reach a compromise. "But it was clear to me that I had reached an acceptable solution by the sheer force of the store's buying power and by my will and determination. By guts, not skill. By force, not finesse," she says. "I had won financial concessions but not a strong relationship. And I was in a business where ongoing relations with vendors was key."

• **Break bread before negotiating.** One way to establish a good working relationship with the opposing side is to treat them to dinner the night before your meeting. When you can relax and enjoy one another's company away from the negotiating table, you build a sense of camaraderie. You're also likely to gain greater insight into your opponents as human beings, and the negotiations are more likely to be amiable.

• **Use silence as a tool.** Susan Pravda tends to let silence mount, a lesson she says she learned the hard way. "Let the other side break it," she advises. "If there is silence, it's because you've reached an impasse, and generally the side that breaks the impasse either has to come up with a compromise or say something to reinitiate the discussion. And more often than not, it's a softening of their position."

Pravda also finds it helpful to use silence as a way of "listening" to the other side. "It's very tough, because in my business, my clients will inevitably want to control things in a way that doesn't let you use silence as well as you can," she admits. "Usually I have to tell them, 'We are not going to say a word about this. We are going to sit there and let it stew and stew and stew until it finally breaks, and the person who breaks is going to be the one who ends up giving in on this. And it happens that way almost every time."

• **When negotiations get stuck and nobody will budge, try initiating a review of how far you've come thus far.** This is particularly effective if your side has conceded more than the other side has. Adopt a "we're-all-in-this-together" attitude, and challenge your opponent to help you brainstorm a creative win-win solution. Even if you can't, your opponent may divulge valuable information in the process. Tell your opponent that you don't know what to do—then ask for advice. Some people find this flattering and will be more willing to compromise when you care what they think.

And if negotiations are at a standstill because the other side won't budge? "I've gotten into situations while negotiating with men, where I realized that they were hearing me, but they weren't *listening* to what I was saying," reports Shadco's Marsha Londe. "Then there's the issue of men stereotyping women. When I realize I'm at a point in negotiations that I've reached a blockade, I'll go around that blockade by appealing to a 'higher authority' to convey my message. Sometimes a man needs to hear from another man."

• **Play "what if."** Come up with compromises that will help you get past no. The best way to do this, according to William Ury, author of *Getting Past No: Negotiating Your Way from Confrontation to Cooperation*, is to ask "what if" questions. These, he says, help encourage a discussion of options.

Suppose, for example, that you're negotiating with your boss to let you hire a full-time assistant. She agrees that your heavy workload merits assistance but refuses your request, explaining that the budget from now until the end of the fiscal year is extremely tight. "Ask me again in three months," she tells you. Instead of giving up, however, you propose, "What if I were to hire a part-time assistant until the new fiscal year? That way we wouldn't have to pay benefits, and I could be training someone to take over full-time when next year's budget goes into effect." Chances are, your boss will be open to your suggestion—or at least willing to propose other alternatives.

• **Dress carefully.** Look important, but don't assume that you need to wear the uniform navy, gray, or black suit. Susan Pravda wears what she's comfortable in, because it makes her feel better about herself and more confident about the negotiations. "I like wearing dresses and bright colors. In a sense, what you wear is a way of making a statement."

• **Close on a high note.** Pravda believes that closing negotiations is an art and recommends not letting the other side walk away feeling defeated. "It may be good to defeat your enemy, but it's not a good idea to let them know it," she says. Pravda avoids this by summing up progress made. "I'll usually say something like, 'Well, I think we made a lot of progress today, and I think we resolved the four issues you had raised as important.' This helps to take the bad taste away if the last thing they gave up was pretty critical."

Above all, be adaptive. "Unlike men, women aren't stuck in a limited number of roles," notes Laurel Bellows. "Men can't smile a lot because other men will think they are weak. But women can smile, be tough and aggressive. Women have a number of roles that they can play, none of which has to carry them through the whole negotiation. They should just get comfortable with a variety of roles."

Shadco's Marsha Londe agrees. "I think that a woman often understands innately and instinctively how to temper her attitude to the person she's negotiating with. I am a strong and assertive woman, and I know there are men with whom I have to make an attitude adjustment and pull myself down to a calmer level, because they can't handle my assertiveness. But there are other men who *want* women to be strong. It's like dressing for success. You know when you can wear a short skirt and when you need to wear a long skirt. You know when you can wear jewelry and when you shouldn't. It's the same thing with your attitude and approach. I find that I intuitively make an assessment about the person and will 'don' a certain attitude in order to relate to that person . . . in order to develop the kind of rapport that I need to succeed. And I think women are better suited to making these adjustments than men are."

Indeed, like dolphins, women possess a negotiating tool that, used correctly, can give them a decisive edge: sonar . . . or intuition.

CHAPTER ELEVEN

Bouncing Back from Adversity

PROFILE

MARILYN MARKS
PRESIDENT AND CEO
DORSEY TRAILERS
ATLANTA, GEORGIA

"I don't believe in making contingency plans, because I don't have time. If I spend too much time playing 'What if it fails?' then that can take on a life of its own. So I never consider 'What if this doesn't work?' I focus, instead, on 'This can work!'"

Marilyn Marks is not a person who fears failure. "I've been given so much freedom in my career, and I've made so many mistakes," she says. "But I've also received the support of so many people to recover from them, and I feel very fortunate about that. In fact, what I've learned is that if people understand what needs to be done, almost anything can be accomplished."

Indeed. Eight years into her career at the Dorsey Corporation, a manufacturer of plastic bottles and truck trailers based in Chattanooga, Tennessee, Marks was asked to oversee the desired sale of Dorsey Trailers, one of the company's subsidiaries. Over the years, Marks had visited Dorsey Trailers and been impressed with the company's truck trailer product, reputation, and extremely dedicated employees. "But I also saw a company where there was a lot of inefficiency, a lot of waste, and a company that had not focused on how it needed to serve the market in an era of trucking deregulation," she recalls. "Also, costs had gotten out of line, and Dorsey Trailers was losing a lot of money at the time."

Nevertheless, Marks decided to take a risk by leading the management of the subsidiary company to purchase Dorsey Trailers. To avoid conflict of interest, she resigned from her job as Vice President of Corporate Planning and was unemployed for six months while she attempted to put the deal together.

It was a risk that paid off. Under her leadership as President and CEO, within two years, sales at Dorsey Trailers had soared from $125 million to $180 million, and the company had upped its ranking to number four in the industry.

The following year, however, not one—but *two*—natural disasters struck the company's key operations in Elba, Alabama. First, a tornado ripped off the front of one of the plant's main buildings and cost the company thousands of dollars in downtime. Then, before Marks even had a chance to get the building repaired, sixteen inches of rain fell on Elba within forty-eight hours, and a levee on the Pea River gave way, leaving the company submerged under fourteen feet of water. "I drove to Elba as soon as I heard," Marks recalls. "The sheriff drove me through the streets in a motorboat to see the plant. The water was so high that I had to duck to keep from being hit by the traffic lights as I looked down on the factory."

Marks soon discovered that thousands of gallons of hazardous chemicals had spilled and that millions of dollars' worth of equipment was floating under fourteen feet of water and mud. Many CEOs might have thrown up their hands in despair, recognizing that the $15 million insurance policy would not begin to cover the damage. But Marks decided to take whatever action was necessary to recover from the crisis—despite the fact that the odds were against her. (The company was also struggling to recover from a desperate cash shortage, brought on by multimillion-dollar losses from a Wisconsin plant closure and difficult industry conditions.)

As the water began to recede, her first priority was to call in safety experts to deal with the chemical spills. Once the area was declared safe, Marks began rounding up employees to help with the cleaning and lubricating of mud-caked motors and equipment to prevent rusting. The problem was, the town's phone lines were down, and many of her employees had lost their homes in the flood. Many, she assumed, likely feared that they had permanently lost their jobs. "I sent my parents out in my four-wheel-drive Jeep to visit as many workers as possible," she says. "They conveyed my message that we were working around the clock trying to save the company." Meanwhile, Marks set out to track down tetanus serum, food, and potable water.

Her employees rallied, as Marks knew they would. "At Dorsey Trailers, we've always had a very participative culture, and in keeping with that, one of the most effective things we did was to get our employees involved in the cleanup as soon as possible."

Another of Marks's priorities was to keep the lines of communication open with the company's vendors. "Within forty-eight hours of the flood, and before we had completely assessed the situation, we faxed them letters explaining what had happened and kept them posted throughout the rebuilding process." Dorsey Trailers' vendors rallied as well, continuing to support the company. Some even started a relief fund for the company's employees who had lost their homes.

Throughout the ordeal, Marks also made it a point to remain as visible as possible and to serve as the company's spokesperson. "Many CEOs might have avoided the spotlight," she acknowledges. "But in this situation, I let the attention focus on me. I felt that if people both inside and outside the company saw that the person who had to make the decisions—and whose name was on the debt—was carrying a lunch pail to work, wearing jungle boots in muddy floodwaters, and fighting off snakes in the plants instead of poring over insurance policies, they would know we were determined to make a go of things."

In those dark days, few besides Marks and her employees believed that Dorsey Trailers could recover—including the banks. "After the flood, the banks continued to cut back on the amount of money they would loan us," she reports. And in fact, at one point Marks did meet with a bankruptcy lawyer. "But I quickly decided that my time would be spent more wisely going the positive route versus the negative route. So I immediately began redirecting my energies to rebuilding the business."

Thanks to Marks's can-do attitude, the dedication of her employees, and a record-setting loan of $25 million from the Small Business Administration, Dorsey Trailers was "up and sputtering by the fall of 1990—and the flood had occurred during the previous spring!" Marks reports. "As early as September, we had recalled all the employees and had even managed a return to profitability." The worst was over . . . or so everyone thought.

Then came the Persian Gulf Crisis, which caused the price of diesel fuel to skyrocket. "The economy slumped, demand for truck trailers took a nosedive, and we were sitting there in the desperately competitive marketplace with a real question mark behind our names as to whether or not we were going to make it." In fact, it wasn't until the company had recovered physically from the earlier crises that she realized just how much damage Dorsey Trailers had suffered in the marketplace. "We had been so internally focused that we had failed to see what had happened in the marketplace," she admits. "And our reputation and market share had really deteriorated." To make matters worse, Marks soon discovered that her competitors had been blasting Dorsey Trailers. "They were telling our customers, 'Dorsey will never make it . . . they'll never pull themselves out of the financial problems exacerbated by the flood.' So what few orders there were, our competitors were managing to snatch up by questioning our long-term viability."

In January of 1991, the company had no choice but to cut its salaried workforce by 20 percent. "Doing that after those same people had worked so hard to keep us alive was devastating," Marks said. But she refused to cut back on her hourly workforce, because she was determined that the plant produce *something* just to keep the doors open.

Once again, despite the odds, Dorsey Trailers rallied. "The people who were left pulled together and said, 'We *will* make this thing work.' We had daily meetings at all management levels to discuss how we could save the plant. And every penny of cash was watched."

A 20 percent reduction in the company's salaried staff also left a lot of voids; yet Marks says her people simply moved in and filled those voids—even though it wasn't their official job. In retrospect, she believes that this unexpected opportunity for cross-disciplinary training turned out to be the silver lining of the company's ordeal. "As a result, we emerged better than any of our competition. Our senior staff now knows so much more about the company as a whole and has developed into a great working team."

In 1990, sales had slumped to $81 million, but by the latter part of 1991, Dorsey Trailers had turned another corner, with sales climbing to $92 million. Consequently, as soon as the company was able, Marks reinstated raises. She also rewarded bonuses of several weeks' pay to her hourly employees for getting the company back into production so quickly.

These days, business is brisk at Dorsey Trailers. Sales in 1993 soared to $175 million, and in 1994 that figure is expected to swell to $200 million. "We have managed to double our sales with fewer people, and we're sold out not only for this year, but well into next year. This is unusual for us—and for the industry. Normally, there is usually a nine- to ten-week backlog, but we're talking a nine- to ten-*month* backlog. So now we're struggling with how we can meet the demand."

It's problems like these that Marks and her staff relish tackling. "As a result of hanging in there and keeping the faith, things have really turned around for us."

Some might assume that the one lesson Marks has likely learned from this ordeal is the necessity of having a contingency plan. Truth is, she doesn't believe in them. "This is a point where I am most criticized," she admits. "But I don't believe in making contingency plans, because I don't have time. If I spend too much time playing 'What if it fails?' then that can take on a life of its own. So I never consider 'What if this doesn't work?' I focus, instead, on 'This *can* work!' "

Not to say that Marks never feels uneasy when things are going well. "Nervous? Absolutely!" she laughs. "I'm always looking over my shoulder for a band of locusts or something. But there is so much more stability and experience now. Having watched what we've been through, we say, 'Hey, it's not going to get any worse than that.' And now whenever a problem crops up, we handle it in stride—piece of cake."

As for what she might have done differently, Marks says she could have done a better job of balancing the internal and external focus of the plant during its crises. "Because we were so internally focused, we did a poor job with the people outside the company— particularly our customers," she admits. "In essence, we ignored them, because we were so busy trying to bandage our own wounds. And that accounted for a big loss in market share, which we should have prevented."

And the greatest lesson Marks learned from her ordeal? "To have faith in people, and the capacity of people to overcome great adversity," she says without hesitation. "And to do it with spirit and to do it as a team. For far too long, it was just one thing after another, and there were many, many weeks when we weren't certain we could make the payroll. But I watched the Dorsey people not give up. They would say, 'This means too much to us. We *can* get through this!'

"Of course, I always did have faith in them," she adds. "But what they did was superhuman."

• • •

Setbacks, crises, and failures—they all come with the territory of being a manager. For example, when researchers at the Center for Creative Leadership in Greensboro, North Carolina, interviewed eighty-six successful Fortune 500 executives about their careers, 66 percent reported either "missing promotions, being exiled to poor jobs, being caught in a major conflict with the boss, contributing to a business failure, or simply being overwhelmed by the enormousness of the job."

Why Managers Need to Stumble

Graduates of the school of hard knocks will tell you that surviving failures, crises, and setbacks makes you stronger and tougher. It can enhance your professional image as well, because it proves that you are willing to take risks. In fact, coming to terms with failure is critical for managers, because otherwise you fear it and end up making safe decisions, which can stymie your career.

Hardships also provide a wealth of learning opportunities according to the Center for Creative Leadership. Data from two studies of general-management-level men and women, all of whom were described by top management as "successful and showing promise for future potential," reveal that hardships gave all of these managers a sense of perspective. It granted them an opportunity to determine not only what was important in terms of their careers and personal lives, but also what their limits and weaknesses were as managers. Moreover, as a result of persevering through setbacks, failures, and traumas, these managers gained confidence in themselves and in their leadership abilities.

Failure is often a stepping-stone to success. After losing an election in 1972, Barbara Boxer was devastated. "It was a big ache because it was a very difficult, year-long campaign. It was a year of my life. I wasn't really prepared for either the campaign or the loss. But it was a tremendously important experience that turned out to be a growth experience. It made me stronger and proved to me that I didn't have to be 'someone' to be worthwhile," she told Dorothy Cantor and Toni Bernay, co-authors of *Women in Power: The Secrets of Leadership.*

"After I lost, I went on to do some really interesting things," Boxer continues. "I became a newspaper reporter. I worked for a Congressman. So it just showed that there is life after losing. When I lost, I faced the pain and reality and found my strengths and weaknesses. It has really given me the courage in my personal life to take risks. I decided to run for the House, and whatever happens, I know I can handle it."

In the 1992 elections, Senator Boxer emerged a winner.

Failure is necessary to appreciate success. Linda Wachner, President of Warnaco, acknowledges, "Victory is so much sweeter when we've failed." In 1979, at the age of thirty-three, Wachner was named President of the U.S. division of Max Factor and Company, where she boosted slipping profits and survived two corporate takeovers before deciding to try and buy the company for herself. When that didn't work out, she resigned and became a managing director of Adler and Shayin, a small New York investment firm. In 1985, Wachner and her partners attempted to buy Revlon's cosmetics unit—but again, the takeover went sour. A year later, however, during her third attempt at a takeover—this time of Warnaco—instead of striking out, Wachner hit a home run.

Wachner credits her success to "an enormous ability to focus for very long periods of time." And not surprisingly, her critics have accused her of being tough. But that's a label Wachner feels comfortable with. "People don't realize that tough is a good thing," she told *Working Woman* magazine in a 1987 interview. "Tough withstands waves. Tough doesn't erode."

A sense of toughness also enables managers to accept defeat in the face of setbacks, crises, and failures—and with their self-esteem still intact. For example, while heading up the YWCA, Gwendolyn Baker was appointed by the mayor of New York City to serve on the city's Board of Education. "I served for five years, and for four of those, I was the only African-American woman on the board," she says. "In my fifth year, which was the beginning of my second term, I was elected board president. Because we had the responsibility of overseeing a budget in excess of $8 billion, it was a very powerful position. Unfortunately, it was the first year that there was an African-American mayor of the city, which not only created a lot of tension, but made it extremely difficult to try to pull people together."

Eventually, "too much political garbage and too much responsibility trying to manage two full-time positions" led Baker to resign from her presidency and the board. "I thought our focus was to be on the schools and to improve the system," she says. "And since I was already putting in ninety to ninety-five hours a week with the YWCA and the school board, I thought the best thing for me to do was to step aside at the Board of Education and let someone else take over who might be able to be more effective."

Later, when Baker was interviewed for her current position as President of the U.S. Committee for UNICEF, the last question she was asked dealt with what she had learned about leadership while serving as president of the New York City Board of Education. She told them, "I think the most important lesson I learned was that when you're really committed to a mission, and you find that you are not able to bring people together to achieve that mission, a good manager will step aside and allow someone else to do it for the sake of the mission. Because leadership is not about power. Leadership is about success at getting people to move with you for the good of the cause."

Bouncing Back: Who Does and Who Doesn't

Some women—like Barbara Boxer, Linda Wachner, and Gwendolyn Baker—manage to rise above setbacks, crises, and failures. Not only are they able to recover from their losses, they manage to turn setbacks into successes. How do they do it? One of the secrets to bouncing back appears to be dependent on the way you *define* failure. "People who rebound well simply never see themselves as failing," says Andrew J. DuBrin, author of *Bouncing Back: How to Stay in the Game When Your Career Is on the Line*. "They perceive a setback as a glitch, a temporary sidestep, a 'no' on the way to 'yes.'"

The ability to bounce back also lies in how managers *perceive* and *react* to failures, setbacks, and crises—and this is where women often run into problems. For example, when Lee Bell and Valerie Young conducted research with working women to pinpoint the kinds of self-inhibiting attitudes and behaviors that typically block women in their work lives, they found that when men fail—even on a task requiring skill—they are more likely to attribute failure to external factors such as bad luck. Women, on the other hand, are more apt to attribute failure to themselves.

Women, they add, are also more likely to "overidentify with failure, to assume more ownership for mistakes, to remember errors longer, and to rebound less quickly from a setback."

Yet another reason failure tends to throw women for a loop is that many of us are perfectionists. But according to New York City career counselor Leslie Rose, "Perfectionist women need to learn the concept of a batting average. Women are taught to do things right—immediately. But from playing sports, men learn that they don't get a hit every time they're up to bat. No one bats a thousand. What's important is to aim for a good average."

Two studies conducted by the Center for Creative Leadership turned up similar results. Comparing data collected from male and female general managers in Fortune 100 sized firms, researchers found that while men and women reported hardship events with equal frequency, women were more likely than men to talk about their mistakes and to agonize over them. They were also less likely to attribute failure to bad luck.

Why does this occur? Bell and Young attribute the phenomenon to the pressures women face while trying to succeed in a male-oriented work world. The way women are treated often fosters insecurity, they theorize. Many women are also perfectionists, and as a result they often don't seek outside help for fear they will be judged incompetent. Moreover, women frequently feel pressured to succeed for *all* of womankind, and failure to them translates into failure for their entire gender.

Ellen Van Velsor and Martha Hughes, researchers with the Center for Creative Leadership, agree and suggest that women's tendencies to perceive failure as a key event, and to attribute it to lack of skill rather than a lack of effort, occurs because they are less likely than men to have learned as children that failure and loss can be survived. "The play of girls tends to focus on taking turns and improving rather than on direct competition, and win/lose situations," Van Velsor and Hughes note in *Gender Differences in the Development of Managers: How Women Managers Learn from Experience*. "So women have had less early opportunity to outgrow the childhood belief that loss or failure is disastrous."

In the Center's Executive Women Project, researchers Ann M. Morrison, Randall P. White, and Ellen Van Velsor studied seventy-six women from twenty-five of the nation's largest corporations and found that women's mistakes *are* often magnified. In other words, high-level managers often operate in a "fishbowl," where their every move is scrutinized. Consequently, the pressures to do everything right can, indeed, be enormous. "As top women in a society where top women are relatively rare, they suffer from what could be called the glasshouse effect. Everything they do is exceedingly visible, and many feel that visibility gives them little room for error without jeopardizing either their own future or the opportunities given to other women in the corporation," the study's authors write.

Perhaps one of the most important findings from the Executive Women Project was that nearly three quarters of the prominent and successful women interviewed reported at least one significant setback. Whether it was not being able to sell an idea or a project, or hiring the wrong people, all gained insight and learned valuable lessons. Moreover, once they had dealt with their failures, many of the executives were grateful at having been given the opportunity to fail. "Through the experience of failing, both male and female executives acquire new skills that help them in their later challenges, such as developing teamwork skills, hiring the right people, and keeping lines of communication open," the authors write. "They also learn something about corporate politics—how things *really* work and how the beliefs of key executives influence decisions. And they learn to lose—even gracefully—and to accept their inability to control all of the world, to expect the unpredictable and to cope with disappointment. These are hard lessons but they build toughness and tenderness and acceptance of imperfection true leaders need."

Bouncing Back

So the trick to managing failures, crises, and setbacks is not to avoid them, but to face them head-on, learn from them, and, when possible, make them work *for* you. Of course, this is no easy task. "Learning how to manage failure is one of the most difficult skills required of a manager," acknowledge Lorne C. Plunkett and Robert Fournier in their book *Participative Management: Implementing Empowerment.* "In a society that worships winners, we have a low tolerance for the losses that lead to winning." Nevertheless, you must learn to manage failure and to take a tough and caring attitude with yourself if you want to be an effective manager. Here are some tips on how to accept failure, setbacks, and crises and to bounce back from them as quickly as possible:

• **When you fail at something, fess up.** Don't get defensive, and don't try to blame others. Be accountable. That way you not only earn the respect of others, you improve your chances of career success. For example, when researchers at the Center for Creative Leadership compared the careers of twenty successful executives to those of twenty who had derailed from the same companies, both types had made mistakes. But while the successful managers faced their errors head-on—by notifying colleagues of the situation, attempting to solve the problems they'd caused, learning from their mistakes, and then moving on—those who had derailed typically tried to deny or cover up their mistakes or pointed the finger at others.

"One of the most important lessons of the workplace is knowing when to ask for help," believes Valerie Wohlleber, former Vice President and Chief Financial Officer of Tenneco Minerals Company. "If I make a mistake, I know the best thing to do is notify people who can help solve it," she writes in an article for *Executive Female.* "If it's something that is relatively small and can be handled internally, solve the problem and then go to your boss to explain what happened and how you have resolved it."

• **Don't ignore a problem, crisis, or mistake in hopes that it will disappear or that someone else will handle it.** Immediately look at what—if anything—you can do to remedy the situation, or at least to minimize the damage. In February of 1991, a USAir 747 jet collided with a Sky West commuter plane at Los Angeles Airport, and thirty-five people died in the ensuing fire. Agnes Huff, Western Regional Manager of Corporate Communications for USAir, rushed to the scene and found fifty to sixty reporters waiting for answers. "I told them I had little information but would go out to the crash site and hold a press briefing as soon as possible," Huff writes in *Executive Female*. "When I got there, I realized it was a bigger disaster than I had imagined." Though the cause of the crash was determined to be an air-traffic-control error, Huff remained at the airport for three days, briefing the press every few hours until the company's CEO arrived from Washington. "There were several things we did right in handling this disaster," Huff believes. "We provided a spokesperson (myself) almost immediately. We involved the CEO, who talked about the backgrounds of the pilots, expressed condolences to the families of the victims, and corrected misperceptions and rumors. We kept updating the press, and we monitored what was being reported so that we could correct inadequacies at the next briefing. If we had hidden from the press and not come out with the facts as we knew them, we could have destroyed our company's good will and reputation."

• **Don't allow yourself to be paralyzed in the face of failure.** Do something—*anything*—to regain confidence. Dawn Steel, former President of Columbia Pictures and now head of her own studio in Hollywood, reveals in an interview with *Mirabella* magazine, "I used to have a sign on my desk at Columbia that said, 'Breathe.' So whenever there was one of those moments where I was faced with bad news or somebody was screaming at me—which happened more often than I can possibly tell you—I took deep breaths a lot."

Besides, if you refuse to let yourself become paralyzed, you may even prevent a disaster-in-the-making from occurring. Marsha Londe, Director of Corporate Accounts of Shadco Advertising Specialties and winner of several national sales awards, offers this story of how clear thinking and quick acting prevented a near-disaster in her business. "A few years ago, one of my customers ordered several crystal awards to be presented at his company's annual awards banquet. The factory said they could deliver on time, and I stayed on top of the situation." The day before the banquet, as a matter of routine, Londe called the customer and told him that the order had been shipped and to expect delivery later that afternoon. But the order did not arrive. "My customer called me, and I immediately called the factory. Their response was, 'Oops, we made a mistake. We're terribly sorry, but there's nothing we can do about it.'

"The president of our company tried to right the wrong by going through the normal channels, but he wasn't getting anywhere," she continues. "So I decided to bypass the normal chain of command and went directly to the manufacturer's vice president—who happened to be a woman. I told her, 'You know me, and you know I don't scream and yell. But I'm very disappointed in what's happened. However, I'm *not* going to disappoint my customer. Now you give me a time frame of how fast you're going to get those awards out here. Call me back and tell me how you're going to ship them and what time they will arrive.' "

The crystal was engraved and sent via Delta Dash that same day. In fact, Londe went to her client's banquet that evening, arriving just in time to personally supervise the receipt and unpacking of the awards for her customer.

• **Don't panic—at least not in front of others.** You need to demonstrate that you *can* take the heat. So focus, instead, on remaining cool, calm, and in control. And if you do feel yourself losing control, call a time-out. Put some distance between you and the problem or crisis. Get some perspective. "I always try to look at a situation and ask myself, 'What's the *worst* thing that could happen here?' " says Londe. "And when I realize that the worst thing is that I might lose the sale, lose the commission, or possibly lose the customer—but I'm not going to lose my life or career over it, it helps me to regain my perspective."

• **Share your blunders with others, so they can learn from them, too.** Grace Pastiak of Tellabs says she recently pulled thirty people together to try a new approach to process management called the Future Search Conference. "The consultant I was working with was not as skilled as she could have been, so I ended up running the conference," she reports. "In many ways, we got a lot out of it, but not what we expected. At the end of it, I asked myself what went right, and there were about two things. Next, I asked what went wrong, and there were about thirty things. I wrote every one of them down. Then I sent out a memo with a cartoon of me with a bag over my head saying, 'Sorry this was such a failure.' "

• **Play "Next time I will . . ."** What's the lesson here? Since 1990, Barbara Carmichael, Vice President of Corporate Communications at Dow Corning, has managed the crisis surrounding silicone breast implants. In *Executive Female*, she writes, "One of the first steps I took when I started this job was to set up a database to monitor all media coverage—both here and overseas. Today the database contains about 7,000 articles, which are classified as negative, positive, and balanced."

After monitoring this extensive database for over a year, Carmichael says she was able to pinpoint the company's biggest problem. "Public perception was that Dow Corning was being secretive," she says. "So with the data I had accumulated, I was able to go to the executive team and say, 'Listen, we've got an issue of corporate reputation on our hands.' This led to the company putting into the public domain every shred of research results it had on implants."

But this focus on the media, Carmichael adds, also caused the company to temporarily lose sight of women with implants. "We were getting too defensive, because people were accusing us of outrageous things," she acknowledges. "Our focus now is back on these women, many of whom have real fears that the product is harming them."

Researchers involved in the Executive Women Project looked at both the kinds of failures respondents encountered on their climb up the corporate ladder as well as the lessons they had learned. The most common setback, for example, was not being able to sell an idea or a project. And the lessons learned? To get others involved and invested in an idea early on, and not to dwell on a failure, but to refocus one's energies into a new idea or project.

Adds management consultant Warren Bennis, "The majority of millionaires that I've interviewed in the last decade and a half said they learned more from failure than from success. The main skill they possessed was the ability to learn from themselves and their mistakes and what they could do to get the best and worst out of people."

• **Brace yourself.** If you've blundered, you should be prepared to take the flak—which could come in the form of your superiors shouting at you, or your colleagues barraging you with constructive criticism. Expect the worst and don't argue or become arrogant or defensive. Take it like a professional. Show some remorse, and apologize if appropriate.

• **Be part of the solution.** If you've screwed up, don't immediately go to your boss with a confession. Instead, think of what you can do to remedy the situation and to prevent others from making the same mistake. Then go to your boss with a confession *and* a plan: "This is what happened, and I apologize. I know we have to deal with this. Here's what I recommend."

• **Recognize that some things can't be fixed.** Feel the pain. Grieve if you have to. Talk about it. Learn your lesson. Then let it go. "To deal with the feelings of loss, it's important to give yourself permission and time to be sad—to go through a miniature mourning process. That grieving, depending on the situation, may take all of five minutes, or you may need to take a couple of days or even weeks to lick your wounds," says Susan Schenkel, Ph.D., a Cambridge, Massachusetts–based psychologist and author of *Giving Away Success: Why Women Get Stuck and What to Do About It.* "What happens to some people however—and this is something women are particularly vulnerable to—is that instead of just letting themselves be sad for a while, they lapse into a pattern of helpless or self-abusive thinking. The helpless thoughts occur first: 'I can't do it' or 'I'll never be able to do it.' You may feel helpless for a short time and then recover. Or your thoughts may then move into self-abusive thinking. These thoughts usually take the form of, 'How could I have been so stupid, lazy, hopelessly naive,' and so on." Yet this can interfere with damage control, she adds, because it keeps you focused internally—on yourself and your flaws—instead of focused externally—on problems and potential solutions.

• **Be caring with yourself.** If you've made a mistake, forgive yourself, as others will likely do. Research conducted by John Skowronski, Ph.D., associate professor of psychology at Ohio State University, reveals that making a mistake doesn't brand us for life and that we can restore our reputation fairly quickly with a single sign of intelligence or competency. When Skowronski asked 120 college students to evaluate people from written reports of their behavior, he found that the majority of people believe that even intelligent individuals can sometimes do really stupid things. But, he cautions, the same is *not* true if you've committed an *immoral* act. "Most believe that honest, moral people always act that way, but one very immoral act, and you're no longer seen that way," he said in an interview with *Psychology Today*. "In fact, those who commit immoral acts must work exceedingly hard to restore their reputations."

• **But be tough with yourself, too.** Refuse to allow yourself to wallow in self-pity. Instead, summon the courage to cope and find a way to convince yourself that you *will* bounce back. As one CEO told Warren Bennis, "When you're in a tough situation, when you've hit rock bottom, that's when the iron enters your soul and gives you resiliency to cope."

Let Your People Fail

Deny your subordinates permission to fail, and they'll adopt a "better safe than sorry" attitude about their work, believes Diane Tracy, author of *10 Steps to Empowerment*. As a result, she adds, "They won't grow and stretch. They'll never go the extra mile. They'll do mediocre work."

Just as managers must allow themselves to fail, so should they allow—even encourage—their subordinates to do so. Not to say that repeated mistakes are acceptable, but if your employees fear failure, they will never take risks, never learn from their mistakes, and never do their best work.

By setting a good example, managers can demonstrate that failures can be survived. This involves regularly sharing your blunders—and lessons learned from them—with your subordinates. And don't worry that admitting your mistakes will tarnish your image. On the contrary, sharing your own setbacks shows that you are human, makes you more approachable, and teaches valuable lessons.

Also teach your subordinates how to *redefine* and *manage* failure. Suzanne Jenniches of Westinghouse, for example, defines mistakes and setbacks as *continuous improvement* versus failure. She has also taught her teams to consistently document lessons learned from projects. This includes not only recording and discussing losses, but carefully analyzing every project once it ends, "because there's never anything that is 100 percent successful," she says. "I believe that even on a project that ends successfully—meaning it made good money, everything shipped on time, the customer was happy, and the quality was outstanding—there are still lessons to be learned on ways to do it better."

In *Participative Management: Implementing Empowerment*, Lorne C. Plunkett and Robert Fournier tell the story of another company that found a unique way to legitimize failure and to encourage discussion and learning from it. "A new column was introduced in the corporate newsletter: 'Failure of the Month,'" the authors report. "It was up to every vice president to contribute to the column, and not to have erred was not to have pushed the limits of business."

CHAPTER TWELVE

Work Smarter, Not Harder

PROFILE

NANCY SINGER
PRESIDENT AND CEO
FIRST OF AMERICA BANK–NORTHEAST ILLINOIS, N.A.
LIBERTYVILLE, ILLINOIS

"I don't run this bank. I create visions and strategic plans for the bank. But more important than anything else, I create the environment in which everyone else can run the bank."

Nancy Singer's secret to working smarter, not harder, is to structure her days so that she's as visible and accessible as possible to everyone in her organization. In fact, Singer spends about 50 percent to 75 percent of her in-office time communicating with employees. And of that amount, 75 percent, she says, is spent listening. "It is much more effective to listen to what someone else has to say than to be talking myself," she reports. "You can learn so much about people and a given situation just by listening to them and asking them questions."

Singer is equally accessible outside of the office. "My employees know they can talk to me anytime, any place," she says. "They know my home phone number, and I encourage them to use it if they want to talk about something in the evening or on weekends. They also know my car phone number. I don't ever want them to feel like they can't get to me, because I believe those folks are my customers. And if I don't treat them with respect and with quality, then how can I expect them to treat our external customers that way?"

Singer's listening philosophy, she says, can be summed up in three words: "integrity, caring, and credibility, but not necessarily in that order. To gain credibility, you need to make sure that your people understand you really *want* to listen to them, and that you won't kill the messenger. They also need to know that you will keep their confidences." For example, when staffers come to Singer with problems, the first thing she does is ask probing questions to make sure that the person hasn't blown things out of proportion. "Then, if it's something that's pervasive or so big that everybody is going to know about it anyway, I'll seek out the people involved to find out more and to pinpoint what went wrong."

But if the problem is something that the employee has told her in confidence, Singer finds a way to forge a solution without revealing her source. "In thirty-two years of banking, I've never yet had a situation where I was told something in confidence, that I couldn't figure out a way to go and ask the right people some questions off the cuff that would bring the problem out on its own without compromising my source. Because the first time you compromise your source is the last time you'll ever get information from anyone."

To demonstrate integrity Singer believes that her people have to know that she's on their side no matter what—that she will listen and not overreact or get defensive. And she practices what she preaches, by backing up her staff—even when they make mistakes. "I tell them, 'Okay, we made a bad decision. Let's talk about what we can do differently, so the next time something like this comes about, we'll know how to handle it.' "

As for the caring aspect of listening, Singer accomplishes this primarily by making herself as visible and accessible as possible. She also tries to keep up with what's going on in her subordinates' personal lives. "You try to remember, for example, that some-body's parents are having a fiftieth wedding anniversary party over the weekend, and you make yourself a little note to inquire on Monday about how it went," she says. "But you don't just ask questions, then turn off your listening skills. You actively listen and ask a question or two. Sure, it takes a few minutes, but it pays big dividends in the long run."

Singer also demonstrates a continuing concern with her employ-ees' professional development and career aspirations. "Corporate goals have to mesh with my employees' goals, not the other way around," she believes. "Because if you can't meet individuals' ca-reer aspirations, they'll find someone else who will."

In fact, Singer encourages her staff to come to her first when-ever they are interviewing for, or considering, another position. "I don't want them to feel they need to go behind my back, because that undermines morale," she says. "Besides, if I know what their career aspirations are—and the employee is a valuable one—I try to find ways to meet those aspirations, whether it's through offer-ing additional training, more responsibilities, or moving people around—whatever it takes—rather than to lose him or her to someone else."

When listening in her office, Singer makes certain that her body language is inviting. "You don't look at your watch or the clock, and you don't shuffle papers," she says. "It's amazing how quickly you can turn an employee off by looking over at a pile of papers or not keeping eye contact with the individual." Singer admits that sometimes it can be difficult to resist eyeing that "to do" stack. "But I really believe that my employees are more important than those papers," she says.

In fact Singer makes it a point, when listening, to shift every-thing that is in the middle of her desk to the side—and if that's not possible, or the discussion is more personal in nature, she moves to the same side of her desk as the employee, or to a conference table or the conference room adjoining her office. "A desk can be intimidating to a lot of people," she believes. "So anything I can do to be on equal ground helps."

Singer is equally considerate of subordinates when they drop by her office and ask if she has a few minutes to spare. If she doesn't, she'll say so, but asks them to come back later on. Then she'll name a specific time and treat that just as importantly as she would a customer or any other appointment.

In fact, when Singer's secretary tells her that an employee needs to see her, she prefers going to their office, "over the intimidation of calling someone to my office. I like to meet them either on a neutral basis, or at least a nonintimidating one. And when we get finished, to make sure that subordinates and I are on the same wavelength, I'll often ask them to recap what we've talked about and what our goals are."

Singer encourages her subordinates to come to her with problems, but she prefers to listen, then have them come up with their *own* solutions. "Sometimes you have to coach people," she says. "So I might say, 'That's an interesting problem that you've presented. What kind of suggestions do you have? If you were in my chair, how would you handle it?' " Then she might suggest that they reconvene the following morning, and adds, "In the meantime, I'll do some thinking, you do some thinking, and let's see if we can't put our heads together and come up with a good solution."

Sometimes, though, people really can't come up with a solution, Singer acknowledges. In which case she might say, "Well, I can think of one thing that we might be able to do." Then she'll encourage the person to think through the various ramifications of solutions by asking questions like, "Well, how do you think so-and-so will react to this? How do you think that will impact productivity? or Do you think we would be able to serve our customers better if we did these things?" But Singer says that she tries never to give orders.

Not to say that Singer lacks a tough side. "I set high and exacting standards, and I expect people to perform," she admits. "My people know that when there's a deadline, it's a deadline. They also know that goals that are set are going to be very aggressive, and that we are *all* going to be stretched to reach them."

If employees don't perform to her standards, Singer says she will go to a certain point in trying to work with them in establishing new goals that play to their strengths and offset their weaknesses.

"But they had better be willing to pay the price for that—which may be lower pay or a lower level job," she says. "And if they choose not to work with the system to make it work, then they're gone. I'm not a callous person when it comes to firing, but if I've given them all kinds of good chances, I see no choice."

Another way subordinates can land on Singer's tough side is to withhold the truth from her about a problem, or try to cover up a mistake. "I stress to my people, 'Don't lie to me. Tell me the whole story, and don't try to cover up something that has happened. Because if that happens, you're going to hear about it . . . in private,' " says Singer, whose philosophy is "praise in public; chastise in private."

But Singer also firmly believes in empowering her employees. "If they make a decision using the best information they had at the time—right or wrong, I will stand behind them 100 percent," she insists. "If it was a bad decision, we may have a discussion in private about what I think they could have done differently. But I will stand behind their decision. I don't run this bank. I create visions and strategic plans for the bank. But more important than anything else, I create the environment in which everyone else can run the bank."

Indeed, considering how accessible and visible Singer makes it a point to be, coupled with her willingness to listen, it's no wonder that the business she oversees has been so successful. Since Singer's arrival twelve years ago, assets at the bank have quadrupled, making First of America the eighteenth-largest of 339 banks in the Chicago area.

And so it appears that Singer's philosophy of "banking on people" has truly paid dividends.

• • •

Technology and a global economy have caused dizzying changes in corporate America over the last decade. Cutbacks, takeovers, and downsizing are rampant, leaving most corporations leaner than ever, with everyone expected to do too much in too little time and with too few resources. Indeed, life on the fast track can quickly lead to burnout, and most likely you know the symptoms: tension, exhaustion, irritability.

The problem is, women don't like to admit they can't do it all. Yet, playing the martyr can be disastrous to your career.

Realizing success on your own terms requires working smarter, not harder. And to do that, you need to sharpen your listening skills, learn to manage your time effectively, and find ways to prevent stress from managing *you*. Here's how:

The Many Benefits of Good Listening

Listening, *really* listening to your subordinates not only makes *them* feel important, it's also a wise investment of time on your part. As Terry Paulson points out in *They Shoot Managers, Don't They?*: "We waste time and money on ill-conceived endeavors that might never get off the drawing board if we encouraged and listened to valid criticism." Not to mention, if you listen, up front, it keeps small problems from escalating into large ones that can demand more of your time.

Moreover, managers who listen well are viewed as far more approachable than those who turn a deaf ear to employees' concerns and ideas. When you're approachable, employees feel safer and more comfortable saying exactly what's on their minds. This, in turn, helps *you* find ways to make changes that can improve both the working environment and your organization as a whole.

Management at Levi Strauss & Co.'s Murphy, North Carolina, plant, for example, launches each new year by setting objectives, then forming committees to make sure all objectives will be met. "We have a committee for everything—from housekeeping and alternative manufacturing to quality and morale—and we give every employee an opportunity to sign up for a committee," says plant manager Tommye Jo Daves. "We believe that if employees are involved in everything that is happening in the plant, our goals are more easily met, and they're more excited about meeting them. This is not a we/they environment. Everything we do here is a team effort, and I'm just a member of the team."

Good listening also enables managers to learn about organizational problems *before* they get out of hand and to get to the root of problems more quickly. And because it empowers employees, good listening also prompts managers to make better decisions—which can often translate into avoiding costly mistakes.

What Kind of Listener Are You?

Effective listening is both an art and a skill that can be mastered—and improved—with practice. What traits separate the unapproachable sharks as listeners from the more accessible dolphins? Here's a roundup of those traits to help you determine the kind of listener *you* may be perceived as by your subordinates.

What Kind of Listener Are You?

Sharks as Listeners	Negative Messages They Send	Dolphins As Listeners	Positive Messages They Send
Poker face; staring at speaker	*I'm bored. Are you almost finished?*	Expressive face; occasionally smiling/nodding	*I'm interested in what you are saying.*
Gazing out a window; glancing at watch; scanning papers on desk	*Can we make this quick?*	Looking speaker in the eye	*You have my full attention.*
Sighing; tapping foot; drumming fingers	*You're wasting my time.*	Murmuring words of encouragement	*I'm attuned to what you are saying.*
Finishing people's sentences; making assumptions	*I know more than you do.*	Paraphrasing speaker's words ("So you think . . .")	*It's important that I comprehend what you're saying.*
Asking pointed yes or no questions/no questions	*Say what?*	Asking pertinent, open-ended questions	*Go ahead. Take all the time you need.*

Leaning back; arms folded tightly	*So, what's so important?*	Leaning forward slightly; loose arms	*I'm open to what you're saying; keep talking.*
Taking excessive notes	*I want to remember everything in case I need to use it against you later.*	Taking notes sparingly	*This conversation is important to me. I want to remember the highlights.*
Pretending to understand when you don't	*Let's just wrap this up as quickly as possible.*	Ending the conversation by summarizing its main points	*Let me be sure I understand where you're coming from.*
Judging/focusing on delivery	*I don't care for (your Southern accent), so I'm tuning you out.*	Judging/focusing on content	*I don't care for (your Southern accent), but I do care about what you have to say.*
Allowing distractions to compete for your attention	*You're not important enough to merit my full attention.*	Ignoring/getting rid of distractions	*I only have ears for you.*
Interrupting to disagree	*You don't know what you're talking about.*	Holding your fire	*I don't agree with you, but I'm willing to hear you out.*
Preparing what you'll say next	*Your opinion doesn't matter to me.*	Giving the speaker your complete attention	*I respect you and your opinions.*
Reacting emotionally	*I don't have to listen to this.*	Focusing on remaining open-minded.	*I want to understand.*
Jumping in to fill conversational gaps	*Come on—let's keep this conversation moving. I don't have all day.*	Using silence to gather thoughts and encourage speaker to keep talking	*Let me think for a minute . . . no hurry.*
Rushing in to correct the speaker or arguing when you disagree	*I don't want to listen to you, because I don't agree with you.*	Keeping thoughts to self until speaker finishes, then calmly stating your views	*I want to find out what is bothering you before I present my point of view.*

No Rest for the Weary

The CFO needs your division's figures for the yearly status report by week's end. Your staff needs instructions before launching a new project. A colleague needs your expertise to land a valuable client. Your appointment book is crammed so tightly that you can barely decipher it, and your phone messages are piling up. You don't know *where* to turn first.

Sound familiar? Women are constantly playing "beat the clock." And burning the candle at both ends. After a long day at the office, many of us work a second shift managing our homes and families. In fact, in her book *The Overworked American: The Unexpected Decline of Leisure*, Harvard economics professor Juliet B. Schor reports that employed women who are also mothers *average* more than eighty hours a week in housework, child care, and on the job. No wonder we feel frazzled!

Although male and female managers are affected by common stressors, women must often deal with a unique set—discrimination, gender stereotyping, and social isolation to name a few.

"Women in a male corporate environment are like strangers in a strange land," says psychologist Susan Schenkel, author of *Giving Away Success*. "They can punt through a lot of things, but subtleties go over their heads, just as they would in a foreign culture. There's great potential for misunderstanding and miscommunication. They have the stress that comes from being an outsider."

Women must also be able to juggle the conflicting demands of family and work life. "Being a mom to my three small children is very important to me," says Karyn Marasco, who often wears many hats in one day: General Manager of the Westin William Penn, baseball team mom, homework coach, cook, *and* housekeeper. "Business travel is a big concern, too," she adds, "and I often feel torn between leaving the children and taking advantage of the opportunity to learn and grow at conferences with my peers and superiors."

Another problem unique to female managers is the incessant need to prove ourselves. And what often happens is that we wear ourselves out striving to reach some unrealistic expectations—usually self-imposed. "It's easy to end up in perpetual motion because as women, we are trying to both catch up and keep up with men," acknowledges Maria Arapakis in *Softpower!* "If we're not careful, our newly found ambitions can land us in the same rat race men have been complaining about for years."

Some women are reluctant to admit they can't do it all and refuse to ask for help—even when overwhelmed. Doing so, they fear, may reveal incompetence. But in reality, *not* getting help shows your superiors that you can't handle your job. Many women also have a tough time saying no on the job. As a result, others take advantage of them. And oftentimes women realize this is occurring, yet they are so conscientious they cannot bring themselves to say no.

"Frequently people expect female managers will nurture them," adds Claire Coyle of SmithKline Beecham. "I do a bit of nurturing if there's a specific manageable need, but I try to keep it to a minimum because it's so time-consuming. I can't be a caretaker for fifty-eight people. I'd go mad. So I keep a business focus and encourage people to be more independent and to make decisions on their own."

Time is a precious commodity, yet the higher up the corporate ladder you climb, the less you seem to have of it. How can you keep time from managing *you*? The trick, according to managers we interviewed, is to find ways to get *more* done in *less* time. And this, they add, involves being tough on time but caring with yourself and others.

Beware: The Time Bandits

Paperwork. Visitors and appointments. Telephone calls. These are a manager's biggest time-gobblers. In a survey of stressful events for managers, ranking at or near the top were these three time crunchers: managing time on the job, demands on time, and interruptions. In fact, studies indicate that the average manager is interrupted *every eight minutes*! But there are ways to handle paperwork, telephone calls, visitors, and appointments quickly and efficiently.

• **Paperwork.** A desk cluttered with papers not only can be distracting, it can overwhelm you to the point of procrastination. Working on a cluttered desk also wastes time. In fact, the average executive wastes forty-five minutes each day searching for something lost on a desk, according to *Executive Female* magazine.

How to tame your desk? As a rule of thumb, try to avoid handling a piece of paper more than once. According to Merrill E. Douglass and Donna N. Douglass, co-authors of *Manage Your Time, Your Work, Yourself,* many managers waste time by repeating work already done. "Many executives read a letter, think about how they'll respond to it, then set it aside until they have more time," the authors say. "Then once they get back to it, they must reread it and rethink their response."

Reshuffling paperwork leads to frustration and clutter. So if it's quick (requires a signature, scribbling a note on the bottom, or making a short telephone call), handle it immediately. But if you're working on something else, and a response requires looking up some data, writing a memo, or calling a meeting, file it in your appropriate "to do" pile for the moment. But first jot down your thoughts in the margins or on a Post-it so that you don't have to start from square one later on.

Grace Pastiak of Tellabs admits that she is extremely organized by nature and, at the age of seven actually wished for a four-drawer filing cabinet as a birthday gift. So it should come as no surprise to learn that she rarely handles paperwork more than once. "One of my bosses along the way once told me that the more you touch a piece of paper, the more it costs the company," she says. "So my philosophy is, if you can get rid of it the first time you touch it, the less it costs the company. And being a responsible manager, that's one of my directives—to be as inexpensive to the company as possible."

• **Telephone calls.** The very instrument that was supposed to be the greatest time-saver in our history has turned into the biggest time-waster. The telephone causes more interruption and generates more stress than anything else in our business environment. Yet there are advantages to communicating by telephone. The trick is to take control and make the telephone work *for* you. How?

First, plan each call just as you would a face-to-face meeting. Draft an agenda. Set objectives. Outline what you want to say. Determine the best time to make the call. And be prepared to answer any questions the caller may have by anticipating questions and gathering all relevant information (files, records) you may need *before* you make the call.

Avoid playing telephone Ping-Pong. Studies indicate that the average businessperson wastes five to seven hours a week playing telephone tag. You can avoid this by scheduling a specific time for callbacks.

Also, know how to hang up on long-winded conversationalists. Many women have been socially conditioned to believe that it is the *caller's* responsibility to end a conversation. But the rules of propriety have changed. No longer must you waste time feeling frustrated because you can't get a caller to hang up. It's perfectly acceptable for *you* to take the initiative.

How? Start speaking in the past tense ("I've *enjoyed* talking to you" or "I'm glad you *called*"). Discuss any action you plan to take ("Let me look into this and get back to you first thing tomorrow"). Summarize any action taken ("I think we've covered everything"). Show appreciation ("Thank you for calling"). Or demonstrate respect for their time ("I know you're busy, so I'll let you go").

• **Visitors and appointments.** On one hand, you want to be accessible to your subordinates. After all, if they are forced to wait around for your input or decisions, not being there for them wastes valuable time. On the flip side though, you don't want people constantly dropping by your office—because then you'll never get *your* work done. "Being accessible has its benefits—strengthens morale and loyalty, keeps up the flow of information between bosses and employees, and enables managers to know about employees' strengths and weaknesses," acknowledges Aileen Jacobson in her book *Women in Charge.* "But there are also costs, particularly if a manager is too accessible. She may not have enough time to plan for the future or to get other tasks done.

This may impede her rise upward because she is overloaded with work and has no time to be creative or to get to know superiors or colleagues. It may also discourage independence in employees."

The trick to keeping interruptions to a minimum is to maintain a balance between the amount of time you spend with your staff and the time you spend tackling your own work. Many managers we interviewed have achieved such a balance by setting aside certain times of the day when employees can feel free to stop by with questions, comments, or just to talk. Others we spoke with achieved the same objectives but used a more formal and structured approach. They set specific office hours and had subordinates sign up for appointments.

In *They Shoot Managers Don't They?*, Terry Paulson tells the story of a manager who used humor to let his subordinates know whether or not he was available to talk. Hanging an antique traffic light in front of his office, "Red meant, 'Unless blood is involved, don't interrupt, or it may be yours.' Yellow meant, 'Caution, use your judgment,' and Green meant, 'I'm open. It's a good time to talk.' He was on green 45 percent of the day, and people appreciated it," Paulson reports. "They never had to guess when it was the right time to approach him."

Several managers we spoke to encouraged their subordinates to use voice mail and E-mail over face-to-face visits when appropriate. Another alternative, suggests Carol Deutsch, President of Communication Seminars in Asheville, North Carolina, is to walk around more. "What this does is condition your employees to talk to you at *their* work sites. It also gives you more control and enables you to call the shots when it comes to ending a meeting with a subordinate," she says.

Stressed for Success?

Rapid advances in technology, coupled with furious restructuring and cutbacks, have caused dizzying changes in corporate America, making life at the office pressure-packed. With companies leaner than ever, managers have more to do in less time and with fewer resources. Throw home responsibilities into the equation, and female managers emerge as perfect candidates for burnout.

A recent large-scale study conducted by the Northwestern Mutual Life Insurance Company in Minneapolis reveals that almost half of American workers feel their jobs are "very stressful" overall. Half also stated that job stress reduces their productivity, and two thirds reported experiencing stress-related physical or mental conditions. Not surprisingly, the study also revealed that women experience more stress than men do on the job. Moreover, according to the study women are more likely to burn out on the job, think about quitting, and experience frequent stress-related illnesses such as headaches and depression.

The problem is, far too many women are hell-bent on being Superwoman at home and Wonder Woman at the office. They mistakenly believe that the more they work, the more they will accomplish and the more efficient they will be. In fact, the reverse is true. "When you're tired, mistakes soar," reports Barbara Mackoff in *The Art of Self-Renewal: Balancing Pressure and Productivity On and Off the Job.* "Lab experiments demonstrate that working too long on complex tasks increases response time by up to 500, percent meaning it takes five times longer to resolve a problem with an exhausted mind."

All Work and No Play

A recent Harris poll indicates that within the last two decades the number of hours the average American worked in a year increased by a whopping 138. Within the same time frame, free time has fallen nearly 40 percent. According to Juliet Schor in *The Overworked American*, women are feeling the time squeeze most of all. Comparing annual hours of paid employment in all industries and occupations over the past twenty years, Schor estimates that "men are working nearly a hundred more hours per year—or an extra two-and-a-half weeks, while women are putting in about 300 additional hours—which translates into an extra seven-and-a-half weeks."

With so much work to do and so little time to do it in, it's difficult—particularly for women—to feel entitled to a little R & R. In fact, when faced with a stretch of free time and nothing pressing to do, instead of relaxing we are consumed with guilt. Our minds churn out the "shoulds" (I *should* be working on that project due next week) and "what ifs" (*What if* I go away to that conference, and my husband or children need me?). And usually when we feel guilty, what we're really saying is, "I don't deserve to enjoy myself."

John Datillo, Ph.D., associate professor in the Department of Recreation and Leisure Studies at the University of Georgia and author of *Leisure Education Program Planning*, acknowledges that many women simply don't feel entitled to R & R. "The concept of free time is elusive to women because, unlike men, there's never been a clear delineation between work and home," he adds. "And while some of today's men are pitching in at home, for most, free time is whatever's left once work is over. For women, however, there's plenty more to do after work. And because they often have more responsibilities, many women rarely have the blocks of free time men enjoy."

Of course, women have also been socially conditioned to be caretakers. Consequently, many of us nurture our bosses, our subordinates, our colleagues, our husbands, and our children, but rarely do we nurture ourselves. "Women feel guilty if they address their own needs, but they're on call for everybody else 24 hours a day," acknowledges Marjorie Shaevitz, author of *The Superwoman Syndrome*.

For many women, career status is the yardstick we use to measure our individual worth. On the job we feel confident, worthwhile, stimulated, and appreciated. And this is healthy—so long as work remains only *one* component of our lives. The problem is, sometimes our identities become so closely tied to our jobs that, when idle, we feel miserable—even lost. So we work until we drop—going in early, staying late, and bringing work home with us to sustain the feeling that we're in control.

Working—both on the job and at home—can also make us feel indispensable, which, in turn, boosts our self-esteem. "While women in this situation often bemoan the pressure, the fact is, they are reluctant to let it go because being indispensable reassures them they are valued and needed," notes Diane Fassel, Ph.D., in her book *Working Ourselves to Death: The High Cost of Workaholism and the Rewards of Recovery.* Yet, this all-work-and-no-play mind-set can quickly lead to burnout.

Stress Can Be Good for You

Stress is a paradox. Properly managed, it can energize and motivate you, as well as jump-start your sense of creativity. Because it gets your adrenaline pumping, it can help you accomplish more than you thought possible. Carole Kitchens of Hoechst Celanese knows the feeling. "I recently had to give a major presentation on global strategy to the highest echelons of the corporation. My stomach was tied in knots, and I was terrified. Everyone on my support staff was working at full speed. Then, once I gave the presentation, and it went well, that was such a high. This was exciting stress, and it was exhilarating. My staff and I were all pumped up and feeling energized, and we were united in a common effort. Plus," she laughs, "I lost three to four pounds—an added benefit."

When it's short-term—and you survive it—stress can also boost your reputation and your self-esteem. It can toughen you and help you develop new skills as well. Even when it's unpleasant, stress can motivate you to stop and analyze what went wrong, plus challenge you to think of ways to bypass similar situations in the future.

But unless you learn how to keep stress to a minimum and find ways to manage it successfully, you'll find yourself in a no-win situation. A life characterized by frantic schedules, overcommitments, and grueling hours can quickly lead to chronic exhaustion and lower your resistance to illness and disease. Moreover, too much stress can make you irritable, cynical, and ineffective as a manager. "It can also be addictive," adds Kitchens, "and if you don't learn to break away from it—if you insist on trying to do it all—you'll end up a workaholic."

Putting the Brakes On

How can you keep stress from becoming an occupational hazard? Here are some "tricks of the trade" the managers we interviewed suggest:

• **Don't get buried in commitments.** Some women have a habit of taking on more than they can handle. Typically, we do this to be nice or to prove ourselves. Fact is, women cannot be *all* things to *all* people without paying a price. So cut yourself some slack and learn how to say no. "Of all the time-saving techniques ever developed, perhaps the most effective is frequent use of the word *no*," believes Edwin Bliss, author of *Getting Things Done: The ABCs of Time Management*. "Learn to decline tactfully, but firmly, every request that does not contribute to your goals," he advises. "Remember, many people who worry about offending others wind up living according to other people's priorities."

The same holds true for commitments outside the office. If you don't have time to take on something—or don't want to—just say no. And as a rule of thumb, before adding a new commitment or activity, subtract an old one. "I'm ruthless with my free time," says Claire Coyle of SmithKline Beecham. "I don't spend my personal time with people I don't care for or in places I don't like to be."

• **Love what you're doing.** Tellabs's Grace Pastiak has a husband, a nineteenth-month-old, a four-year-old, and a five-year old. She is also in the process of building a house. "I have a tendency to take on more and more projects," she admits. "But I take things minute by minute. I think that it's important no matter what you do, to love what you're doing," she adds. "And if you don't, get out."

• **If you have children, maintain a balance.** Many of the managers we spoke with are also mothers, and many also insist that having children not only makes them better time managers, but that having youngsters to care for keeps them sane. Cynthia Danaher of Hewlett-Packard is a good example. "People often say to me, 'I don't understand how you can do this job with three children.' And my response is always, 'I don't know how anyone could do this job *without* three children, because you could drive yourself crazy. You *need* that balance.' "

• **If overwhelmed, consider adjusting your working hours.** When Bridget Shirley, an industrial engineer and Project Manager at Johnson Wax, decided that she wanted to have a second child, she intentionally took on a special assignment. "My goal was to work full-time on that project for a year or so, then turn it into a part-time position once I got pregnant," she says. "That way, when I went on maternity leave, it wouldn't jeopardize my standings." After giving birth, Shirley opted for the maximum (five months) maternity leave Johnson Wax allows and enjoyed every moment of it. "You can do it all, and if people choose that option, I think that's fine," she says. "But to me, it was too much of a strain."

And in the fall of 1993, Laura Meier and Loriann Meagher successfully lobbied Xerox to let them share a sales-management slot—a first for Xerox at this level of the corporation. Both Meier and Meagher were mothers of young children unwilling to give up either the challenge of working or the joys of spending quality time with their youngsters. Today the former rivals operate as a team and rank among the top, nationally, in sales. The pair say they have also discovered unexpected advantages from their partnership. "We've each doubled our connections and problem-solving resources within Xerox," they report. "And while we used to go home and talk to our husbands when we had something pressing on our minds, now we have someone to talk to who really understands and who we can bounce ideas around with."

• **Pinpoint your biggest time-wasters and find alternative solutions to help you work more quickly and more efficiently.** Is your desk always cluttered? Are you too accessible to subordinates and colleagues? Are you a perfectionist? When overwhelmed, do you tend to procrastinate? Do you jump from project to project? Are you indecisive? Are you reluctant to delegate? "I struggle with perfectionism," says Johnna Howell of Westin Hotels and Resorts. "I work long hours to achieve the best product that I believe I can personally develop. The only time this is a problem is when it affects other aspects of my life such as relationships with my family or staff. At that point, I adjust my priorities, remind myself that *people* are more important than *things*, and get my life back in balance."

• **Set realistic objectives.** Make daily and weekly "to do" lists, estimating the amount of time you figure it will take you to accomplish each goal. That way, if you consistently miss the mark, you will learn to adjust your timetable accordingly. In *The Superwoman Syndrome*, Shaevitz advises also making a "not-to-do" list. "Include tasks that can be delegated, things done just to please others, and jobs whose completion is of very little consequence. What would happen if someone else did the job or if it wasn't done? If the answer is 'nothing,' cross it off."

Divide remaining tasks on your list into "must do" and "would like to do," and attempt to cluster similar tasks together. This saves time and helps you keep the momentum going from project to project. Next, set priorities, and handle tasks in order of importance, but be flexible. Sometimes priorities must be flip-flopped according to the workload.

• **Go to the office early or stay late.** Hanne Dittler, Vice President of Technical Services at Westin Hotels and Resorts, says she accomplishes a great deal of work by going to the office early in the morning before the phones start ringing.

• **Build a social support system.** When swamped with responsibilities both at work and at home, social activities are frequently the first to go. Yet friends can be great supporters in times of stress—even if all you do with them is commiserate.

When Rosa Gatti, now a senior vice president of ESPN, first started her career at Loyola University, she found the transition into the male sports world to be a tough one. "Being the only female, I didn't have anyone to turn to for advice," she says. "For instance, when I traveled with men's teams, there were no other women to ask, 'What are you going to wear? Should I sit in the front of the bus or in the back?' or 'How should I handle an inappropriate comment?' " Gatti says that it was her friends and family who helped her get through those trying times. "They couldn't share my experiences directly, but they listened and lent their support to what I was doing. There is no doubt that my success has been largely due to the support provided by my family and friends."

In time, more women entered Gatti's domain, providing her with an opportunity to share and compare experiences as well as comradeship. "I often tell other women, 'Look, we need to help one another,' " she says. "When I got into the business, I often heard people say that women don't help other women. But I decided early on that that would not be the case with me. I am determined to help other women. It's key. We've got to support one another. No woman is an island."

• **Cultivate interests outside your job.** Doing this not only enriches your life, it offers you something to look forward to and provides you with energy to better cope with on-the-job stressors. "There are more sources of self-esteem and fulfillment open to managers who lead a well-rounded lifestyle," claims Joan Kofodimos, author of *Balancing Act: How Managers Can Integrate Successful Careers and Fulfilling Personal Lives.* "In addition a person who is attuned to his or her deepest personal aspirations, values, and purpose is more likely to make choices that fit those that satisfy external pressures. And he or she is likely to have a broader repertoire of leadership behaviors which are in short supply in today's organizations—such as concern with coworkers' needs, a desire to collaborate, and the ability to relinquish control."

Helen Pastorino of Alain Pinel Realtors and her husband live on a ranch in Los Gatos with thirty Andalusian horses, four llamas, four goats, three potbellied pigs, six turkeys, four peacocks, four dogs, and a handful of cats. Pastorino says she begins and ends each day with her menagerie. "My animals help ground me to nature, to reality," she explains. "I learn by observing them. They don't have a spoken language, and they don't have hidden agendas. They just live."

Tellabs's Grace Pastiak, who likes a lot of variety in her life, dabbles in calligraphy and cartooning. She also recently coordinated a show for seventy-five sculptures from around the world. "I once read that we only use 10 percent of our brains, so my goal in life has been to use 11 percent," she quips.

And Karen Himle of the St. Paul Companies is a well-known personality *outside* her office, having hosted a weekly local public television interview program in the Twin Cities. She also often serves as a moderator on public television discussion programs. "I'm involved with a hospital board and the YMCA board in Minneapolis," she adds. "But I try not to take on too much. Part of it is a corporate responsibility now that I am in this position. But I would do it, regardless, because I think you need that kind of balance. If all you have is work, work, or work, and then you run home, I think you're missing some opportunities. Besides, I've probably learned as much in my nonprofit work that I've been able to apply on the job, as much as I've been able to offer the boards I serve on. So it really is a two-way street."

In fact, as Phyllis Moen, associate professor of human development and family studies at Cornell University, has learned from her studies of women and employment over the life cycle, women who complement their careers with volunteer work enjoy better physical and mental health. "The notion that you have some control over what you do, when you do it, and how much you do is beneficial to overall health and well-being," she notes in an interview with *Working Woman* magazine. But Moen cautions women *not* to turn volunteer work into yet another obligation, as this defeats the purpose.

• **Take advantage of high-tech "toys."** Karen Walker of Compaq has a laptop computer that keeps her from putting in twelve-hour days at the office. "With my laptop, I can put in a fairly normal workday, then tackle an hour's worth of work at night or on weekends from my home."

Adds Kodak's Candy Obourn, "I can remember when I was a

staff assistant to the CEO coming in at 4:00 A.M. so I could get my work done and still have time for the family." Now Obourn has a second office—at home—which she has equipped with a fax machine and computer so she can bring work home with her and still have family time. Obourn also has a car telephone, and frequently uses travel time to return calls.

Work smarter, not harder, and you may likely discover that you are a far more effective manager. Carol Orsborne, author of *How Would Confucius Ask for a Raise? Exploring Spiritual Values in the Business World,* recalls the days when she and her husband both worked seventy-hour weeks in their jointly owned San Francisco public relations firm. "Then we decided to work to live, not live to work," she recalls. After mutually deciding they could get by on a lower income, the couple opted to cut back their work schedule to thirty hours a week. Then a funny thing happened: Profits soared. "I think we worked so hard because we thought we had to," Orsborne says. "Many of the things we believed we had to do turned out to not be necessary at all."

These days, the Orsbornes live and work in Nashville, Tennessee, and continue to limit their working hours so as to have the luxury of spending more time with each other and their children. Carol is also the founder of Overachievers Anonymous (originally called Superwoman's Anonymous, but changed when so many men asked to join) and frequently lectures on how to replace destructive patterns of ambition driven by fear and insecurity with success guided by spiritual principles and fueled by inspiration.

Above all, keep in mind these words of wisdom from Lily Tomlin, who once said, "The trouble with the rat race is that even if you win, you're still a rat."

CHAPTER THIRTEEN

Climbing the Corporate Ladder: Getting Noticed and Promoted

PROFILE

KRYS KELLER
DIRECTOR, AFFILIATE RELATIONS
ABC TELEVISION NETWORK
NEW YORK, NEW YORK

"Women are still outnumbered, and men are still calling the shots. And because we are playing their game on their field, you won't ever get them to see your point of view without finding some common ground. Once you're accepted, however, there's more of a willingness to listen to you on other issues."

If you want something, you've got to ask for it." Growing up, you probably heard this from your mother more times than you care to remember. But by heeding this advice, Krys Keller, Director of Affiliate Relations at ABC Television Network, has managed to significantly increase her visibility.

Four years ago, shortly after assuming her position at the network, Keller decided that she wanted to join the New York City Chapter of American Women in Radio and Television (AWRT), a women's professional group. "But I wanted to do it only if I had the support of ABC—both financially and in terms of resources," she says. So Keller approached her boss, who was familiar with the organization, and her request was soon granted. "As it turns out, I was the first person on the staff who had ever asked for corporate support for professional membership."

Keller now believes that her request not only sent a signal that she was willing to commit her time to enhance ABC's visibility *outside* the corporation, but that it set off a domino effect of opportunities to become more involved *inside* the corporation as well. "Soon after I joined AWRT, I was asked to serve on the Capital Cities/ABC Women's Advisory Committee," she recalls. "This twelve-member committee is made up of women who represent various aspects of the company's corporate structure, including its radio stations, magazines, newspapers, and the network itself. The committee wanted someone from AWRT to serve, so the timing worked out well for me."

In 1992, Keller was also tapped to participate in Capital Cities' pilot mentoring program, designed to expose women in middle management to high-level company executives with whom most would not ordinarily have contact. "Being selected for the first 'class' of this program was a tremendous honor," Keller says.

Keller's mentor encouraged her to apply for a position she never would have otherwise considered. "They wound up hiring someone much more senior than me, but considered me because of my mentor's recommendation. And again, during the interview process, I met another senior executive who is now supportive of my efforts."

Keller's knack for striking up comfortable conversations with male colleagues is considered an asset. Her secret weapon? "Sports," she says. "I'm fortunate. I have a son who plays college fooball. I understand the sport by osmosis, and this is helpful. Men may not work with me any differently because of it, but it provides a common interest."

When it comes to increasing visibility on the job, Keller believes that finding a way to ease the comfort level between men and women is critical in *any* organization. "It is something very simple and elementary. It can't be forced. But women are still outnumbered, and men are still calling the shots. And because we are playing *their* game on *their* field, you won't ever get them to see your point of view without finding some common ground. Once you're accepted, however, there's more of a willingness to listen to you on other issues."

Networking is yet another strategy Keller recommends. Describing herself as an "equal opportunity networker," Keller says, "I think it's to your advantage to get to know a broad range of people—men, women, young, old, junior level, senior level. It can be fascinating to find out what people are all about. The term 'networking' may be somewhat trite now, but I don't know what other word to use. It's important to guard against being short-sighted—against falling into a rut or being tunnel-visioned about dealing with only the people you need to get the job done. I firmly believe you can do your job better when you know more about life in general. And it certainly is broadening to learn about others and have insight into what they do."

Keller says she uses the same approach to networking with both men and women. "I can talk sports, politics—you name it," she says. "Of course, all of my supervisors have been men, so I've been thrust into a situation of 'sink or swim, pal.' But I also believe that for any female manager, if you can't schmooze with men, you can't do your job. So again, success falls back on the ability to establish that comfort level when talking to, and working with, men."

Image, too, is important for visibility, Keller believes. "In the television business, image is crucial. It's very important to develop presentation skills and to try and carry yourself in a manner that suggests you know what you're talking about—even though you may not all the time. But in the end, your image is only as good as what you can deliver—and that means doing the job and doing it very well."

Another key to increasing visibility is risk-taking. And the biggest risk she ever took was accepting her current position. In 1989, Keller was living comfortably in Dallas, working for the Coca-Cola Company. "I had every reason to believe that I would ride out my future there. I liked the corporation. I liked living in Dallas. I had tremendous benefits and great opportunities for long-term growth." Then Keller was offered the job at ABC in New York.

Initially, the opportunity overwhelmed her. It was a move to a city where she knew virtually no one and would live a lifestyle 180 degrees different from the one she had grown accustomed to in Dallas. "It was a big risk. But I knew that if I didn't do it, I would regret it forever."

In retrospect, Keller reports the move *was* difficult on a personal level. "I had to deal with the loneliness of a living in a big city." But professionally, the move was worth the effort. "Work was always the reward—a reminder that I did the right thing," she says. "And the fact that I was doing a good job and being recognized for it kept me going."

But Keller has never been one to rest on her laurels. "Things have gone well for me at ABC," she acknowledges, "but I have never lost sight of what I'm here for—and that is to be the best director of affiliate relations that this company has ever had."

• • •

What does it take to get noticed and promoted in corporate America, and are the requirements for promotion different for women than they are for men?

Who gets ahead and why have been the focus of a number of studies conducted in recent years. A team of researchers at the Center for Creative Leadership, for example, interviewed sixty-six managers (eighteen of whom were women) from three Fortune 500 companies who had recently been promoted. Also interviewed were their bosses, their bosses' bosses, and in many instances a human resource person involved in the promotion process. Their findings? Many factors influencing promotions may be out of your control, but there are still ways to boost your promotability: by stepping out of the pack, by positioning yourself to move up, by soliciting feedback from others on your strengths and weaknesses, by not feeling discouraged if you get passed over for a promotion, and by continuing to do the best job you can.

A study conducted by Rose Mary Wentling and reported in *Business Horizons* magazine turned up similar results. Following personal interviews with thirty women holding middle-level management positions in fifteen Fortune 500 companies located in the Midwest, Wentling found that the majority of those who moved up worked extremely hard, had mentors, displayed strong interpersonal/people skills, and demonstrated competency on the job, as well as a willingness to take risks.

Finally, a recent *Fortune* poll asked CEOs, "What should female executives be doing to get to the top?" Respondents' answers included: Develop a broad base of experience, excel at what you're charged with, and be more visible and assertive.

Combining advice derived from these polls and surveys, along with tips from managers featured in this book, we have compiled a list of strategies that should prove helpful in *your* efforts to get noticed—and promoted:

• **Know your company inside out.** What makes it tick? Who typically gets promoted? Who makes promotion decisions? Make it your business to understand *all* aspects of the company you work for. The more you know—about the business *and* the people running it—the better. Tellabs's Grace Pastiak, for example, believes that one good way to learn more about the company—and to simultaneously increase your visibility—is to help others. "Whenever someone has asked me for assistance, I've always tried to be of service. Just by helping others, you gain more visibility because you learn about other groups, and you learn more about the company."

• **Ask for feedback.** What are your strengths and weaknesses—not as *you* see them, but as viewed by your superiors? What expectations do your boss and your boss's boss have of you, and how can you best fulfill these expectations? Where do you fit into the big picture? Questions like these should always be asked during your performance evaluations, but don't wait. Ask for feedback continuously—after completion of every project, following a presentation, after leading a meeting. Women *assume* that promotions will be handled fairly, so they don't ask questions. Men *always* ask what they need to do to move up.

• **Help your boss meet his or her objectives.** Find out what your boss's objectives are, then look for ways to help him or her achieve them. "My boss likes to be kept well informed, so I make sure that I keep him in the loop or up-to-date on projects/assignments in which I'm involved," says Laura Martin of Westin Hotels and Resorts. "In return, I've found that this works well to ensure that he is supportive of decisions I'm making along the way. It also helps in building his trust, so that he tends to delegate more decision-making authority to me."

• **Let others know that you're eager to broaden your responsibilities.** When it comes to speaking up—and particularly telling others what we want—women tend to be timid. But according to Toni Bernay, co-author of *Women in Power*, "Timidity does us in more than aggression, because we become invisible."

One of the best ways for women to gain visibility and to move up the corporate ladder, according to Kathleen Williams of Atlantic Gelatin, is to find a way to move from a staff to a line job. Williams, who made the leap herself in 1991, reports in an article she wrote for *Working Woman* magazine, "During performance reviews, which are held several times a years, I reinforced in my boss's mind that I was interested in new challenges. I also welcomed every opportunity to stand in for him at meetings and on business trips." If you're interested in broadening your responsibilities, Williams suggests, "Offer to do something extra that will get you beyond the sphere of your daily duties and into areas that appeal to you. And at appropriate times (like a performance review), tell your supervisor that you'd like to take on more responsibilities and move within the company when the opportunity arises."

• **See a need and fill it.** Find ways to contribute to the company's bottom line. Look for weaknesses within your company, then develop plans to address them. Pay attention to what customers are demanding, and find a way to fill those needs. Initiate proposals that will help save the company money, or bring in new business. Suggest new approaches to problems. Become an expert in an area that's important to your company. Create a niche for yourself.

Tommye Jo Daves, for example, found an unusual way to demonstrate her management skills and increase her visibility. She set up a successful employee-training and adult education program when she was at Levi Strauss's Blue Ridge, Georgia, plant—a program that has since been replicated at all thirty-one Levi Strauss plants in the United States. Her idea also earned her the Daniel E. Koshland Award, the highest honor Levi Strauss bestows to an individual—"for outstanding leadership above and beyond the call of duty." "We felt that if we offered the opportunity, individuals (operators as well as supervisors and management) would take advantage of it to advance themselves," says Daves, who is now plant manager at the company's Murphy, North Carolina, plant.

• **Take on high-profile projects.** Volunteer to take responsibility for projects that will showcase your skills. Several of those promoted in the Center for Creative Leadership's study, for example, helped to implement quality programs or other organizational initiatives that exposed them to a large number of executives. "These responsibilities required them to network with, make presentations to, and participate in meetings with senior executives," the research team reports. "As a result, these people became known as capable, and it helped them to get mentioned at promotion time."

Volunteer for, or get assigned to special projects and task forces—even when they aren't high-profile—just to get your name and face known in the company. "I often volunteer to take on assignments that may not be technically or professionally challenging, but may increase the number of people with whom I have contact throughout the company and/or hotels," says Laura Martin of Westin Hotels.

• **Be in the right place at the right time.** When researchers at the Center for Creative Leadership asked the superiors of sixty-six recently promoted managers the reasons for promotion, many cited circumstances beyond an individual's accomplishments. For example, availability (an assignment had come to an end) and vacancies created by reorganization and retirements were often key factors in promotions. That's why it's critical for female managers to speak up and let their goals and ambitions be known—particularly when they have just completed a major long-term project, or when they notice an unanticipated vacancy in the company.

When Rosa Gatti graduated from Villanova University in 1972, she took a temporary job as a secretary in the Sports Information Office at the university. "I had studied languages, but had always been a sports fan," she says. "And this job enabled me to discover a career I never knew existed: sports public relations. I threw myself into it and learned everything I could." Two years later, Gatti's boss left in the middle of football season, and Gatti was the only other full-time person in the office. "They asked me to hold down the fort, to be acting director, while they decided what to do. So suddenly there was that window of opportunity." Today Gatti is Senior Vice President of Communications for ESPN.

• **Develop good people skills.** Establish positive working relationships with colleagues, subordinates, and superiors. An earlier study conducted by the Center for Creative Leadership compared female managers at or near the general management level of Fortune 100 sized corporations to male general managers from another study done at the center. In an effort to pinpoint various factors that contributed to success or derailment, researchers also interviewed twenty-five "savvy insiders" at ten of the same companies—sixteen men and six women responsible for identifying and selecting executives for top jobs. These insiders were asked to come up with an example of a woman they knew who had made it—as well as an example of one who had derailed—and to describe the qualities and characteristics that had helped or hurt these women. One success factor that stood out was "superior people skills."

"Several insiders commented on high morale in these women's groups," the researchers also report. "They were also particularly impressed when women earned the trust and respect of seasoned and/or male subordinates. One insider noted, 'She's very demanding, somewhat unforgiving, but she also looks after her people. They trust her.' "

"When I was named Acting Director of Sports Information at Villanova University, I suddenly found myself in an all-male environment, which tended to be very macho," says ESPN's Rosa Gatti. "I'm petite in size, and my nature was to be very feminine. In fact, I had studied ballet for years." Being constantly surrounded by men, however, caused Gatti to deal with some important issues. "Could I be feminine and still be taken seriously in the sports world?" she wondered. "Later, I went through a kind of identity crisis. Should I be wearing slacks instead of a skirt? Should I wear high heels? I wrestled with questions like that for a while, then realized that I had to be me. I couldn't worry about how people would judge me, and that was the most important lesson I learned: that I could be feminine *and* professional."

• **Do outstanding work.** "The big secret is to always deliver," believes Mylle Bell, Executive Vice President of Strategic Management at Holiday Inn Worldwide. "Do what you're supposed to do, and do it extraordinarily well. Look for that extra mile, and go for it willingly. This means not just meeting your budget, but exceeding it."

Rosa Gatti agrees. "After working at Villanova University for a few years, Brown University called and wanted to hire me. I had no intention of taking the job, but when I went to the interview, I was impressed. I also felt it would be a good growth experience to go someplace where I didn't know anyone, so I took the job," she says. During her four years at Brown, Gatti hosted national championships, served on several national sports committees, and was selected to serve as vice president of the national organization. "ESPN was covering one of the national championships we hosted in 1980," she recalls, "and that was during the network's first few months of operation." The ESPN producer covering the event went back to his president, who was looking for a public relations specialist, and recommended Gatti as a candidate. "It's the age-old story: If you do the job well, you get noticed."

Indeed, women who succeeded in the center's study had superstar track records. "These women always stood out in the assignments they took, through their technical competence, professionalism, ability to anticipate and head off problems, or leadership," the researchers report.

In fact, performing outstanding work virtually guarantees visibility. "I've seen people in my company say, 'Gee, what kind of visibility can I get if I take on this project?' " says Grace Pastiak. "But I don't think that way. I say to myself, 'Yeah, I think I can make that happen.' Then, I almost always find that the challenge of doing the job well provides me with more visibility than I need to go look for."

• **Project a professional image.** Thankfully, strict dress codes for businesswomen have all but vanished in corporate America, leaving women free to express their individuality—within limits. So find a style that works for you, yet implies substance and confidence. Your image should convey the message "I'm in control."

"Everything you do makes a statement as you are rising through the ranks," believes Jane Evans of U.S. West Communications. "The way you dress is particularly important, and I like to dress with flair, having come out of the fashion business. But that doesn't mean gaudy. In fact, I've always cautioned young women not to wear their cleavage to work. Part of me is the way I look, feel, talk, and act—all of that is bundled up in image. And I believe you should have a signature."

Dawn Steel agrees. "The most important thing is to feel great, whatever it takes. If you feel completely confident, you'll get attention," she told *Mirabella* magazine. "On the other hand, if you walk into a board room and everyone's staring at you because you're dressed in some unorthodox way, then they're not going to listen to you. And I, for one, don't want there ever to be any excuses about why they're not listening to me. Because the most important thing in terms of being in a man's world—where we all are—is that you don't want men to be uncomfortable, either."

• **Be determined to succeed.** Women in the Center for Creative Leadership study who succeeded possessed a passion for success.

"These women worked hard, seizing more responsibility, pushing and persisting until the job was done," the researchers note.

Ella Williams's story is a good example. Thirteen years ago, Williams had an idea for a business: an engineering support and computer services firm that would work exclusively with the defense industry. But her salary as a secretary for an oil refinery, which she supplemented by collecting aluminum cans, made starting this new venture a real gamble. In fact, about all she had going for her were a dozen years' worth of professional contacts made while working for Hughes Aircraft—and the determination to succeed.

Nevertheless, by taking a second mortgage on her home, this divorced mother of two managed to raise $65,000 and began pounding the pavement. Her first three years were rocky, primarily because few in the industry took her seriously. Instead of giving up, however, Williams, who had no training in marketing, came up with a unique strategy to hook clients. She began baking breads, cheesecakes, and muffins to leave behind when she visited clients. Soon, clients were calling her back for a second visit, and within a year she landed an $8 million contract to test and evaluate missile systems for the Department of Defense. Today, Aegir, Williams's Oxnard, California–based company, is a multimillion-dollar concern with clients including such industry giants as Lockheed and Northrop. Moreover in both 1989 and 1990, the U.S. Small Business Administration named Aegir its "Small Business Prime Contractor of the Year." And in 1993, Williams was named one of "The Nation's Ten Most Admired Women Managers" by *Working Woman* magazine.

• **Be yourself.** Williams believes that her personality is her strongest selling point. "I'm not afraid to be a woman," she says. "There is power in femininity, not in emulating men. I am very nurturing, but there's power in nurturing. That's our orientation as women, so why go against the grain?"

• **Strive for continuous self-improvement.** Successful managers do whatever it takes to assure that they have cutting-edge work skills. They also choose extracurricular activities that will not only sharpen their managerial skills but increase their visibility. Jane Evans, who has enjoyed high visibility throughout her stellar career—which has included serving as president of I. Miller Shoes at the age of twenty-five, as president of Butterick/Vogue at the age of thirty, as executive vice president of General Mills, and as president of the InterPacific Retail Group—says, "In whatever town I've lived in, I've served on the boards of major museums and theaters. I've also been active in the United Way. I do a lot of things in the community that give me a great deal of visibility and an opportunity to network, particularly with the male leaders of the community."

Borden's Karen Johnson is also active in her community. "I'm on the hospital board, where I try to lend my skills," she says. "What I find is that women who possess specific skills can apply them anywhere. If you're good at problem-solving or have good people skills, for example, go and apply them in a different arena. It's not only rewarding, it helps sharpen your skills at your full-time job."

• **Don't get too comfortable.** When Catalyst, a New York-based research and advisory group that tracks the progress of women in business, recently asked a group of senior managers, "What advice would you give to people who want to advance?" survey participants stated, "Most people stay in jobs long after they've quit learning. If you're on the road to a goal, you can't afford to be lazy." They also advise women eager to climb the corporate ladder to "leave a foundation job—one in which you develop critical skills—as soon as you've mastered the challenges. But remember that it's not always necessary to change organizations to find opportunities."

The point here is to avoid resting on your laurels. Instead, look for opportunities to stretch and grow. Several managers in the Center for Creative Leadership study, for example, were promoted because they had initiated new projects that were a bit beyond the scope of their jobs. Consequently, researchers at the center advise that if you feel you are stagnating in your current position, try reaching beyond your responsibilities to make contributions in other areas.

If there are no opportunities to shine inside the company, try looking outside. Teach a course. Run for political office. Become active in a professional organization. Get published in trade journals. Head up a community charitable solicitation.

• **Increase the comfort level between you and male superiors, colleagues, and subordinates.** "The women who make it to the very top first are going to be the ones with whom the men are most comfortable," says Laurel Cutler, a member of the board and the management committee of Foote, Cone & Belding Communications.

Shadco's Marsha Londe, whose largest customer hauls cars and trucks, agrees. "As part of this company's safety and incentive program, they wanted to provide monthly gifts to their truck drivers, and I was asked to suggest appropriate incentives. To do this, I realized how important it was to meet and talk with the truckers themselves. My goal was to find out what their needs and interests were so that I could suggest gifts that would best motivate them."

To meet with the drivers, Londe had to be at the terminals at the crack of dawn. "These were bright men," she says. "They also liked to tease and joke around. They wanted to show off and show me everything—which gave me an ideal opportunity to ask lots of questions." Londe sat in their rigs, drank coffee with them in their break rooms, and spoke to them in groups as well as one-on-one. "I asked for their opinions and listened to their jokes," she says. "I found out what they liked and didn't like. I also learned what kinds of gifts would have meaning for them."

The truckers, Londe discovered, had received lots of sweatshirts, but what they really needed was rain gear or hooded sweatshirts to wear while loading and unloading their rigs. "I learned that they would welcome a quality tool kit for their rigs— and not the cheaper standard kit they'd already been given," she adds. "I also found out that they wouldn't mind gifts they could take home to their wives. In fact, many, I discovered, would be happy with something as simple as 'his and her' key tags, so that they could keep one and give the other to their wives."

• **Don't be discouraged if you're passed over for a promotion.** "Our study showed that contextual reasons often drive promotions," the researchers at the Center for Creative Leadership say. "This means that if you've been passed over, it may be a reflection of someone else's situation, not your abilities." So sit tight, don't make a scene. Do, however, feel free to ask *why* you were not promoted. That way if it *is* due to a professional weakness, you can begin work on changing and improving yourself immediately.

• **Master your corporate culture.** Ignore the way things are in your company, and you'll achieve visibility for all the wrong reasons. "When I was first named vice chief of radiology, I started attending Medical Executive Committee meetings," says Dr. Kathleen McCarroll, Chief of Staff at Detroit Receiving Hospital. "Eager to participate, I would either come up with an idea, or there would be an agenda item, and I would put my hand up and start discussing it. But no one else would discuss it. In fact, no one else ever said *anything*. And whenever there was a motion on the floor, there would essentially be no discussion. Everyone would just put their hand up and vote. I couldn't figure it out."

Finally, McCarroll's boss gave her some advice: "Never surprise anyone at a meeting. Never bring up something that hasn't been discussed *before* the meeting. If you're going to make a motion or build on an agenda item, you must discuss it with all the other pertinent parties *before* the meeting."

"What I learned is that while it may be a sham democracy, this is the way a lot of boards work," McCarroll continues. "If you go to a meeting and make a motion during new business, ten-to-one, the motion gets tabled, because nobody's had time to jawbone it around outside of the public forum. But even worse, by speaking up before conferring with others, you show everyone that you're out of the loop . . . out of the power structure."

• **Take credit for your achievements.** Women often feel uncomfortable boasting about their accomplishments, but men don't hesitate to proclaim theirs. In her study of college students, for example, Cheryl Olson, Ph.D., a social psychologist at Allegheny College, found that when women were asked to *write* about their achievements, they matched the men in their readiness to take personal credit. But when they had to *describe* their accomplishments in a face-to-face job interview, they, unlike their male counterparts, minimized their abilities by attributing their success to outside factors such as luck or timing. "Women are taught that it's unattractive to be up-front about their accomplishments," writes Olson in an article for *Glamour* magazine. "But in the long run, this attitude can be damaging to your career. Someone who uses this strategy all the time stands a chance of being seen as less confident rather than humble. Moreover, research shows that employers award fewer promotions and attractive assignments to employees who are supposed to have succeeded through luck rather than ability."

Women also tend to wait to get noticed for their achievements— but it's not likely to happen. Make it a habit to keep track of how much money you save or bring into the company, of projects you take on and their successful results, and of problems you solve. Highlight these accomplishments at your performance reviews or when you're up for a raise or promotion. But don't wait until then to do so. Submit periodic progress reports to keep your superiors up-to-date on projects you're overseeing and to remind them of your contributions. Also send brief memos to your bosses when projects are completed.

• **Ask questions.** Cultivate good working relationships by asking others' advice when you have a problem. Most people will jump at the chance to offer their expertise and will feel flattered that you've asked for their input.

• **Take risks.** Thanks to social conditioning, women, as a rule, prefer playing it safe. In fact, when Paul Slovic, professor of psy-

chology at the University of Oregon, studied the risk-taking behavior of children between the ages of six and sixteen, he found
no difference between the youngest boys and girls. But by the
age of nine, boys took more risks than girls did. "This leads me
to believe that women may take fewer risks because our culture
doesn't encourage them to," says Slovic.

Jeanette Scollard, author of *Risk to Win: A Woman's Guide to
Success*, agrees. "The very word scares women. When I give a
lecture, I sometimes ask what risk means to my audience. Invariably, the men answer 'success' or 'opportunity,' but the women
say 'fear' or 'failure.'" Indeed, the word "risk"—which comes
from the Italian word "risco"—means unknown origin. And unfortunately, women frequently fear the unknown. "But every
woman in business today needs to take risks, because it means
you're moving, growing, changing," adds Scollard. "And things
do change—your company, the way it does business, the marketplace. If you don't take chances, if you bury your head, you'll be
obsolete and out the door. Today, it's inactivity that's the real
risk."

Marsha Londe of Shadco agrees. "Some years ago, I tried to
sell a national grocery store chain a nationwide calendar program.
I was new on the job and had been told I didn't have a chance in
hell of closing that deal, and that I was wasting my time and money
flying to the company's headquarters. My husband's attitude was,
'What's the worst thing that can happen?' I thought for a minute
and said, 'I'll lose the money I paid for the airline ticket.' And he
said, 'Right, but you're going to play with the big boys and see
what you can learn.' So I went for it . . . and got the order."

Adds Jane Evans, "You've got to try new things. That's the only
way you get noticed and accepted in a company." Within days of
being named President of I. Miller Shoes at the age of twenty-
five, Evans had received more than enough publicity—but for all
the wrong reasons. Having joined the company just out of college
as an assistant buyer, Evans had moved quickly up the ranks. But
she had barely gotten her feet wet when the company's chairman
of the board decided that since the company was largely in the
business of selling to women, that women should be in positions

of authority and responsibility. His choice for a new president was Evans, who says, "He threw me to the sharks. But at the time, I. Miller had already had something like eleven presidents in fourteen years. So I think they turned to me and said, 'How bad can she be?' "

That was in 1970, and Evans was one of few females running a company. "Consequently, I had the attention of the national press at the age of twenty-five—and only for that reason." Later, Evans received even more media attention—but for the right reasons—when she took a risk that paid off. "We did some marketing research, and every time we asked somebody about I. Miller shoes, you could be sure they were going to say, 'Oh, my mother used to wear your shoes.' So it was obvious that we had to do a tremendous job of repositioning ourselves. I took a rather bold step at that time of hiring a designer to come up with a package of shoes geared to younger customers. Soon after that, we opened a store called the Miller Eye and began to cater to that working woman who was just beginning to enter the workforce in droves. And we did it without a whole lot of research." When the risk paid off, it not only increased Evans's visibility, it caused a lot of talk in the industry about the revitalized I. Miller. Since then, Evans says she has never looked back.

Can Having a Mentor Make a Difference?

In a study of 106 businesswomen conducted by Joan Jeruchim and Pat Shapiro, co-authors of *Women, Mentors, and Success*, only 23 percent reported *not* having a mentor. And while those without mentors had achieved success on their own, most felt they would have climbed the corporate ladder faster had they had one.

Indeed. In a *Fortune* survey of CEOs, one third of the respondents said they believed that women's careers often stall out for lack of the informal advice and sponsorship that men typically get from one another. Countless other studies have also confirmed that women with mentors enjoy greater job success and satisfaction than those who do not have one.

The problem is, many women don't actively seek mentors. Instead, they *wait* to be chosen. Or, they often fall into mentoring relationships without fully understanding the concept and are not comfortable being coached.

Yet the benefits of having a mentor are legion. Mentors can provide sponsorship, feedback, expertise, and encouragement. They can boost your self-esteem, show you the ropes, and increase your visibility by ensuring that you get credit for good work. They offer acceptance and often have the power to open doors that might otherwise be closed to you. "Mentoring is especially helpful for women because women typically define themselves through relationships, and these relationships give them strength," note Jeruchim and Shapiro. Moreover, the authors add, mentors can help women fight discrimination—to break into the old boy network and to crack the glass ceiling.

"My mentor gave me my first big job when he threw me to the wolves by making me president of I. Miller," says Jane Evans. "Mentors are important, particularly if they will give you straight talk and really help you understand the ropes."

According to Jeruchim and Shapiro, as many as a third of the country's major companies have now set up formal mentoring programs. If your corporation has one, do whatever it takes to get involved. Otherwise, try to find a mentor on your own by approaching senior people in your company whom you respect and admire and asking for their support.

Are there advantages to having a male mentor over a female one? Of the 106 protégées Jeruchim and Shapiro interviewed, 49 percent had male mentors, 19 percent had female mentors, and 32 percent had both. As for differences between genders, the authors note, "Male mentors tended to give practical advice and support, while female mentors—usually in less powerful positions—were more responsive to emotional needs." And when asked to identify the mentoring functions that had been most helpful to them, 85 percent of the women in the authors' study cited "advice and information," while 80 percent said "personal support."

But Jeruchim and Shapiro add that neither quality alone will suffice and that, in addition, most women have different needs at different stages of their careers. "A woman in her twenties, intensely focused on her career, may need an aggressive male mentor; in her thirties, as she tries to combine work and motherhood, she may prefer guidance from an older career woman with children of her own," they explain.

In other words, finding the best mentor for you should depend on where you are in your career and what your greatest needs are at the time. And don't get discouraged if men you'd like to have as mentors don't appear interested in taking you on as a protégée. "There was one great lawyer at my old firm that I always wanted to work with," says attorney Susan Pravda. "But it was clear that he was just never comfortable working with me. Finally, I gave up and figured, 'This is not going to get me where I want to go. I'm better off finding people who are comfortable working with me and who are going to push for me.'"

The Kiss of Death

What are the quickest ways to get noticed for all the *wrong* reasons? In its three-year study of top female executives in Fortune 100 sized companies, the Center for Creative Leadership attempted to pinpoint factors that had contributed to the derailment of female executives. Researchers came up with three factors: performance problems, wanting too much, and the inability to adapt—or trying too hard to be one of the boys. "It was essential that these women contradict the stereotypes that their male bosses and coworkers had about women," the researchers noted. "They had to be seen as different, better than women as a group. But they couldn't go too far and forfeit all traces of femininity because that would make them too alien to their superiors and colleagues."

In other words, a dolphin trying to impersonate a shark was the "kiss of death," because too tough was considered offensive, macho, alienating, and overly aggressive. Tough enough was okay, however—even desirable. In fact, success required being "comfortable, natural at being tough."

Dabney Mann's managerial style underscores these findings. While working as Director of Advertising and Promotions at Turner Program Services in Atlanta, one of Mann's major responsibilities was to manage a slew of outside vendors. "I basically handled all the trade and consumer support for programs that Turner Broadcasting System sold to independent stations," she says. "My vendors ran the gamut from printers and producers, to convention coordinators and exhibit companies." Mann attributes her success in this position to the fact that she didn't try to micromanage these vendors. "I treated them as extensions of my department and worked hard to develop loyalty and good personal relationships with them," she reports. "Had I been demanding and unpleasant to work with, I believe that would have been reflected both in their performance and price. For example, I could just have easily insisted, 'I'm not going to do this or that until you give me such and such a price.' Most vendors desperately want Ted Turner's business, so I was in a position where I *could* have acted that way. But I believe that that kind of attitude will ultimately come back to haunt you. Of course, if vendors were disloyal or tried to gouge me, they'd have to answer to that—and I can be *very* tough. But that only happened to me once."

Another of Mann's responsibilities as Director of Advertising and Promotions was to work closely with stations to help them promote programs. Having worked equally hard at establishing good relationships with this group as well has paid off for Mann, who was recently promoted to a sales position. "Now I'm on the other side of the desk—selling to these same people I've supported all those years," she says. "Had I been difficult to work with, they probably wouldn't even give me the time of day now. It just goes to show that you never know. The tougher you are, and the more people you alienate, the harder it will be for you to do a good job in the long run. In other words, what goes around, comes around."

CHAPTER FOURTEEN

Moving Up:
Obstacles Women Face

PROFILE

JAN THOMPSON

VICE PRESIDENT, SALES OPERATIONS
MAZDA MOTOR OF AMERICA
IRVINE, CALIFORNIA

"Those of us who started out in the 1970s have a chance of breaking through in the 1990s. But I think the real opportunities lie with the next generation of women—the ones who are now in their thirties."

Growing up, Jan Thompson always knew that she would ultimately choose a career that was nontraditional. "Not because I wanted to make a political statement," she says. "It was just my nature."

And, in fact, upon graduating from Western Michigan University with a degree in marketing in 1972, Thompson returned to her hometown of Detroit in search of a job with one of the Big Three automakers. Ford wasn't hiring at the time. Working for General Motors was out of the question, since that would have meant moving to Flint, and Thompson was already working nights on her MBA degree at the University of Detroit. That left

Chrysler, where Thompson was soon accepted as the company's first female management trainee. "At the time, there weren't any women in management at GM or Ford either," she reports. "So it was a real breakthrough deal."

Despite her minority status, Thompson says she never felt uncomfortable being Chrysler's token woman. Which isn't surprising since she grew up with three brothers and a sister in a family where everyone was equal, and everyone played sports. Moreover, Thompson had often been the only female in her college classes. "So I was used to hanging out with guys," she says. "Of course, had I gone into Chrysler's management program as Miss Fluff or something, they probably would have taken me apart." Instead, Thompson became fast friends with the majority of her male peers. "Today, most of the guys I trained with are now at the senior levels of management in the automotive industry, and we're all *still* good friends."

In 1974, after two years of rigorous management training, Thompson was eager to branch out and begin working in the field. "Unfortunately Chrysler was dragging its feet over whether or not it was appropriate to appoint a woman to be a district sales manager," she recalls. A few of Thompson's male colleagues had also tried to dissuade her. "Early on, one had told me that an MBA degree was an absolute prerequisite for becoming a district sales manager. He didn't know that I was going to graduate school at night, so I told him, 'Great, I'm working on it right now!' But the funny thing was, once I got into that position, I discovered I was the *only* one with an MBA, And in fact, most of the male district sales managers I was working with had undergraduate degrees in the oddest subject areas . . . like geology."

On one hand, Thompson believes that her pioneer status as Chrysler's first female district sales manager worked to her advantage. "There were zero expectations of me," she explains, "so I had nowhere to go but up." On the flip side, however, she had to work incredibly hard to prove that she was as good as—if not better than—her male counterparts.

Surprisingly, the warmest reception Thompson received came from the company's dealers. "These are the people you'd *think* would ask, 'Gee, what are they sending a broad in here for? She doesn't know anything about this business.' But I was devoted to them. I took care of all the little things for them that the men in my position didn't want to be bothered with. For example, if a dealer couldn't find where he'd been paid on some rebates, a male district manager's attitude was typically, 'Hey, I don't have time for that. Have your office manager call the regional office to check on that.' But *I* would help them out—and they loved it."

From 1974 to 1981, Thompson bounced around the Midwest, then settled in Orange County, California. Along the way, she worked in various sales positions, always meeting—or exceeding—her quota and increasingly gaining the respect of her peers and superiors.

But in 1984 she came to a crossroads in her career, when Chrysler requested that she return to Detroit. Having grown accustomed to the California life-style, Thompson turned them down. Meanwhile, friends of hers at nearby Toyota had been begging Thompson to come and work with them. "I figured I'd been working in the trenches long enough," she says. "It was time I got some corporate experience."

Thompson joined Toyota as video communications and field training manager, then quickly became the company's national truck advertising manager. In 1986, she was tapped to create, from scratch, the entire marketing concept for Toyota's first luxury car, the Lexus.

Two years later, a headhunter called to tell Thompson that Mazda was looking for a vice president of marketing. At first the position didn't interest her in the least. "Then I found out that they were getting ready to simultaneously launch the Miata and the MPV minivan—and that they had no marketing department, no nothing," she says. "That was too much of a challenge to walk away from."

Challenge is something Thompson relishes, and these days one of her biggest challenges lies in coming up with new ways to sell cars so that Mazda can hold on to its market share. "The appreciation of the yen has been a real killer for us," she reports, "and we can't subsidize prices, because then we're accused of dumping."

Another challenge Thompson has taken on is finding ways to

break the male hold on the automotive industry. "Women buy half the cars in America, but they are still not taken seriously on the car lots. They are either ignored, or salesmen want to know where their husbands are. It's amazing to me that this stuff still happens."

To date, thanks to Thompson's marketing strategies, Mazda has made great strides in targeting women as customers. In recent years, the company's name has been synonymous with the Ladies Professional Golf Association championships and Mazda's Tennis Classic for Women. Thompson is also working hard at helping her dealers sell more cars to women. "We've done lots of training classes," she reports. "But the problem is, turnover at dealerships is close to 100 percent a year."

Thompson believes that the ideal way both to combat this high turnover rate *and* to make it easier for women to feel comfortable buying cars is to dramatically increase the numbers of women *selling* cars. "Women have a tendency to be more loyal—they don't quit as often as men do," she says. "But you have to give them flexibility, because they do have families. They can't work twelve-hour days like the guys do. And maybe if we changed the way we do business—paid a salary instead of 100 percent straight commission—we would attract more women."

Having more women on the lots would also help to clean up the image far too many people have to the sleazy car salesman. "I recently saw a story on CNN where a nun, dressed in street clothes, was selling cars at a dealership," Thompson reports. "She was kicking the tires and pointing out features, and I thought, 'Wow, this is brilliant! Who *wouldn't* buy a car from a nun?' I'm always telling my dealers, 'Get people with credibility representing you. Recruit more women!' "

In fact, Thompson's dealers insist that they, too, want more women selling cars. "But women tend to cancel themselves out. They say, 'Gee, we don't know how to fix cars.' And that's a huge misconception. I don't know how to fix cars either—and believe me, 90 percent of the guys I work with probably couldn't change their oil. But anyone can read those brochures and do their home-work. Women can easily make $75,000 to $85,000 a year in this profession."

Women could also change the way people sell cars. "We have a female dealer in San Jose whose sales manager is also a woman. Theirs is a one-price selling store—so there's no haggling—and they have been reasonably successful. If I were out car shopping, I wouldn't go anyplace else."

The question is, would women selling cars be taken seriously? Thompson acknowledges that the expectation that men know a lot more about cars than women do may be an obstacle. But from her vantage point, the acceptance of women in *all* fields is changing for the better. "There's a whole different political relationship among the young men and women coming out of college today," she observes. "They are far more equal than when I graduated, and they work together extremely well."

In fact, Thompson finds this new breed of women particularly refreshing. "I have to admit that when I first started in this business, I thought I had to be like the guys. There were certain expressions I had to use, and I had to swear and do other things the guys did. After all, my role models were all men," she explains. But eventually Thompson learned that she could set her own rules and embrace the fact that she was female. Now she encourages the women who work for her to wear their gender proudly on their sleeves. "I tell them, 'You don't have to hide anything. You don't have to take a back seat to anyone.'"

Thompson also bends over backward to help the new breed of women entering her industry to succeed. She has been instrumental in many of their promotions. She has also served as a mentor to them. "These women always tell me that having a role model and someone to talk to has made a lot of difference to them," she says.

Thompson's willingness to help women succeed reaches beyond her industry. One project she is particularly proud of, for example, is the Mazda Golf Clinics for Professional Women. Created by Thompson and her marketing staff, these clinics are held annually in nine cities across the United States and are designed to help professional women master a sport that businessmen often rely upon for schmoozing and networking.

Thanks to role models and mentors like Thompson, the glass

ceiling is becoming thinner. "Those of us who started out in the 1970s have a chance of breaking through in the 1990s," Thompson believes. "But I think the real opportunities lie with the next generation of women—the ones who are now in their thirties."

And despite the fact that Thompson continues to be a minority—at least in the executive suite—in her industry, she has managed to turn what others might have seen as obstacles into advantages. How? For starters, she paid her dues willingly. "To climb the ladder, you've got to come up the field ranks. You've got to be in the trenches, work with the dealers, and *earn* those stripes before you can gain the respect of your superiors."

Consistent hard work has paid off as well. "Jan's the kind of person who will roll up her sleeves and delve into what needs to be done," reveals one of her former supervisors at both Chrysler and Mazda. "People tend not to look at Jan as a woman in business, but as a person in business. And that's saying a lot, because she's working in an environment that doesn't welcome women."

Thompson's willingness to take risks has also likely played a factor in her success. "Maybe being a woman presents that opportunity," she says. "Just being a woman in this industry already makes me a risk, something different, so I can take advantage of that by breaking other conventional rules."

But perhaps Thompson's greatest strength lies in her ability to make the men around her feel comfortable—even the Japanese. Indeed, Thompson's warm personality and healthy sense of humor have made her a legend of sorts among Mazda's executives in Japan. Prior to one Far East trip, for example, Thompson had one of her Japanese assistants compose a phonetically spelled poem in Japanese that she could recite during her presentation. "I rehearsed it over and over again until I got the cadence down." The gimmick was a huge hit. "They loved it," she reports. "They were applauding like crazy."

And on a more recent trip to Japan, Thompson ended up on stage at a geisha bar with eight male colleagues crooning "Love Me Tender." "The Japanese love my silly gestures, because it shows I take the time to try and understand them," she says.

Taking the time to understand and get to know her dealers has endeared Thompson to this group as well. "It used to be that you took dealers out and wined and dined them or boozed it up with them—things a woman couldn't do as well as a man," Thompson says. "But the dealers didn't expect that of me, so I could change the rules." Instead, Thompson would play golf or tennis with her dealers. She also forged personal relationships with them and their wives. "Now they all treat me as part of the family," she says. "They'll say, 'Come on home with me . . . Mary Lou wants to cook for you.' Or they'll say, 'I want my daughter to meet you.' And because the relationship I have with them is more personal, it probably gives me an edge."

Thompson has managed to forge equally personable relationships with her male co-workers. As a result, she says she has never felt excluded from the old boy network. "What I *have* done, though, is exclude myself," she says. "When we go to Japan, for instance, the men often want to cruise the geisha bars after dinner, and sometimes I'll bow out—because I don't drink, or maybe because I'm just too tired. And in fact, I think they appreciate it when I duck out every now and then. I know what they do, and, frankly, I'm just not interested."

Oddly enough, Thompson reveals that her chosen nontraditional career tends to confound women more frequently than it does men. "All too often, I meet women who ask me what I do for a living, and when I tell them I get a puzzled look in response," she says. "Then they'll ask, 'Well, do you *like* doing that?' " And even after Thompson explains that she has been in the industry for twenty-three years, she'll inevitably be asked something like, "Well, *why* do you like it?"

Perhaps the best answer Thompson could give would be to recite the popular Mazda slogan she created . . . because "It Just Feels Right."

• • •

Exclusion from the old boy network. Unsupportive bosses and dinosaur companies. Sexual discrimination and male chauvinism. The infamous glass ceiling. These are just a handful of the obstacles female managers face in their climb up the corporate ladder. Yet a majority of the successful managers we interviewed said they had not encountered such obstacles. "They may have been there, but I just didn't see them," remarked Mylle Bell of Holiday Inn Worldwide. "Of course I didn't really look for them, either. I was too busy trying to do excellent work."

Adds ABC's Krys Keller, "I have not felt discriminated against at all. Maybe it's because I've had the confidence and wherewithal to go after what I wanted."

Even managers who said they had encountered obstacles refused to be sidetracked—either by ignoring these obstacles or by finding ways to get around them. In fact, many of the managers we interviewed felt that what often separates "victims" from those who refuse to be waylaid is attitude. "It's important for women not to have a chip on their shoulder," says Katherine August, Executive Vice President of First Republic Bancorp in San Francisco. August suggests that generally you can create the environment you want. "You can often create change by owning up to your role in the situation," she believes.

Janice Scott, a sales representative for Zep Mfg. Co., agrees. "My diverse customer base includes municipal sewage treatment plants and a variety of industrial manufacturing facilities, which, needless to say, are all old boy arenas." In fact, oftentimes when Scott gives her business card to a secretary, the person she's trying to see will come out and meet Scott just out of curiosity. And their standard line? "What's a nice girl like you doing in a place like this?" Moreover, many of the male sales reps in Scott's field hand out girlie calendars or tickets to ball games to win a sale. As for Scott, she wins clients' trust through demonstration and product knowledge and application, and being able to answer clients' technical questions. "When an engineer recently commented, 'Oh, I just love it when Janice talks technical,' I took it as a compliment— that as a woman, I have as much technical knowledge as any man my clients deal with."

Determination to succeed is another important factor. Krys Keller, for example, feels that her passion to always perform her best, coupled with a determination to perfect her communication skills and try to make others feel comfortable around her, has been key in helping her to avoid obstacles.

Besides, as Holiday Inn's Mylle Bell points out, many obstacles managers face on the way up may not even be gender-related. "There are always things in life that can get in the way if you let them. It doesn't matter if you're a man or a woman. If you sit around and look for things, then you'll probably find them. How does that saying go . . . 'Careful of what you want—you may get it'?"

Not to say that obstacles for female managers in corporate America don't exist . . .

OBSTACLE: Women Must Work Harder to Prove Themselves

In her study of thirty women holding middle-management positions in fifteen Fortune 500 companies, Rose Mary Wentling concluded that women are under enormous pressure to do outstanding work continuously and must consistently demonstrate competency on the job.

"Female managers have to work harder to gain credibility," acknowledges Jane Evans of U.S. West Communications. "We're still at a stage where true equality is not out there. We have to work harder to be noticed, and just to prove that we are able to handle the job, the family, and everything else."

But all that may be changing. "Women have to be really good at what they do. They can't be mediocre, or they will get lost in the shuffle," says Krys Keller. "But is it really any different for men? Men are no longer promoted based on gender alone. *Nobody* can be dead weight on the job anymore. These days, with downsizing and lots of middle managers being eliminated, *everyone* has to perform well to survive."

Keller speaks from experience. "When I came to this department four years ago, I was one of six directors responsible for twenty-eight stations. Now I'm one of two responsible for over one hundred stations, and the other person who's still here has been with the department for twenty-five years. The fact that I survived the downsizing, I think, is a clear indicator that job performance is what counts—male, female, it doesn't matter."

OBSTACLE: Exclusion from the Old Boy Network

The managers Wentling interviewed also reported feeling hindered because they were often excluded from their organizations' informal power structures—the networks composed of men who play golf, attend sporting events, and go out for lunch and drinks together. Being left out, these women felt, kept them from taking part in valuable informal business discussions. It also prevented them from being privy to important inside information that might have helped them to position themselves to move up.

"One female manager told me, 'I am more at a disadvantage than my male peers because I am excluded from the old boy network. This network is crucial to assessing information about implicit norms and power coalitions. In short, this network is vital to knowing what is going on and understanding the implications of operating within the political environment.' "

Nancy Hamlin, president of Hamlin & Associates, a management consulting firm based in Marblehead, Massachusetts, has spent over twenty-five years as an advisor on gender issues to such blue-chip corporations as Hewlett-Packard, Digital Equipment, and Kinney Shoes, as well as the U.S. Postal Service and the U.S. Coast Guard. She says that old boy networks exist even in the most progressive corporations. But, she adds, "Men don't do this on purpose; they just don't *think* about it. It's simply not in their level of consciousness."

How can women become members of these insiders' clubs? Women in politics are beginning to adopt an "If-you-can't-beat-'em-join-'em" attitude. After her election to Congress in 1992, Lynn Woolsey went to Washington and immediately signed up to play on the congressional basketball team—a first on Capitol Hill. That same year, Representatives Maria Cantwell (Washington), Ileana Ros-Lehtinen (Florida), and Blanche Lambert (Arkansas) became the first women to step up to the plate in the Roll Call Congressional Baseball Game. "I've warned 'em; I'm coming to win," Lambert told reporters.

Finding a mentor who is part of the old boy network can also help. In *Women, Mentors, and Success*, Joan Jeruchim and Pat Shapiro acknowledge that a mentor can often be a political ally. "Mentors can open doors, introduce you to the power holders, promote you within the corporation, and help you understand the subtleties of the corporate culture."

Learning to relate to male colleagues on their level—which again, leads back to establishing that comfort level—can be beneficial as well. "But you can't push your way into the old boy network," cautions one manager we spoke with. "You can, however, ease your way into it. First, do whatever it takes to get on committees and task forces that involve the men who are part of these networks. Next, learn how to carry on a good conversation with men—at meetings, at company social events, even at the water cooler. Once you get to know some of these men, invite one or two of them to lunch. Chances are, once they feel comfortable with you, they'll be less likely to exclude you."

Lyn Wylder, Chief Rail Engineer for the Metro Atlanta Rapid Transit Authority (MARTA) and the only woman in the country overseeing the design and construction for a major mass transit system, agrees. Before landing a job with MARTA in 1982, Wylder worked as a consultant with several different firms, but despite her talent and enthusiasm, she faced more than her fair share of obstacles. "They wouldn't let me travel because they didn't know what to do with me," she told a reporter with *The Atlanta Journal*. "They wouldn't let me go into the field, because I guess I was supposed to be a dainty Southern lady."

Having graduated from Georgia Tech when the male to female ratio was eighty to one, however, Wylder says she was used to living in a "guy's world." And while she still gets the occasional sideways look from contractors accustomed to dealing with men,

Wylder doesn't let it bother her. "I learned a long time ago just to ignore it," she says. "It's not my problem, it's theirs."

Recently Wylder agreed to help her alma mater launch a mentor program designed to attract young women to the male-dominated field of engineering. "It's high time that women made friends with slide rules and came storming over the artificial barricades that have kept them away from engineering."

Doing your job exceptionally well may help you win the old boys' approval and acceptance. And in some instances, a simple demonstration can be a valuable tool for securing a new clients. Zep Manufacturing's Janice Scott, for example, once tried to get into a television production studio to sell them some cleaning and maintenance supplies. When she couldn't get past the secretary at the front door, she managed to gain entry through the vehicle maintenance garage, then asked to speak to the manager of operations. "He came out, and within seconds, I could tell that he was uncomfortable talking with me," she recalls. "He refused to look me in the eye, and he kept fidgeting." As Scott talked, she took out some putty and began rolling it around between her fingers. "The crack in your garage door needs to be repaired," she said as she proceeded to fill in the crack. When she was finished with the job, she turned and said, "This will harden in fifteen minutes, and in an hour will be completely cured, at which point you'll be able to paint over it." To which the operations manager sarcastically responded, "Sure." But the putty did harden, the manager did paint over it, and Scott ended up with a new client. "You've got to do what it takes to demonstrate competency," she believes, "because that's what will get you over the hurdles of sexual stereotyping."

And if none of these strategies helps you gain entrance to the club, learning to deal with the exclusion—and succeeding in spite of it—may be the best way to invest your time and energy. Carole Kitchens, for example, is one of four managers—and the only female of the bunch—to head up the Sunette Division of Hoechst Celanese Corporation. Consequently, she has faced a number of obstacles. "Usually it's subtle," she says. "The other three managers will go to lunch, and unless I happen to be there when they're making plans, I don't get invited. Or I'll find out there was a brainstorming meeting on a strategic change, and they'll offer, 'We knew you weren't in this afternoon,' or whatever, as an excuse. They respect very much what I do, but they can't imagine that I know anything about real business. And that's such a joke, really, because there's *never* been a session in *any* area that I haven't been able to make a contribution. In fact, at the risk of sounding egotistical, I'm usually far ahead of them on a lot of things."

Five years ago, when she was appointed to her position, Kitchens says she was far too defensive. "I'd say, 'Get off my case. I know what I'm doing here,' " she reports. "But I've since become much more politically astute. I've learned not to internalize all the slights. Now I'll say to myself, 'Well, look at who's doing the slighting. Do you really think this person is a paragon?' And if so, I might be hurt. But if not—which is usually the case—then I ask myself, 'Why am I worried?' "

This mellowing, Kitchens adds, has made her more effective at getting things done. "If you spend too much emotional energy fretting about the snubs, you're not going to be successful and get where you want to go."

OBSTACLE: Unsupportive Boss/ Dinosaur Company

One way to avoid the obstacles that female managers typically face is to make the right choices regarding where you work and who you work for. "Find an environment that's supportive," recommends Katherine August of First Republic Bancorp. "Early in my career, in each place I worked there was someone who was very supportive. That support gave me confidence."

Jane Evans of U.S. West Communications agrees. "I suggest that young women just entering the workforce look to see if a CEO has daughters who are of college age and beyond, because those are usually the ones who have had personal experience with discrimination. And if their darling daughters have come up against it, they quickly become very sympathetic."

In Rose Mary Wentling's study, several of the women interviewed reported having bosses who had difficulty working with women or who did not believe in the advancement of women. As a result, these bosses withheld guidance and encouragement.

What can you do if you're stuck with a boss who doesn't support your professional growth and development? Warren Bennis, management consultant and author of *An Invented Life: Meditations on Leadership and Charge*, advises, "Talk to the boss directly one-on-one. And if that doesn't work, go around and talk to other people and maybe even to the boss's boss." And if that doesn't work? "You have to leave," Bennis believes. "In the long run, that business is going to fail if it doesn't change its ways, so the end result is the same. Either way you go."

The problem is, many women stay with unsupportive bosses and try to tough it out. They *hope* that things will change, or they blame themselves. Meanwhile, they waste precious time stuck in dead-end jobs and often damage their self-esteem in the process. "It's not unlike staying in a bad marriage because you're frightened by the prospect of being too old to remarry, and not being in a financial position to strike out on your own again," says Bennis. "So you stuff it all down and say, 'I'm just going to stay in a lousy relationship because the alternatives are worse. But too often, I'm afraid, the alternatives are better. It's just that people aren't acting upon them."

OBSTACLE: Sexual Discrimination/ Male Chauvinism

"When I was assigned to my current position from a position in another part of the company, I felt that my credibility was frequently challenged—either indirectly or through passing comments—during the first several months," says Laura Martin of

Westin Hotels. "And I was certainly qualified for the position, having had extensive experience in accounting." Martin's problem was compounded by the fact that her position had originally reported to a vice president who had a reputation for hiring young females to fill positions outside of their former disciplines. "Before any of these women had a chance to prove their abilities in their new jobs, it was not uncommon for them to be discredited as being appointed simply because the vice president liked surrounding himself with a female staff."

Once, while at a conference, Martin had a hotel general manager ask her point-blank if she was one of "Charlie's Angels"—a term frequently applied to this group of women.

Male chauvinism still accounts for a significant part of the obstacles women face in the workplace. Case in point: Despite the fact that 1992 was dubbed the "Year of the Woman," stories from the 1992 elections served as a harsh reminder of the double standards that women must contend with. A handful of examples stand out. Democrat Gloria O'Dell, a Democratic senatorial candidate from Kansas, was branded a lesbian by her primary opponent, Fred Phelps—a reverend no less. At one rally, Phelps's supporters held signs calling the forty-six-year-old divorced mother "Bull Dike O'Dell."

In a column for *The Washington Post,* Jack Anderson and Michael Binstein criticized Illinois senatorial candidate Carol Moseley-Braun for "looking more and more like just one of the boys." And when Katie Couric interviewed presidential candidate Ross Perot in June of 1992, Perot had nothing but praise for the popular anchorwoman. "Can you imagine if I had Katie as a running mate?" he remarked. Yet in a second interview three months later, when Couric pressed him to clarify his positions on the issues, Perot accused Couric of "trying to prove her manhood."

Other common misconceptions men continue to have of women: When the going gets tough, women fall apart. We are indecisive, inconsistent, moody, and too emotional. We are pushy, difficult to work for, and make things more complicated than they need be. We are not good team players, nor are we capable of seeing the big picture. Does any of this sound familiar?

These common prejudices some men have of women in the workplace are usually based not on experience, but on ignorance. For example, when attorney Rita Page Reuss began her career as a trial lawyer in Ohio, she was the first female to argue cases in that state's Court of Appeals. In fact, Reuss has been a pioneer almost everywhere she has worked—from the Ohio Attorney General's Office to Land O'Lakes, where she is now an officer and Vice President of Public Affairs for the corporation. And not surprisingly, she has encountered more than her fair share of obstacles. "In the early years, the prevailing attitude was, 'This is no place for a woman . . . women can't litigate . . . women don't understand finance and business matters . . . and I don't want to be involved with bringing the first woman in this business to meetings.' And overcoming these obstacles was a challenge. To succeed, you couldn't have a chip on your shoulder. You had to be strong, positive, aggressive, and very well prepared. But in all fairness, you also had to give people a chance to get to know you and to understand the different ways in which you worked." Reuss did just that and adds, "After a while, I ended up becoming good friends with most of the people who initially didn't want me there at all. It takes time."

In fact, according to Michael S. Kimmel, a sociologist at the State University of New York at Stonybrook and author of *Manhood: The American Quest*, the invasion of women in the workplace and the near extinction of the all-male arena in corporate America has thrown many men for a loop—particularly those who've grown accustomed to, and who support, the old ideologies. "Such a shift in the workplace has helped to change some old prejudices, but it has also produced a new tension between the sexes, as some men complain that women are competing for 'their' jobs," writes Kimmel in an article for *Harvard Business Review*. "Sexual harassment has become a way for men to remind women that they are, after all, 'just' women, who happen to be in the workplace but don't really belong there."

But the real reason for such bitterness and uncertainty, Kimmel adds, "lies not in the supposed new power of women, but in the rapid changes taking place in today's corporations—furious, fast-paced restructuring and reengineering." Yet as more and more women move into leadership positions, research suggests that men's sexist attitudes are softening. In a recent study of managerial men in corporate America, for example, male managers who had worked with women as peers were less likely to stereotype women as unfit for managerial roles than were those who had only worked with women as subordinates. In other words, familiarity appears to breed less contempt.

ESPN's Rosa Gatti agrees. "Today, people are more aware of issues surrounding women, but we still have a long way to go. You don't find as much blatant discrimination today, but you do find more subtle bias."

To be successful, then, women must learn how to deal with gender stereotyping in acceptable ways and refuse to let it keep them from reaching their goals. How? The managers we interviewed used a number of different strategies. Laura Martin, for example, has found that the most effective response for her is to do her job and let her successes speak for themselves. "However, I do believe that just forging ahead quietly, just minding my own business isn't enough," she adds. "Although it was a bit daunting, my response to the general manager who asked if I was one of 'Charlie's Angels,' was to let him know how unfortunate I thought it was that such an unflattering label had been applied to some very talented women."

Before graduating from Harvard Business School and landing a job at Hewlett-Packard, Cynthia Danaher worked in sales for General Electric. "I was the only woman in the local sales office, and my colleagues were twice my age. I didn't have anything in common with them, and they did not take me seriously," she recalls. "But I was extremely well respected and received a lot of support from the corporate headquarters, so I chose to focus on that. In fact, that's what ultimately drove me to apply to business school. I realized that I needed to gain credibility, and doing that would either take time or undertaking something impressive— like going to business school for my MBA."

Cynthia Carlson, Chairman of the Carlson Group, a training and development firm based in Charlotte, North Carolina, acknowledges, "I have a corporation with my last name on it, yet I can walk into a meeting where I have planned and arranged every detail—including scheduling the participants—and if there are men from outside my company in attendance, they are going to talk to my male employees first. It happens. But I've learned to accept it and find ways to work around it. You have to be able to deflect sexist attitudes and comments and get on with doing your job."

Gwendolyn Baker recommends facing prejudices head-on. "As an African-American woman, I get it across the board," she says. "It's just systemic, and you have to realize that this is the kind of world we live in. I deal with it by being very open and very candid about it. I've also found that a lot of one-on-one is helpful. If I have a man who is resisting me because I am a female, I can accomplish so much by just saying, 'Will you have breakfast with me?' or 'Let's go to lunch.' Then we'll sit and talk—not about sexism, but about issues that are common to both men and women—families and backgrounds, for instance."

As you develop your own strategies for dealing with male chauvinism and sexual discrimination, keep in mind that a lot of it is simply oneupmanship. "A competent woman is a formidable challenge to men," believes Carole Kitchens. "Men are accustomed to sometimes losing a battle to another man, but they don't quite know how to play the same game—which usually involves putting someone down—with a female. Consequently, they're at a little bit of a loss. In my case, if I get into a heated discussion with a male colleague, chances are I'm going to win, because I'm more verbal and quicker at thinking on my feet than my male co-workers are. The problem is, they don't quite know how to deal with that kind of competition. So what do they do? They use exclusion as a weapon. Or they try to put me down. And that's fair. It's naive for we females in the workforce to think that the guys are going to give up all the goodies just because we're here now. It's not going to happen. We have to learn to go for whatever we want on our own terms."

Also, keep in mind that while there will always be some men who'd simply rather not work alongside—and particularly for—

a woman, it appears that these attitudes are waning. Recruiter Peter Maher, managing partner at Deven International in Verona, New Jersey, recently noted in an article for *Management Review*, "Fewer men are lobbying against the hiring of women managers because they're discovering that reporting to a woman is 'not a bad deal.' "

OBSTACLE: The Fast Track Versus the Mommy Track

Some companies are reluctant to hire women of childbearing age to fill high-level positions for fear that they'll want to start families. Many also hesitate to *promote* women for the same reason. Their rationale: "She's probably going to have children—which will involve a long maternity leave. And once she has kids, she won't be too serious about her work."

Of course, countless women in corporate America today have already proven that motherhood need not be detrimental to on-the-job excellence. For example, when Janice Scott set her sights on becoming a sales representative for Zep Manufacturing, the vice president of the company tired to talk her out of it. "This job is so demanding, and the success rate for women with children is not high," he told her. "I strongly advise you to rethink this decision."

Instead, Scott was more determined than ever to take the job— and to succeed. And, in fact, her track record has been so impressive that she is repeatedly asked if she'd be interested in moving up to a sales management position. "I tell them, 'I *am* a manager. I have over six hundred accounts, a husband, two children, and a dog.' Besides, I already earn more than my sales manager does!"

The key to Scott's success is organization. "I'm very regimented," she reports. Indeed, Scott is out of bed by 4:45 A.M. and works out for a half hour to "get my blood pumping," she says. She and her husband employ a nanny during the summer and have hired a private tutor to help their children with schoolwork, particularly on the nights before heavy test days. Scott does a lot of paperwork at home on the weekends. She's also a fanatical list-maker and loves checking things off. "Believe me, this juggling act gets stressful, and sometimes you just want to pull your hair out. But I've always had a passion for success, so I try not to think so much about the responsibilities. I just do what I have to do."

Scott is fortunate in that she can set her own hours for the most part. "That way, if there's an important event at my children's school, I can plan my work schedule around that."

Some women, however, don't have the luxury of setting their own schedule. But if they have a proven track record, that often makes it easier to build in flexibility. "I always advise young women just entering the workforce that if they plan to be mothers, they should stay at a company long enough to grow roots before having children," says Hewlett-Packard's Cynthia Danaher. "That way, you don't have to hop on an airplane all the time to gain credibility. You can get a lot of things done by phone." Growing roots makes a big difference when you need flexibility later on, she adds. "And I'm happy I stayed here long enough to do that."

Because female managers like Danaher have firsthand knowledge of the stresses that come with the territory of trying to manage a family *and* a career, they are far more empathetic with their subordinates who are also parents. "Basically, men want the same things in a work environment that women do," believes Danaher. "At Hewlett-Packard, we have a lot of young parents, and I understand that they want to spend time with their children. So when they're traveling all the time, I'll often ask, 'Do you *really* need to go, or can this be handled another way?' And I'll usually see this instant relief in their eyes, because that was a question they were rarely asked before."

Mazda's Jan Thompson is equally flexible with her subordinates. Though not a mother herself, she says, "I have a lot of compassion for working mothers. If my staff needs to take off to meet with teachers, see their children in a school play—whatever, they just go. It's not a problem, because these women always pay me back tenfold."

As more and more women climb the corporate ladder, we predict that more and more companies will become family-friendly. In the meantime, the law of supply and demand is on our side, forcing companies to rethink the issue of excluding working mothers (or potential mothers) from top-level positions. Not because it's the right thing to do, mind you, but because it makes good business sense.

OBSTACLE: The Infamous Glass Ceiling

In a 1992 *Fortune* poll of 201 chief executives of the nation's largest corporations, 92 percent of the respondents said that the number of female managers at their companies had increased, and 18 percent reported the numbers had stayed about the same. But only 16 percent believed it "very likely" or "somewhat likely" that they would be succeeded by a female CEO within the next decade. And a mere 18 percent thought it would be "very likely" that even after twenty years a woman would be tapped to run their companies.

Findings from businessman and sociologist Allan J. Cox's study of the career advancements of American males are a bit more encouraging. Eighty-five percent of top male executives said their companies were eager to promote women to middle management positions. But only 68 percent supported women moving to top management slots. What gives?

"Chemistry in the race for top management positions plays a pivotal role," writes Patti Watts in an article for *Executive Female*. "And chemistry in corporate America has meant the quality of being most like the person—the CEO, the board member—who's doing the choosing. This is a real barrier for women. But as younger male managers continue to incorporate female qualities into their management styles and move up the ranks, choosing a woman for the top spot should come naturally."

Jane Evans at U.S. West Communications agrees. "As you get closer to the top, there's still very much a glass ceiling," she acknowledges. "People like to be around people who are like themselves. And we're just not like them. But I think that as this younger generation begins to take over corporate America—you know, men who have had working wives, been to business school with women, grown up with more equality—we're beginning to see some cultural changes. People are really pushing to get women and minorities into top positions. Still, I think the barriers will exist as long as we have the older generation running corporate America."

The grapevine also plays an important role, in that those who *win* top positions are often those who have been *told* about existing vacancies—and women and minorities are frequently left out of the loop. "The people who learn first about an opening or executive-level hiring need are usually management's business associates, friends, and often their executive recruiters," acknowledges Susan Khoury, a principal at Dieckmann & Associates, an executive search firm based in Chicago. "And because of the way society is structured, these people tend to be white males." For years, Khoury and her colleagues have been trying to break that chain—at least where talent is concerned. "The candidates we present are there because they make good business sense for the company, not because we feel any great obligation to advance a social initiative," says Khoury. "Thinking in terms of 'affirmative action' focuses on the hiring of executives as a problem; thinking in terms of productivity, no matter what gender, focuses on the hiring of executives as an opportunity."

From her vantage point at ABC, Krys Keller also agrees that the glass ceiling exists—but not necessarily from a negative standpoint. "I've been with my company long enough to have developed some credibility, visibility, and to find my comfort level. And I'm ready to move up," she says. "But in an era of corporate retrenching, right now I'm looking at a scenario where someone needs to die or retire for me to do that. In other words, I'm in a waiting mode. So today— when women talk about glass ceilings, it may not be for gender reasons. It's because there are only so many possibilities within their organization, and they may have to wait."

Yet even when opportunities to move up *are* available, when it comes to advancing their careers, women tend to move at a snail's pace compared to men—and not by choice. According to *The Cox*

Report on the American Corporation, 40 percent of the top executives and 43 percent of middle managers polled acknowledge that women are likely to advance more slowly than men. Perhaps this is another area where mentoring can help.

Self-Imposed Obstacles

Some of the hurdles women face, however, we bring on ourselves. For example, in an article for *Executive Female,* M. June Smith, Vice President of Coors Ceramicon Designs in Golden, Colorado, writes that some women have not yet unlearned the limiting belief systems we were raised with. These, she explains, run the gamut from "Women don't traditionally succeed in that field" and "Women just don't get to be officers in corporations" to "I'm sure I won't succeed" and "I'm just not smart enough." These beliefs, she adds, have been instilled in many of us from childhood. "Our parents, teachers, friends, bosses, and so on all reinforce negative beliefs that limit our ability to succeed. And what's worse, we buy it!"

As little girls, many of us were taught to be "seen and not heard." Consequently, as adults our communication skills tend to be more tentative than men's, and as a result we are interrupted more and are often viewed by men as "invisible." For example, at meetings women frequently wait until the "right moment" to present ideas—and then do so without conviction and confidence. What happens then is we are often ignored, not taken seriously, or we don't get credit for our ideas.

"Often a woman at a meeting will make a comment that is ignored; later a male colleague makes the same point and it's discussed, taken seriously, and ultimately attributed to him," acknowledges Deborah Tannen in *You Just Don't Understand.* "Part of the reason may be that the woman presented her point in a stereotypically feminine way— she spoke briefly, phrased it as a question, spoke at a low volume, and a high pitch. If the man who followed her used a stereotypically masculine style of speaking—he spoke at length in a loud, declamatory voice—his message was the same, but the metamessage was different: 'This is important.' "

Speaking up—with confidence and conviction—won ESPN's Rosa Gatti the respect and comradeship of her male cohorts a few years ago. "We were working on a boxing event that Don King was promoting, and there I was at a high-power meeting with representatives from ABC, ESPN, and the Don King boxing contingent—all males except for one other woman and me," she recalls. "Don was extremely concerned because he felt that we weren't giving him enough publicity on this particular event. 'This is bigger than Wimbledon . . . bigger than the World Series,' he screamed at us. But no one said a word. Now whenever someone challenges me or gets in my face, I rise to the occasion. And granted, King was addressing everyone in the room, but I was the only one who decided to speak up. 'Don, if this is such a big event, where are the boxing writers, and why aren't *they* writing about it?' I asked. Dead silence followed initially, but soon we were able to proceed with our discussions. Meanwhile, I wondered if I'd done the right thing, and as it turns out, I did. When we walked out of the meeting, several of the men slipped me a high five, and said, 'Way to go!'"

As little girls, many of us were also raised to be consensus-seekers. This can be a positive trait, but can also translate into indecisiveness on the job. According to Debra Benton in *Lions Don't Need to Roar*, indecision on the job can be deadly. "Unsolved problems get worse, conflicts recur, and you look wishy-washy," she says. Moreover, indecision drives men crazy.

Women are taught to play it safe as well—to always obey "the rules." Consequently, as adults, many of us not only emerge reluctant to take risks, we often lack the backbone and know-how to make our own rules. Not Dawn Steel, who played by her own rules and wound up becoming the first female president of a Hollywood studio. "Actually, I think I broke rules all the time, because I didn't even know what the rules were—which is a distinct advantage," she told *Mirabella*. "I had the benefit of having no idea what the parameters were, so I didn't know what I couldn't do." Ignorance is often bliss.

Yet another reason women are held back is because many of us are oversensitive. Attorney Susan Pravda believes that women must develop a thick skin to survive in corporate America. "Once you're far enough up on the ladder where you are truly measured for your skills, I don't think it's as hard. But getting there can be frustrating," she says. "People would always accuse me of being too tough a negotiator, and I think I was labeled that way because I was a woman. If I'd been a man, it wouldn't have evoked a comment. In fact, I think it was used as a way to try to get me to back down. But I believe you have to be able to ask yourself, 'Am I really too tough, or am I just doing a good job?' You have to look at criticism fairly and consider the source. For instance, people I respected used to tell me, 'Susan, you have to learn to listen better.' And they were right. But I *wasn't* too tough. I was just doing a good job. And you have to get comfortable with that."

Not surprisingly, women are often held back in corporate America because they lack self-confidence. And considering the hoops that female managers must jump through to get noticed and promoted, it's no wonder that our expectations of success are lower than are men's.

"I'm nearly fifty, and have been dealing with peers who are, for the most part, businessmen from the old school," says Carole Kitchens. "I've been on the pioneering edge, and it's been very painful at times. But these days, I'm seeing a new breed of men and women coming through. The men have working wives and help take care of their children. They're also very comfortable working with women." And the new women? "They are much better equipped than I was in terms of confidence and self-esteem. They come in expecting and demanding to be treated with respect. And it works."

Indeed, as women gain clout in corporate America and our numbers escalate, so will our confidence levels. Meanwhile, those of us who don't feel confident must learn to fake it till we make it. For example, in her climb up the ladder to become the first female president of a Hollywood studio, Dawn Steel told *Mirabella*, "Actually one of my great tricks was that before I walked into a room, I would picture the people in it applauding me—you know, for whatever— I had done something that made them welcome me into the room. And so when I got to the room, I had made myself more comfortable by that image that I kept in my head. And it always worked. I would take a deep breath and play a part."

Finally, many women fail to get noticed and move ahead because they fear—or misunderstand—power. In an article for *Working Woman* magazine, Maureen Dowd, who covers the White House for *The New York Times*, notes, "Men have never had any trouble with the concept of power. They want it purely, directly, unapologetically, libidinously. It is their entitlement and driving force. But for women, power has always had a negative aroma. It has been considered an acid that corroded femininity and sexual allure, an isolating force. The role models for powerful women were all claws and black arts—Lucrezia Borgia, Lady Macbeth. Women were raised to believe that they should get their way indirectly, through cajoling and flattery."

Authors Dorothy Cantor and Toni Bernay agree. "Women mistakenly believe that power is unfeminine," they note in *Women in Power*. Moreover, the authors add that women's fear of power hinges on the belief that having power will destroy their relationships—and relationships are critical to women.

But before women can embrace the concept of power, perhaps they must *redefine* it and discover how power can be used to *help* others. "Women can redefine power as a caring kind of power—not self-serving, but directed toward advancing an agenda," the authors note. And women are generally comfortable with this definition of power because it encompasses the notion of empowering others. "This power integrates typically female qualities with some male characteristics," explain the authors, "and it values both kinds of attributes equally."

Of course, on the flip side, there are women who embrace power—the old definition of it, that is—a bit too eagerly and emerge as male clones. And while it used to be that women who wanted to advance in corporate America had no choice but to become sharks, nowadays taking a command-and-control approach to management may be the kiss of death for both male *and* female managers.

CHAPTER FIFTEEN

Swim with the Dolphins

Corporate America is just now beginning to realize that effective managers must possess the right technical skills to get the job done, as well as the right people skills to assure a sense of cohesiveness in the workplace and to keep morale high. These managers strike an appropriate balance between considering the needs and concerns of subordinates and making decisions on their own. They are competitive *and* cooperative, versatile *and* flexible. They are considerate and sensitive and yet are able to roll with the punches.

Strength in Numbers

This realization, coupled with the fact that women fit the bill, is literally changing the demographics of corporate America. For example, 60 percent of corporate boards now include women—up from 11 percent in 1973. And according to Ralph Dieckmann, a principal with the executive search firm of Dieckmann & Associates, "Ten years ago, few women surfaced in the normal course of searches. In recent years, however, there's been a demand for women executives—and more importantly, the availability of talented women at senior executive levels has risen dramatically."

This is sweet music to the ears of women who for decades have been repeatedly told that their skills had no place in the corporate halls of America. Even sweeter is the fact that capable women are not only getting noticed, they are being wooed—and for all the *right* reasons.

Lynn Bignell, a principal with Gilbert Tweed & Associates in New York, confirms, "When women and minorities were hired eight to ten years ago, it was generally because of affirmative action. Now companies are hiring women and other minorities as senior executives so that they can be role models and act as bait in a work force that is diversifying. Today, hiring women managers is a totally *business-driven* initiative."

Moreover, evidence continues to mount that more and more women are climbing the corporate ladder and making substantial progress in their assault on the glass ceiling. According to *American Demographics* magazine, the number of female executives rose 14 percent between 1987 and 1991, from 5.9 million to 6.7 million. (Simultaneously, the number of male managers increased 3.5 percent, from 8.8 million to 9.1 million.) In addition, the number of women placed in senior managerial positions (senior vice president and up) by Korn/Ferry International, the world's largest executive search firm, increased from 5 percent of the total in 1982 to 16 percent in 1992. Alan S. Neely, Managing Director of the Atlanta office of Korn/Ferry, notes, "Since women account for over half of the graduates of U.S. graduate business schools, we expect the number of women placements into senior executive positions to increase dramatically over the next ten years."

Hopefully all of this progress *will* have a ripple effect, and for those waiting in the wings, it will simply be a question of momentum and a matter of time before they join the upper ranks.

Sandra K. Woods, Vice President of Adolph Coors Brewing Company, agrees. "I truly believe that we will see change in this decade," she says. "Women have entered management in large numbers over the past several years, and business cannot afford not to take advantage of this training and experience. It takes a chief executive fifteen to twenty-five years or more to reach the top, and many women managers are just now reaching that stage of their careers from their entrance in the late 1960s and 1970s."

Granted, women currently hold less than 7 percent of the top Fortune 500 positions. But Patricia Aburdene and John Naisbitt, co-authors of *Megatrends for Women*, predict that today's Fortune 500 will not resemble the list for the year 2002. "Today's senior executives will retire in the 1990s," they believe. "Just below them is a cadre of female talent ages 35–45 that will break into CEO and senior executive positions by decade's end."

Researchers Roy Adler, Ph.D., professor of marketing at Pepperdine University, and Rebecca Yates, Ph.D., director of the MBA program at the University of Dayton, are equally optimistic. In a recent study, they tracked the careers of male and female MBA students over a twenty-five-year period and found that nearly three times as many of the women with MBAs had reached top management spots than had men. The researchers conclude that by the year 2000, 20 percent of the Fortune 500 companies' top slots will be held by women. "The number of women entering senior management is extraordinary," says Adler, "and it's accelerating."

Ready When They Are

Smart companies are just now beginning to recognize the strengths of female managers, and once they get a taste of our talents and capabilities, our numbers *will* swell.

We've paid our dues. We've proven our worth. We're exactly what American corporations—and its workers—need to remain competitive in the 1990s and beyond. We recognize—and even accept—the fact that moving up the ranks may involve a few hurdles, but for the most part will simply require playing the waiting game. And that's okay. Because, like dolphins, women are persistent. And tough. And patient if need be.

But no longer are we willing to impersonate sharks, jump through hoops, or be dominated and manipulated simply for the sake of pleasing others. We're proud of our species and eager to share our strengths with all the other fish in the sea . . . but *only* on our own terms.

Bibliography

Introduction

Ciabattari, J. "The Biggest Mistake Top Managers Make: A Surprising and Disturbing Report on American Corporate Management." *Working Woman*. October 1986, pp. 47–54.

Fruehauf, V. "Are You and Your Employees on the Same Wavelength?" *BPI News*. January 1978, p. 5.

Modic, J. "How's Your Quality of Work Life?" *Industry Week*. June 15, 1987, p. 7.

CHAPTER ONE: The Shark Attack Is Over

Jerome, R. "The Dolphin Treatment." *People Weekly*. October 25, 1993, pp. 175–78.

Lenz, E., and B. Myerhoff. *The Feminization of America: How Women's Values are Changing Our Public and Private Lives*. Los Angeles: Jeremy P. Tarcher, 1985.

Nathanson, D. Interview. January 14, 1993.

World Book Encyclopedia. 1988, Vol. 5, pp. 298–302.

CHAPTER TWO: Steel and Soul: Power Tools of Dolphins

Ash, M.K. *Mary Kay Ash on People Management*. New York: Warner Books, 1984.

Autry, J.A. *Love and Profit: The Art of Caring Leadership*. New York: Avon Books, 1991.

Beatts, A. "Q&A with Dawn Steel." *Mirabella*. October 1993, pp. 38–40.

Berglas, S. Interview. February 9, 1994.

Caggiano, C. "What Do Workers Want?" *Inc.* November 1992, p. 101.

Ciabattari, J. "The Biggest Mistake Top Managers Make: A Surprising and Disturbing Report on American Corporate Management." *Working Woman.* October 1986, pp. 47–54.

Fraser, J.A. "Women, Power and the New G.E." *Working Woman.* December 1992, pp. 59–96.

Glaser, C.B., and B.S. Smalley. *More Power to You! How Women Can Communicate Their Way to Success.* New York: Warner Books, 1992.

Hartman, C., and S. Pearlstein. "The Joy of Working." *Inc.* November 1987, pp. 61–68.

Hellwig, B. "Executive Female's Breakthrough." *Executive Female.* September-October 1992, p. 43.

Komaki, J. Interview. January 18, 1994.

Levering, M., and M. Moskowitz. *The 100 Best Companies to Work for in America.* New York: Doubleday/Currency, 1993.

Lundin, W., and K. Lundin. *The Healing Manager: How to Build Quality Relationships and Productive Cultures at Work.* San Francisco: Berrett-Koehler, 1993.

McFarland, L.J., L. Senn, and J.R. Childress. *21st Century Leadership: Dialogues with 100 Top Leaders.* Los Angeles: The Leadership Press, 1993.

Modic, J. "How's Your Quality of Work Life?" *Industry Week.* June 15, 1987, p. 7.

Nelton, S. "Men, Women and Leadership." *Nation's Business.* May 1991, pp. 16–23.

Saltzman, A., and K. Horan. "The New Meaning of Success." *U.S. News & World Report.* September 17, 1990, p. 56.

Tannen, D. *You Just Don't Understand: Women and Men in Conversation.* New York: William Morrow, 1990.

Tracy, D. *10 Steps to Empowerment: A Common-Sense Guide to Managing People.* New York: William Morrow, 1990.

Verespej, M.A. "Workers Rate Their Bosses." *Industry Week.* August 3, 1992, p. 31.

Welch, M. "The Secrets to Their Success." *Georgia Trend.* December 1993, pp. 62–66.

CHAPTER THREE: Great Beginnings: When You're the New Boss

Benton, D.A. *Lions Don't Need to Roar: Using the Leadership Power of Professional Presence to Stand Out, Fit In, and Move Ahead.* New York: Warner Books, 1992.

Francis, S. "So Now You're the Boss." *Cosmopolitan.* March 1991, pp. 116–19.

Glaser, C.B., and B.S. Smalley. *More Power to You! How Women Can Communicate Their Way to Success.* New York: Warner Books, 1992.

Grove, A. *One-on-One with Andy Grove: How to Manage Your Boss, Yourself, and Your Co-workers.* New York: G.P. Putnam's Sons, 1987.

Harvey, J. *If I'm So Successful, Why Do I Feel Like a Fake?* New York: St. Martin's Press, 1985.

Hill, L.A. *Becoming a Manager: Mastery of a New Identity.* Boston: Harvard Business School Press, 1992.

Hunsaker, J., and P. Hunsaker. *Strategies and Skills for Managerial Women.* Cincinnati: South-Western Publishing Company, 1986.

Kruger, P. "What Women Think of Women Bosses." *Working Woman.* June 1993, p. 40.

Payne, T. *From the Inside Out: How to Create and Survive a Culture of Change.* Albuquerque: Lodestar, 1993.

Plummer, W. "Woman Among Wildcats." *People Weekly.* March 22, 1993, pp. 51–52.

Powell, G.N. *Women and Men in Management.* Newbury Park, CA: Sage Publications, 1988.

Shannon, E. "Those Kids Are So Eager. Interview with Janet Reno." *Time.* July 12, 1993, p. 24.

Vennochi, J. "What They Don't Teach You at Harvard Business School." *Working Woman.* February 1993, pp. 52–59.

Watts. P. "I'm the New Boss. What's the Best Way to Take Charge?" *Executive Female.* January-February 1992, pp. 67–68.

Watts, P. "Off to a Flying Start." *Executive Female.* January-February 1993, pp. 42–45.

Williams, K. "A Different Route to the Top." *Working Woman.* December 1992, pp. 42–44.

CHAPTER FOUR: Attracting, Hiring, and Keeping Good Employees

Bone, D. *The Business of Listening: A Practical Guide to Effective Listening.* Los Altos, CA: Crisp Publications, 1988.

DeCamp, D.D. "Are You Hiring the Right People?" *Management Review.* May 1992, pp. 44–47.

Elsea, J.G. *The Four Minute Sell.* New York: Simon & Schuster, 1984.

Fallon, W.K. *Effective Communications on the Job.* Los Altos, CA: Crisp Publications, 1988.

Glasser, C.B., and B.S. Smalley. *More Power to You! How Women Can Communicate Their Way to Success.* New York: Warner Books, 1992.

Greathouse, C.L. "10 Common Hiring Mistakes." *Industry Week.* January 20, 1992, p. 22.

Houston, P. "The Smartest Way to Build Company Loyalty." *Working Woman.* April 1992, p. 72.

Jacobson, A. *Women in Charge: Dilemmas of Women in Authority.* New York: Van Nostrand Reinhold, 1985.

Lammer, T. "How to Read Between the Lines: Tactics for Evaluating a Résumé." *Inc.* March 1993, p. 105.

Levering, M., and M. Moskowitz. *The 100 Best Companies to Work for in America.* New York: Doubleday/Currency, 1993.

Macan, T.H. Interview. January 20, 1994.

Moskal, B.S. "Company Loyalty Dies, a Victim of Neglect." *Industry Week.* March 1, 1993. pp. 11–13.

Leeds, D. *Smart Questions: A New Strategy for Successful Managers.* New York: Berkley Books, 1988.

Peters, T. *Thriving on Chaos: Handbook for a Management Revolution.* New York: HarperCollins, 1987.

Powell, G.N. *Women and Men in Management.* Newbury Park, CA: Sage Publications, 1988.

Spragins, E. "Hiring Without the Guesswork." *Inc.* February 1992, p. 80.

Thompson, C. "How to Fire." *Inc.* May 1992, p. 66.

CHAPTER FIVE: From Staff to Team: The Dolphin As Coach

Altany, D. "Women Managers: A Vibrant Force." *Industry Week.* March 2, 1992, p. 25.

Bennis, W. *On Becoming a Leader.* Reading, MA: Addison-Wesley, 1989.

Hammer, M., and J. Champy. *Reengineering the Corporation: A Manifesto for Business Revolution.* New York: HarperCollins, 1993.

Leeds, D. *Smart Questions: A New Strategy for Successful Managers.* New York: Berkley Books, 1988.

Peters, T. *Thriving on Chaos: Handbook for a Management Revolution.* New York: HarperCollins, 1987.

Petersen, D.E., and J. Hillkirk. *A Better Idea: Redefining the Way American Companies Work.* Boston: Houghton Mifflin, 1991.

Tracy, D. *10 Steps to Empowerment: A Common-Sense Guide to Managing People.* New York: William Morrow, 1990.

Watts, P. "Free Advice (from Paula Nesbitt, M. June Smith, Judy Woodruff and Others)." *Executive Female.* January-February 1990, pp. 41–45.

CHAPTER SIX: Sharing the Workload

Autry, J.A. *Love and Profit: The Art of Caring Leadership*. New York: Avon Books, 1991.

Drennan, D. "How to Get Your Employees Committed." *Management Today*. October 1984, pp. 121–26

Hunsaker, J., and P. Hunsaker. *Strategies and Skills for Managerial Women*. Cincinnatti: South-Western Publishing Company, 1986.

Leeds, D. *Smart Questions: A New Strategy for Successful Managers*. New York: Berkley Books, 1988.

Milwid, B. *Working with Men: Professional Women Talk About Power, Sexuality, and Ethics*. Hillsboro. OR: Beyond Words Publishing, 1990.

Prendergast, A. "Learning to Let Go." *Working Women*. January 1992, pp. 42–45.

Tracy, D. *10 Steps to Empowerment: A Common-Sense Guide to Managing People*. New York: William Morrow, 1990.

CHAPTER SEVEN: Good Employees Are Made, Not Born

Brown, D. "So You Want to Start an Incentive Program." *Management Review*. February 1992, pp. 43–45.

Drennan, D. "How to Get Your Employees Committed." *Management Today*. October 1984, pp. 121–26.

Holmes, R.H. How to Motivate Your Employees." *Business Age*. August 1989, pp. 40–41.

Levering, M., and M. Moskowitz, *The 100 Best Companies to Work for in America*. New York: Doubleday/Currency, 1993.

Louio-George, W. "What Motivates Best?" *Sales & Marketing Management*. April 1992, pp. 113–15.

McAfee, R.B., and M. Glassman. "It's the Little Things That Count." *Management Solutions*. August 1988, pp. 32–37.

McClenahen, J.S. "It's No Fun Working Here Anymore." *Industry Week*. March 4, 1991, pp. 5–8.

Modic, J. "How's Your Quality of Work Life?" *Industry Week*. June 15, 1987, p. 7.

Prokesch, S.E. "Battling Bigness." *Harvard Business Review*. November-December 1993, p. 143.

Rifkin, G. "The 'Iron Lady' Keeping Lotus on Track." *New York Times*. January 23, 1994, p. F-10.

Verespej, M.A. "Workers Rate Their Bosses." *Industry Week*. August 3, 1992, p. 31.

CHAPTER EIGHT: The Lighter Side of Managing People

Barreca, R. *They Used to Call Me Snow White . . . But I Drifted: Women's Strategic Use of Humor*. New York: Viking Press, 1991.

Basso, B. with J. Klosek, *This Job Should Be Fun: The New Profit Strategy for Managing People in Tough Times*. Holbrook, MA: Bob Adams, 1991.

Cantor, D., and T. Bernay. *Women in Power: The Secrets of Leadership*. New York: Houghton Mifflin, 1992.

Fassihi, T. "Taking Humor Seriously." *Executive Female*. November-December 1990, pp. 13–14.

Freiberg, R.A. Interview. January 30, 1994.

Houston, P. "The Smartest Way to Build Loyalty." *Working Woman*. April 1992, pp. 72–77.

Ivins, M. *Molly Ivins Can't Say That, Can She?* New York: Random House, 1991.

Kushner, M.L. *The Light Touch: How to Use Humor for Business Success*. New York: Simon & Schuster. 1990.

"Last Laugh." *Psychology Today*. January-February, 1993, pp. 16–17.

Levering, M., and M. Moskowitz. *The 100 Best Companies to Work for in America*. New York: Doubleday/Currency, 1993.

Mackoff, B. *What Mona Lisa Knew: A Woman's Guide to Getting Ahead in Business by Lightening Up*. Los Angeles: Lowell House, 1990.

McClenahen, J.S. "It's No Fun Working Here Anymore." *Industry Week*. March 4, 1991, pp. 5–8.

Monroe, V. "Men and Women." *Mirabella*. December 1992, p. 25.

Paulson, T.L. *Making Humor Work: Take Your Job Seriously and Yourself Lightly*. Menlo Park, CA: Crisp Publications, 1989.

Rosenberg, L. Interview. January 18, 1994.

Schwartz, M., and C.R. Babcock. "Arizona Senate Hopeful Banks On Her Up-Front Approach." *Washington Post*. September 24, 1992, p. A-10.

"Sick Jokes, Healthy Workers." *Psychology Today*. July-August 1993, pp. 16–17.

Solomon, F. Interview. February 15, 1994.

"State's First Female D.A.: 'I'm Plenty Tough.' " *Atlanta Constitution*. September 10, 1991, p. C-2.

Tavris, C. *Everywoman's Emotional Well-Being*. New York: Doubleday, 1986.

Wilson, S. *The Art of Mixing Work and Play*. Reynoldsville, OH: Advocate Publishing Group, 1992.

"Women in Washington: How Are We Doing?" *Lear's*. January 1994, p. 53.

"Women of the Year." *Glamour.* December 1992, pp. 114–15.

Young, S. "Laugh—It's Healthy." *Glamour.* December 1992, p. 33.

CHAPTER NINE: Managing Conflict and Difficult Employees

"Apology: Timing Is Key." *Working Woman.* August 1991, p. 78.

Arapakis, M. *Softpower! How to Speak Up, Set Limits, and Say No Without Losing Your Lover, Your Job, or Your Friends.* New York: Warner Books. 1990.

Autry, J.A. *Love and Profit: The Art of Caring Leadership.* New York: Avon Books, 1991.

Deep, S. *Smart Moves.* Reading, MA: Addison-Wesley, 1990.

Jacobson, A. *Women in Charge: Dilemmas of Women in Authority.* New York: Van Nostrand Reinhold, 1985.

Koltnow, E., and L.S. Dumas. *Congratulations! You've Been Fired.* New York: Fawcett Columbine, 1990.

McGarvey, R. "You Can Take off the Gloves. You Can Criticize Your Boss Without Coming to Blows (Or Jeopardizing Your Job)." *Executive Female.* November-December 1989, pp. 34–58.

Moskal, B.S. "An Age of Realism: Managers and Subordinates Think More Alike." *Industry Week.* December 14, 1987, p. 18.

Paulson, T.L. *Making Humor Work: Take Your Job Seriously and Yourself Lightly.* Menlo Park, CA: Crisp Publications, 1989.

Paulson, T.L. *They Shoot Managers Don't They? Managing Yourself and Leading Others in a Changing World.* Berkeley, CA: Ten Speed Press, 1991.

CHAPTER TEN: Win-Win Negotiating

Kasten, B.R. "Separate Strengths: How Men and Women Manage Conflict and Competition." In L.L. Moore (ed.), *Not As Far As You Think: The Realities of Working Women.* Lexington, MA: Lexington Books, 1976.

Leeds, D. *Smart Questions: A New Strategy for Successful Managers.* New York: Berkley Books, 1988.

Nelton, S. "The Womanly Art of the Deal." *Nation's Business.* January 1993, p. 58.

Schapiro, N. *Negotiating for Your Life: New Success Strategies for Women.* New York: Henry Holt, 1993.

Ury, W. *Getting Past No: Negotiating Your Way from Confrontation to Cooperation.* New York: Bantam Books, 1991.

Williams, M. "How I Learned to Stop Worrying and Love Negotiating." *Inc.* September 1987, pp. 132–34.

"Women at the Table." *Psychology Today*. September-October 1992, p. 11.

CHAPTER ELEVEN: Bouncing Back from Adversity

Beatts, A. "Q&A with Dawn Steel." *Mirabella*. October 1993, pp. 38–40.

Bell, L., and V. Young. "Imposters, Fakes and Frauds." In L.L. Moore (ed.), *Not As Far As You Think: The Realities of Working Women*. Lexington, MA: Lexington Books, 1976.

Cantor, D., and T. Bernay. *Women in Power: The Secrets of Leadership*. New York: Houghton Mifflin, 1992.

DuBrin, A.J. *Bouncing Back: How to Stay in the Game When Your Career Is on the Line*. Englewood Cliffs, NJ: Prentice Hall, 1992.

Kiechell, W. "When a Manager Stumbles." *Fortune*. November 12, 1984, pp. 265–68.

Morrison, A.M., R.P. White, and E. Van Velsor. "The Glass House Dilemma: Why Women Executives Dare Not Fail." *Working Woman*. October 1986, pp. 110–12.

Plunkett, L.C., and R. Fournier. *Participative Management: Implementing Empowerment*. New York: John Wiley & Sons, 1991.

Schenkel, S. *Giving Away Success: Why Women Get Stuck and What to Do About It*. New York: HarperPerennial, 1992.

Smalley, B.S. "Bouncing Back from Failure." *New Woman*. July 1989, pp. 102–7.

Sobkowski, A. "Damage Control When a Crisis Hits." *Executive Female*. May-June 1992, pp. 67–68.

"Stupidity, Sí, Villany No." *Psychology Today*. July-August 1993, p. 24.

"A Talk with Warren Bennis." *Psychology Today*. November-December 1993, pp. 30–31.

Tooley, B. "Turning Trials into Triumphs." *Working Woman*. January 1987, pp. 66–70.

Tracy, D. *10 Steps to Empowerment: A Common-Sense Guide to Managing People*. New York: William Morrow, 1990.

Van Velsor, E., and M.W. Hughes. *Gender Differences in the Development of Managers: How Women Managers Learn from Experience*. Greensboro, NC: Center for Creative Leadership, 1987.

Watts, P. "Yikes! I Made a Big Mistake. Now What?" *Executive Female*. November-December 1991, pp. 17–19.

CHAPTER TWELVE: Work Smarter, Not Harder

Arapakis, M. *Softpower! How to Speak Up, Set Limits, and Say No Without Losing Your Lover, Your Job, or Your Friends.* New York: Warner Books, 1990.

Bliss, E. *Getting Things Done: The ABCs of Time Management.* New York: Charles Scribner's Sons, 1991.

Datillo, J. Interview. September 16, 1992.

Douglass, M.E., and D.N. Douglass. *Manage Your Time, Your Work, Yourself.* New York: AMACOM, 1980.

Fassel, D. *Working Ourselves to Death: The High Cost of Workaholism and the Rewards of Recovery.* New York: HarperCollins, 1990.

Jacobson, A. *Women in Charge: Dilemmas of Women in Authority.* New York: Van Nostrand Reinhold, 1985.

Keyes, R. *Timelock.* New York: HarperCollins, 1991.

Kofodimos, J. *Balancing Act: How Managers Can Integrate Successful Careers and Fulfilling Personal Lives.* San Francisco: Jossey-Bass, 1993.

MacKoff, B. *The Art of Self-Renewal: Balancing Pressure and Productivity On and Off the Job.* Los Angeles: Lowell House, 1992.

McGee, K.G. "How to Beat the Time Crunch." *New Woman.* January 1993, pp. 44–47.

Meier, L., and L. Meagher. "Teaming Up to Manage." *Working Woman.* September 1993, pp. 31–108.

Orsborne, C. *How Would Confucius Ask for a Raise? Exploring Spiritual Values in the Business World.* New York: William Morrow, 1994.

Paulson, T.L. *They Shoot Managers Don't They? Managing Yourself and Leading Others in a Changing World.* Berkeley, CA: Ten Speed Press, 1991.

Schor, J.B. *The Overworked American: The Unexpected Decline of Leisure.* New York: Basic Books, 1991.

Shaevitz, M. *The Superwoman Syndrome.* New York: Warner Books, 1988.

Smalley, B.S. "Do You Need to Take a Break?" *New Woman.* November 1992, pp. 121–25.

Tooley, J.A. "8 Minutes Worth of Work." *U.S. News & World Report.* May 22, 1989, p. 81.

Tooley, J.A. "Rough Day at the Office." *U.S. News & World Report.* May 22, 1989, p. 81.

Wein, B. "Job Stress? We Can Work It Out." *New Woman.* April 1993.

Wylie, P., and M. Grothe. "How to Listen so Your Staff Will Talk. *Executive Female.* July-August 1992, pp. 27–32.

CHAPTER THIRTEEN: Climbing the Corporate Ladder: Getting Noticed and Promoted

Beatts, A. "Q&A with Dawn Steel." *Mirabella*. October 1993, pp. 38–40.

Cantor, D., and T. Bernay. *Women in Power: The Secrets of Leadership*. New York: Houghton Mifflin, 1992.

Collins, N. *Professional Women and Their Mentors*. Englewood Cliffs, NJ: Prentice Hall, 1983.

Dumas, L. "Taking Risks in Business: Are Women Getting the Hang of It?" *Cosmopolitan*. June 1991, p. 228.

Fisher, A.B. "When Will Women Get to the Top?" *Fortune*. September 21, 1992, pp. 44–56.

Jeruchim, J., and P. Shapiro. *Women: Their Mentors and Success*. New York: Fawcett Columbine, 1992.

Kennedy, M.M. "Where Do You Want to Be 10 Years from Now?" *Glamour*. August 1992, p. 123.

Morrison, A.W., R.P. White, E. Van Velsor. "Executive Women: Substance Plus Style." *Psychology Today*. August 1987, pp. 18–25.

Morrison, A.W., R.P. White, E. Van Velsor, and the Center for Creative Leadership. *Breaking the Glass Ceiling*. Reading, MA: Addison-Wesley, 1987.

Olson, C. "Don't Let Modesty Keep You from Taking Credit." *Glamour*. October 1992, p. 140.

Ruderman, M.N. "Who Gets Promoted?" *Executive Female*. May-June 1992, p. 33.

Scollard, J. *Risk to Win: A Woman's Guide to Success*. New York: Macmillan, 1989.

Slovic, P. Interview. February 15, 1994.

Wentling, R.M. "Women in Middle Management: Their Career Development and Aspirations." *Business Horizons*. JanuaryFebruary 1992, p. 47.

Williams, K. "A Different Route to the Top." *Working Woman*. December 1992, p. 42.

CHAPTER FOURTEEN: Moving Up: Obstacles Women Face

Beatts, A. "Q&A with Dawn Steel." *Mirabella*. October 1993, pp. 38–40.

Benton, D.A. *Lions Don't Need to Roar: Using the Leadership Power of Professional Presence to Stand Out, Fit in, and Move Ahead*. New York: Warner Books, 1992.

Bliss, E. *Getting Things Done: The ABCs of Time Management*. New York: Charles Scribner's Sons, 1991.

Brownmiller, S. *Femininity*. New York: Simon & Schuster, 1984.

Cox, A.J. *The Cox Report on the American Corporation*. New York: Delacorte Press, 1982.

Dowd, M. "Power: Are Women Afraid of It—Or Beyond It?" *Working Woman*. November 1991, pp. 98–99.

Fisher, A.B. "When Will Women Get to the Top?" *Fortune*. September 21, 1992, pp. 44–46.

Goldberg, D. "Hard-hatted Woman." *Atlanta Journal/Atlanta Constitution*. November 28, 1993, p. E-8.

Hellwig, B. "Executive Female's Breakthrough." *Executive Female*. September-October 1992, p. 43.

"How to Win Influence." *Psychology Today*. July-August 1993, p. 20.

Jeruchim, J., and P. Shapiro. *Women: Their Mentors and Success*. New York: Fawcett Columbine, 1992.

"Katie Couric." *People Weekly*. December 28, 1992, pp. 74–76.

Kimmel, M.S. "What Do Men Want?" *Harvard Business Review*. November-December 1993, pp. 50–63.

Lenz, E., and B. Myerhof. *The Feminization of America: How Women's Values Are Changing Our Public and Private Lives*. Los Angeles: Jeremy P. Tarcher, 1985.

Levering, R., and M. Moskowitz. *The 100 Best Companies to Work for in America*. New York: Doubleday/Currency, 1993.

Lindsey, K. "The End of the Mommy Track." *Georgia Trend*. December 1993, p. 27.

Maning, M. *Leadership Skills for Women*. Los Altos, CA: Crisp Publications, 1989.

Perry, N.J. "If You Can't Join 'Em, Beat 'Em." *Fortune*. September 21, 1992, pp. 58–59.

Powell, G.N. *Women and Men in Management*. Newbury Park, CA: Sage Publications, 1988.

Richardson, E. "Catfights." *Mirabella*. December 1992, p. 58.

Schneider, K. "Women Candidates Face Old Story: The Double Standard." *Athens Daily News/Athens Banner-Herald*. September 20, 1992, p. D-10.

"A Talk with Warren Bennis." *Psychology Today*. November-December 1993, pp. 30–31.

Tanenbaum, J. *Male and Female Realities: Understanding the Opposite Sex*. Sugarland, TX: Candle Publishing, 1989.

Tannen, D. *You Just Don't Understand: Women and Men in Conversation*. New York: William Morrow, 1990.

Tucker, C. "Breaking Free from the Feminist Stereotype." *Atlanta Constitution*. October 18, 1992, p. H-2.

Watts, P. "Free Advice (from Paula Nesbitt, M. June Smith, Judy Woodruff and Others)." *Executive Female*. January-February 1990, pp. 41–45.

Watts, P. "Men Who—Gasp! Manage Like Women." *Executive Female*. September-October 1991, pp. 31–34.

Wentling, R.M. "Women in Middle Management: Their Career Development and Aspirations." *Business Horizons*. January-February 1992, p. 47.

CHAPTER FIFTEEN: Swim with the Dolphins

Aburdene, P., and J. Naisbitt. *Megatrends for Women*. New York: Villard Books, 1992.

American Demographics. Interview. February 22, 1994.

Bignell, L. Interview. January 18, 1994.

Dieckmann, R. Interview. January 18, 1994.

Hogarty, D. B. "Cracks in the Glass Ceiling?" *New Woman*. February 1994, p. 42.

Neely, A. S. Interview. February 22, 1994.

Nichols, D. "Job Candidates Wanted: Talented Women Please Apply." *Management Review*. March 1992, pp. 39–41.

Acknowledgments

With special thanks to the Dolphins who contributed to this book:

Christine Anderson
Christine Anderson & Associates
Dabney Arthur
Turner Broadcasting System
Katherine August
First Republic Bancorp, Inc.
Sue Baird
Browning Management
Gwendolyn Calvert Baker
U.S. Committee for UNICEF
Colleen Barrett
Southwest Airlines
Mylle Bell
Holiday Inn Worldwide
Laurel Bellows
Bellows & Bellows
Cindy Bender
Meridian Travel
Mary Black
Super Wash
Emma Lou Brent
Phelps County Bank
Randi S. Brill
The Quarasan Group
Nicole Browning
MTV Networks
Sue Brush
Westin Hotels and Resorts

Cynthia Carlson
The Carlson Group
Claire Coyle
SmithKline Beecham
Julie Culwell
Atlanta Committee for the Olympic Games
Helene Dahlander
Westin Hotels and Resorts
Barbara Behrman Dan
Jimmy Dean Foods
Cynthia Danaher
Hewlett-Packard
Tommye Jo Daves
Levi Strauss & Co.
Carol Deutsch
Communication Seminars
Charlotte Dison
Baptist Hospital of Miami
Hanne Dittler
Westin Hotels and Resorts
Maggie Elliot
Walt Disney Imagineering
Jane Evans
U.S. West Communications
Debbi Fields
Mrs. Fields Cookies
Cynthia Fontayne
The Fontayne Group

Betty Forbes
Central Fidelity Mortgage Corporation
Ronna A. Freiberg
Kenetech Windpower, Inc.
Rosa Gatti
ESPN
Susan Groenwald
The Barter Corporation
Donna Hansen
Ft. Myers Police Department
Karen Himle
The St. Paul Companies
Johnna Howell
Westin Hotels and Resorts
Katherine Hudson
W.H. Brady Company
Suzanne Jenniches
Westinghouse Electric
Karen Johnson
Borden, Inc.
Krys Keller
ABC Television Network
Carole Kitchens
Hoechst Celanese Corporation
Susan Lang
Aldus Corporation
Harriet Gerber Lewis
Gerber Plumbing Fixtures
Marsha Londe
Shadco Advertising Specialties
Alice Lusk
EDS
Dr. Kathleen McCarroll
Detroit Receiving Hospital
Kim McCaulou
Westin Hotels and Resorts
Karyn Marasco
Westin Hotels and Resorts
Marilyn Marks
Dorsey Trailers
Laura Martin
Westin Hotels and Resorts

Loriann Meagher
Xerox Corporation
Laura Meier
Xerox Corporation
Sherry Mosley
Corning, Inc.
M. Colleen Mullens
AT&T Business Communication Services
Debbie Newport
Federal Express
Candy M. Obourn
Eastman Kodak
Victoria Ogden
Cape Cod Community Newspapers
Nanci O'Neill
Westin Hotels and Resorts
Carol Orsborne
The Society for Inner Excellence
Linda Pacotti
Schering-Plough
Grace Pastiak
Tellabs
Helen Pastorino
Alain Pinel Realtors
Mary Pierce
American Express Personal Financial Planning
Susan Pravda
Epstein, Becker & Green
Lisa Resnick
The Prudential Preferred Financial Services
Rita Page Reuss
Land O'Lakes
Lynn Richardson
Xerox Corporation
Anna Rolphe
Century Publishing
Morene Seldes-Marcus
Hi-Fi Buys
Janice Scott
Zep Mfg. Co.
Bridget Shirley
Johnson Wax

Nancy Singer
First of America Bank—Northeast Illinois

Dorothy Smiley
Westin Hotels and Resorts

Dee Thomas
Thomas & Ewing

Carolyn Thompson
CBT Training Systems

Jan Thompson
Mazda Motor of America

Karen Walker
Compaq Computer Corporation

Virginia Walker
Scios Nova

Virginia Weldon
Monsanto Company

Ella Williams
Aegir

Sandra K. Woods
Adolph Coors

Author's Note

Connie Glaser is available for keynote presentations and seminars based on *Swim with the Dolphins*. For more information, call (404) 804-0318 or (706) 613-7237.

Index